FISCAL AUSTERITY AND INNOVATION IN LOCAL GOVERNANCE IN EUROPE

Fiscal Austerity and Innovation in Local Governance in Europe

CARLOS NUNES SILVA
University of Lisbon, Portugal

AND

JÁN BUČEK
Comenius University, Slovakia

Routledge
Taylor & Francis Group

LONDON AND NEW YORK

First published 2014 by Ashgate Publishing

Published 2016 by Routledge
2 Park Square, Milton Park, Abingdon, Oxfordshire OX14 4RN
711 Third Avenue, New York, NY 10017, USA

First issued in paperback 2016

Routledge is an imprint of the Taylor & Francis Group, an informa business

British Library Cataloguing in Publication Data
A catalogue record for this book is available from the British Library.

The Library of Congress has cataloged the printed edition as follows:
The Library of Congress Cataloging-in-Publication Data has been applied for.

ISBN 13: 978-1-138-27364-1 (pbk)
ISBN 13: 978-1-4724-3243-8 (hbk)

Contents

List of Figures

List of Tables

Note on Contributors

Boris Bakota, PhD, is Associate Professor of Administration and Administrative Law, Head of Chair of Administrative Sciences, Faculty of Law, Josip Juraj Strossmayer University, Osijek, Croatia, and Visiting Teacher at the University of Applied Sciences in Vukovar, Croatia. He is the President of Strasbourg-based ENTO (European Network of Training Organizations for Local and Regional Government). He is member of the Board of Croatian Institute of Local Government, full member of the Croatian Academy of Legal Sciences and member of the Editorial Board of Croatian and Comparative Public Administration. His research interests are mainly focused on local and regional government, ethics in public administration and on animal law and welfare.

Anja Brauckmann, Dipl.-Ing. Spatial Planning, Research Institute for Regional and Urban Development, Dortmund, Germany. Her research interests are mainly focused on sustainable urban development, costs and benefits of urban development projects, demographic change, residential choice and household mobility.

Ján Buček, PhD, is Associate Professor and Head of Department of Human Geography and Demography at the Comenius University in Bratislava. He holds a PhD degree in Economic Geography (Comenius University, 1996). His research focuses on various governance and development issues at the local/urban and regional levels. Currently he is the Chair of the International Geographical Union Commission on Geography of Governance (since 2008) and Vice-President of the Slovak Geographical Society (since 2010).

Milan Bufon, PhD, is Professor of Human and Political Geography at the Faculty of Humanities of the University of Primorska (Koper, Slovenia). He also served as the Director of the Institute for Mediterranean Humanities and Social Studies at the Science and Research Centre of the University of Primorska (1996–2006). His main research interests are interaction between social and spatial processes in Europe, and particularly border studies. He published several books and scientific articles in both domestic and international journals and organized various international conferences in Slovenia and abroad. He was Vice-Rector for research at the University of Primorska and is currently President of the Slovene Research Institute in Trieste (Italy).

Blanka Marková, Mgr. is a PhD student at the Department of Human Geography and Regional Development at the Faculty of Science at the University of Ostrava.

Her research interests include Tourism Management, the role of culture and cultural events in regional development and multi-level cultural governance, with a particular focus on the European Capital of Culture. She also works as a project manager at Masaryk University in Brno.

Carlos Nunes Silva, PhD, is Professor Auxiliar at the Institute of Geography and Spatial Planning, University of Lisbon, Portugal. His research interests are mainly focused on local government policies, history and theory of urban planning, urban and metropolitan governance, urban planning ethics, urban planning in Africa, research methods, e-government and e-planning. His recent publications include the books *Citizen e-Participation in Urban Governance: Crowdsourcing and Collaborative Creativity* (2013), *Online Research Methods in Urban and Planning Studies: Design and Outcomes* (2012), *Handbook of Research on E-Planning: ICT for Urban Development and Monitoring* (2010) and *Portugal: Sistema de Govern Local* (2004). He is member of the Steering Committee of the International Geographical Union Commission 'Geography of Governance' (2012–16), and the founding Editor-in-Chief of the 'International Journal of E-Planning Research' (IJEPR).

Ilona Pálné Kovács, PhD, graduated as a lawyer, defended her PhD in political science and was elected as a corresponding member of the Hungarian Academy of Sciences in 2013. She is a scientific adviser in the Institute for Regional Studies, Centre for Economic and Regional Studies, HAS, and Professor at the Department for Political and International Studies at the University of Pécs. She is a leader of the PhD programme in political science also at the University of Pécs. Her scientific interests are regional governance and local governments, management of regional policy teaching and public administration and constitutional law. She was leader and participant of many domestic and international research projects among several EU framework programmes.

Bahdan Sarazhynski is a postgraduate student of International and European Law, LLM Programme at the European Humanities University, Vilnius, Lithuania. He is a *cum laude* graduate of International Law, LLB, also at the European Humanities University. During LLB studies he spent two semesters as an exchange student at the University of Deusto, Bilbao, Spain. His research interests are mainly focused on administrative law, sports law, EU law and international trade law. He served as a news block subeditor at EHU law magazine *Jus Gentium*.

Andrej Sopkuliak is a PhD student at the Department of Human Geography and Demography, Comenius University, Bratislava, Slovakia. His research activities are mainly focused on local finance, decentralization and local economic development.

Stephanie Steels, PhD, is Lecturer in Social Work in the School of Healthcare at the University of Leeds. She completed her PhD in Public Health at the University of Manchester. Her doctoral research was centered on investigating the potential health implications of urbanization in Vietnam, in addition to exploring NGO engagement with policymakers and government authorities in implementing public health policy. Her research interests focus on health inequities and intersectoral action within the urban context. She previously held positions at the World Health Organization, University of Manchester and the University of Liverpool.

Iva Tichá, Mgr. Ing., is a PhD student at the Department of Human Geography and Regional Development at the Faculty of Science, University of Ostrava. Her research is focused on the governance of ageing, social exclusion and its impact on city finance (case study: city of Ostrava). She also works as a junior researcher at the Faculty of Social Studies at the University of Ostrava, Czech Republic, and is engaged in the activities of the European Research Institute for Social Work and Institute for Sustainable Urban Development.

Hellmut Wollmann, PhD, Prof. Emeritus, was a student of law and political science at Heidelberg and Wesleyan University, Connecticut, USA (1956–63), and a Kennedy Memorial Fellow at Harvard University (1970–71). He was Professor of Public Policy and Public Administration at Freie Universität (1974–93) and at Humboldt University (1993–2001), both in Berlin. His research is mainly focused on comparative public policy and public administration. He is editor of numerous publications: *Comparing Public Sector Reform in Britain and Germany* (2000), *Evaluation of Public Sector Reforms* (2003), *Provision of Public Services in Europe* (2010) and *Comparative Public Administration in Europe* (with S. Kuhlmann, 2014).

Preface

As local governments across Europe increasingly face financial constraints in their capacity to act and to meet all their functional responsibilities, institutional reform and policy innovation became, perhaps more than ever before, keywords in the national and local political agendas across the continent; although the evidence suggests a process with multiple facets, with both ruptures and continuities, and highly differentiated among European countries.

The book, the outcome of the work of researchers from different academic backgrounds, offers an overview of some of the problems and challenges faced by local governments in Europe as well as an outline of some ongoing institutional reforms and innovations in these countries. It is the result of the scientific cooperation developed by the authors under the auspices of the International Geographical Union (IGU) Commission on Geography of Governance.

Fiscal Austerity and Innovation in Local Governance in Europe explores some of these changes and the new challenges confronting local self-government in the field of local governance in Europe. The book explores four dimensions of this process of institutional reform and innovation associated with the context of fiscal austerity experienced by local self-government in Europe: i) the impact of the economic and financial crisis on local finance systems (for example, Slovakia), or the impact of economic adjustment programs in the reform of local government institutional architecture (for example, Portugal); and the new institutional arrangements associated with the move from public to private provision of local public services; ii) cross-border regional and local cooperation and the reform of meso level territorial administration which has been partially impacted, constrained or stimulated by the current economic and financial crisis (for example, Hungary, Croatia, Belarus); iii) innovation in policy tools, such as a new role for NGOs, and new fiscal instruments for sustainable urban development; iv) the impact on specific policy sectors (for example, social policy).

The book is intended for scholars, researchers, students and policymakers in the field of local governance, broadly defined, and in particular for those working in the fields of Public Administration, Geography and Political Science. We trust the book will add new data and insights to the literature on local governance in Europe, in particular to the literature on the impacts of the current economic and financial crisis on local government.

In sum, this collection of chapters illustrates the diversity of problems, barriers and constraints confronting local self-government in Europe and at the same time exemplify the transformative potential of some institutional and policy innovations being experimented in this field. For that reason, we hope that academics, policymakers and other readers will find these chapters motivating for the development of new solutions for the current challenges.

Carlos Nunes Silva and Ján Buček

Chapter 1

Introduction

Carlos Nunes Silva and Ján Buček

Local self-government throughout Europe has been unevenly impacted by the economic recession and fiscal austerity that some European countries experienced in the last years, in particular since 2008. Whilst these European governments make cuts to reduce budgetary deficits and public indebtedness levels, these in turn impact on local self-government budgets in a way that in some countries is leading to deep reforms in its structure and functional competences. With reduced income, local self-government across Europe is increasingly faced with the pressure to provide more for less, which calls for new policy approaches and innovative policy tools. However, this has not been a uniform process so far, as local self-government has been impacted differently by the economic and financial downturn, and for that reason have different experiences of fiscal austerity and tended to adopt different responses. The austerity impact is stronger in countries under international bailout and with a declining economy, as is the case of Portugal in this period, and less in countries with relatively better economic performance, as is the case of Germany.

The current wave of fiscal austerity that affects European countries, within and outside the Euro zone, and the policy responses adopted, are too complex or wicked to be addressed in a single volume. However, this mosaic of ongoing reforms on local self-government found in Europe provide an opportunity in which to explore the potential of engaging other stakeholders in local policies and an opportunity to experiment innovative policy tools and other institutional innovations. The following chapters aim to add new data and insights to the existing research on the ongoing changes in the local governance model in Europe in a selection of countries that provide a reasonable coverage of the diversity found within the European model of local governance. The book also contributes to debate on various forms of decentralization, multilevel governance and their confrontation with current public finance stress. The approaches of the central state to sub-state governments are more complex and new strategies are adopted, either interim or longer term. A new wave of central-local negotiation is in process, also leading to new outcomes.

In the book we seek to answer five main research questions related to the impact of fiscal austerity on local self-government and local governance in Europe:

1. How does fiscal austerity, in particular the budgetary and sovereign public debt and the external pressures in the Euro zone, affect the local government finance system and the local government institutional reforms?

2. To what extent did the current public finance crisis (budgetary/sovereign debt crisis) impact on the model of local public services provision, and to which degree and why has the process shown cross-country and cross-policy convergence or divergence?
3. Is the meso level of self-government able to play a positive role in the new governance model, offering a real opportunity to shift power among administrative tiers and stakeholders?
4. With cross-border integration increasing in Europe, to what extent can cross-border regionalism be an element of the new multilevel governance model in Europe, incorporating national, regional and local institutions and stakeholders, and how can it help to tackle the complex challenges that result from the current fiscal austerity context?
5. What is the impact of public expenditure cuts in specific local government policy sectors – social services and sustainable urban development – and what innovative policy tools have been developed and applied?

The book has 12 chapters including an Introduction and a Conclusion. Part I deals with the institutional and financial changes in local government and seeks to answer the first two research questions. In Chapter 2 ('Local Self-Government Finance in Slovakia During the 2008–11 Crisis'), Ján Buček and Andrej Sopkuliak evaluate the financial situation of Slovak local self-government during the economic, financial and subsequently fiscal and debt crisis over 2008–11. One of the main findings in this chapter is the flexible way with which local government in Slovakia dealt with the effects of the crisis, underlying previous findings that there is no single governance model that can fit all, suggesting instead that local socio-economic conditions and political culture are key determinants to be considered. This is followed in Chapter 3 ('The Economic Adjustment Program Impact on Local Government Reform in Portugal') by an overview of the current reform of local government in Portugal, seen as one of the consequences of the economic adjustment program signed between the Portuguese government and the European Commission, the European Central Bank and the International Monetary Fund, in 2011, confirming an overall trend towards increased administrative centralization, a reversal from networked governance towards the old hierarchical model of public administration bureaucracy, and a reversal in the model of public service provision towards privatization along the neo-liberal governance model. In Chapter 4 ('Public Services in European Countries: Between Public/Municipal and Private Sector Provision – and Reverse?'), Hellmut Wollmann discusses, based on the case of the UK, France, Italy and Germany, the development of the organizational forms – public sector versus private sector – and the underlying operational logics – political and economic – in the service sectors of water and energy provision, over the last century, examining whether to which degree and why this process has shown cross-country and cross-policy convergence, offering a number of insights that ought to be considered by all those engaged in the design and implementation of the new wave of local government reforms across Europe and in other regions of the world.

Part II deals with issues of territorial administrative division and multilevel governance and the potential and actual impact of fiscal austerity in the reforms being devised in several European countries and seeks to answer the third and fourth research questions mentioned above. In Chapter 5 ('The Role of Local Governance in Strengthening Cross-border Cooperation'), Milan Bufon 'discusses problems and challenges that emerge from an intensified cross-border integration, particularly in Europe, which is creating a sort of "cross-border regionalism" that might be sought as a new constituent part of a complex, multi-level system of governance incorporating not only national, but also local and regional agents'. The author mentions cross-border cooperation and integration as one of the most challenging innovations linked to the 'Europeanization' of policy-making and regional and local planning, having its natural and real base, as well as instrumental form focused on EU funds access. This process of increasing sub-national cooperation across borders seems to be the reversal of what appears to be emerging at the meso level as reported in the following chapters of this section. Ilona Pálné Kovács, in Chapter 6 ('Failed Rescaling of Territorial Governance in Hungary: What Was the Gist?'), analyses the motivations and forces behind the various reform measures implemented or postponed in Hungary in the last two decades in the field of regional meso government and likely to continue to determine policy outcomes in this domain despite the external pressures from the current fiscal austerity context. Deep structural and organizational changes as such could not change the legacy, the culture and the mechanisms of the past, leading to inefficient reforms. Chapter 7 covers an analysis of the administrative division reforms in Croatia ('Local and Regional Government Reform in Croatia: Subsidiarity and Innovation in an Era of Austerity'). Boris Bakota confirms that structural administrative changes have been difficult to implement in the country, admitting that the current economic and financial crisis and the solutions being experimented in other European countries should be considered in the reform of local governance in Croatia. The chapter also explores possible solutions for the future territorial administrative restructuring of the country. Bahdan Sarazhynski examines and discusses local governance institutions in the Republic of Belarus in Chapter 8 ('Local Governance in Belarus: the Impact of the Economic and Financial Crisis on the Administrative Division Reform'). The author identifies several problems such as lack of local autonomy, overlapping powers or unsuitable territorial-administrative division. The chapter explores the potential impact of the current economic and financial crisis on the centrality of this reform within the Belarus national political agenda.

Part III comprises three chapters on new local/urban management tools aimed to address weaknesses found in the current governance model, as is the case of the new roles that should be assigned to NGOs, as Stephanie Steels exemplifies in Chapter 9 ('Non-Governmental Organizations (NGOs) and Citizen-Authority Engagement: Applying Developing World Solutions to Europe in an Era of Fiscal Austerity'). She explores the potential opportunities that exist within the UK for NGOs to support health providers under the new health reforms, particularly in the urban environment. New fiscal tools are discussed by Anja Brauckmann in Chapter 10 ('Regional Effects of Urban Development Projects: an Innovative Tool to Support Fiscal Sustainable Urban Planning'). It calls for more complexity and regional cooperation in evaluation of urban development projects from the fiscal point of view, carefully considering costs and benefits for single municipalities. In Chapter 11 ('The Economic Crisis Impact on the Social Policy of Ostrava City'), Blanka Marková and Iva Tichá illustrate the kind of impacts the current fiscal crisis and public expenditure cuts can have on specific local social policy issues in an old industrial and mining city.

The book concludes with Chapter 12, in which the conclusions are presented and further research directions are identified and discussed.

PART I

Chapter 2

Local Self-government Finance in Slovakia During the 2008–11 Crisis

Ján Buček and Andrej Sopkuliak

Introduction

The impact and success in coping with the economic and financial crisis varies across states, regions and partial markets, as well as across individual local governments. It offers an important challenge to scientists in many disciplines, including geographers. Despite increasing attention on the current economic and financial crisis, or 'the geography of crisis', there prevails a focus on the financial markets, banks, states and housing issues (for example Aalbers, 2009; Lee et al., 2009; Harvey, 2011). Attention paid to the impact of the crisis on local government financing and functioning is also growing. However, as this was not a mainstream issue, it started with a certain delay. Taking into account the important role of local governments in contemporary society is a very useful research orientation. A large number of local governments had been seriously hit by the direct impacts of the crisis through losses in own capital investments, limited access to borrowing or facing a sudden decrease in own revenue (summarised for example by CEMR, 2009). Besides such immediate impact of the crisis, wide-ranging and longer term difficulties have emerged. They are related to the financial scarcity that spread across public finance in general, and accompanied by the inevitable fiscal consolidation not only at central but also at sub-national levels of government. This development has motivated the expansion of analytical works that focus on local governments' financial situations and their responses to the pressure generated by the crisis.

We have to be aware that financial scarcity is not new to local governments. There have been numerous experiences with a lack of resources caused by various circumstances accumulated over the past decades. Besides the not-so-frequent global crises situations, there have been experiences with regional as well as national crises. Financial scarcity can also be the result of specific central-local financial relations, leaving or transferring fewer resources to local governments. It has been a familiar situation in post-socialist countries. Many local governments suffered long-term fiscal scarcity caused by general public finance shortage. We cannot overlook the troubles of individual local governments caused by collapsing local economic and social environments (for example in systems with more direct links between the local economy and local revenues). Not so rare have been the cases of local governments facing critical financial situations caused by own mismanagement (bad investments, long-term high deficits and extreme local debt). The situation related to the global financial and economic crisis that started in 2008 is both more specific and dangerous for local governments. Due to the global nature of crisis, it concerns numerous local governments in many countries. It is also longer term and multiplied in effect by the extensive shift of the crisis into the public finance of many countries, accompanied by various levels of fiscal stress and austerity. It means that under this kind of crisis, opportunities for external support and consolidation are limited. Under financial pressure are banks, the private business sphere, as well as higher levels of government, and ordinary citizens. The search for a balanced response in the sharing of related burdens while sustaining the provision and development of local public services is not an easy task.

Fiscal stress and austerity, related strategies and measures at the local level have been widely debated in literature in recent decades. Well known and extensive was publication activity in the field of fiscal austerity and urban innovation 'initiative' (for example Clarke, 1989). Local austerity policies were examined by Lobao and Adua (2011) in the USA during 2001–08. Coe (2008) focused on opportunities for the supervision and assistance of states to local governments in fiscal trouble. Besides the increasing number of academic papers focusing on the crisis at the local level, we cannot overlook the reports prepared within various institutional settings (international, non-governmental organisations). Such are for example the cases of the White Paper focusing on strategies for local leaders during the crisis prepared by Miller and Svara (2009), or the Council of European Municipalities and Regions (CEMR, 2009) report on the impact on and responses of local governments in the early stages of the crisis. It is also the case of Pailais' (2009) analysis of local governments and the crisis performed for Cities Alliance. Among the latest initiatives we have to mention the activities of the Council of Europe, expressed for example in texts and recommendations edited by Davey (2011). If we concentrate on the crisis in Central and Eastern Europe (CEE), more studies quickly emerged (for example Smith and Swain, 2010; Staehr, 2010). Among the most comprehensive attempts, we can mention the effort to monitor the crisis in CEE countries and their regions in the volumes edited by Gorzelak and Goh (2010), and Gorzelak, Goh and Fazekas (2012). To date, less attention has been paid to local government during the crisis in Central and Eastern Europe. A rare case of such research is the early assessment of crisis responses in CEE countries prepared by Sedmihradska, Bobcheva and Lados (2011). Of course, many practical reflections can also be found in printed and electronic resources of the directly involved associations of local governments, or individual global cities.

The study of crisis in the context of local government offers many important research topics. Among which the most critical are the basic dimensions of the crisis, for example the depth of consequences and duration. Sensitive issues are its impact on local service provision and administration. The crisis is also a challenge to local representatives to adopt reasonable responses. There are multiple opportunities in strategies and measures that could be used to mitigate negative effects. It also concerns intergovernmental co-ordination, which is hardly avoidable. Researchers should not shy away from the discussion about the contribution of local governments to the economic recovery. It is a question whether they can provide or contribute to economic stimulation during the crisis. Standard attention should be paid to the study of best practices, organisational adjustment, prevention and so on. Very positive outcomes can be provided by analyses of the development and efficiency of responses over a longer time. Such can offer valuable knowledge concerning the dynamics of the crisis and the evolution of the situation and responses of local governments. We can consider various general as well as individual factors that influence success in crisis mitigation.

The crisis situation in such a scale is quite unique also for local self-governments in Slovakia. It is true even despite the financial scarcity that emerged in the first half of 1993, related to the difficult public finance situation of the newly established Slovak Republic (Buček, 1993). However, at that time it had been a short-term lack of resources, and the powers of local self-governments were reduced. They were also less autonomous and more dependent and interlinked to the central state. Not surprisingly, we can also find experiences of individual self-government that faced serious problems in financing as a result of their worse financial management during the second half of the 1990s. Such local financial difficulties were also faced by large Slovak cities such as Košice and Banská Bystrica, due to too excessive borrowing (Kling and Nižňanský, 2004). This led to the introduction of stricter limits on local borrowing by central state legislation since 2005. Although the majority of local self-governments experienced financial scarcity during the transition period, they are less experienced in coping with the consequences of unexpected, deep and longer term crisis. Despite the strong impact of the crisis on local government finance in Slovakia, there has been a lack of systematic attention to the study of this issue until now. Among few cases we can mention is Buček (2011) who focused on the specific issue of municipal property during the crisis period in Bratislava. More practically oriented debates among practitioners and policymakers can also be found.

The main aim of this contribution is to analyse and evaluate the financial situation of Slovak local self-government during economic, financial and subsequently fiscal/debt crisis over 2008–11. After outlining the main features of the economic crisis in Slovakia, we focus on selected items of local budget developments with the intention of revealing the impact of crisis on budget financing. Our objective is also to identify local self-government techniques in coping with fiscal stress, as well as the related important contextual factors. We would also like to reveal the character of co-ordination and cooperation between the central state and local self-governments in resolving the public finance imbalance by tracing their relationships. Our contribution concludes with a debate concerning the sensitivity and adaptation of local self-government finance to crisis.

As main sources of information we used legislative and financial documents concerning central, as well as local government – especially the final accounts of the Slovak Republic (focusing predominantly on local finance data 2008 to 2010), macroeconomic data according to the Statistical Office of the Slovak Republic and tax data provided by the Financial Directorate of the Slovak Republic. The interplay between central state and local government had been studied by tracing and interpreting documents and the statements of the main representatives of both levels. The central state represented the central government and the Ministry of Finance. On the opposite side were associations of local self-governments. They are represented by two main associations – The Association of Towns and Communities of Slovakia (in Slovak – Združenie miest a obcí Slovenska – ZMOS) with more than 2,700 members (there are almost 2,900 local self-governments in Slovakia), and The Union of Cities of Slovakia (in Slovak – Únia miest Slovenska – UMS) with about 70 members (including the largest cities). As an important source of information, we used the main weekly newspaper that focuses on local self-government issues – *Obecné Noviny*. From the terminology point of view, we use the term 'local government' in a more general and international context. We prefer the term local self-government (in Slovak – miestna samospráva) which respects the tradition and terminological accuracy in the Slovak context.

Basic Features of Economic and Public Finance Development During the Crisis

Slovakia could not avoid the crisis that hit global finance and the economy mostly since 2008. After an era of spectacular economic growth exceeding during short periods even 10 per cent of GDP (see Figure 2.1), the first effects of the economic and financial crisis emerged in October 2008. The decline in production of many sectors culminated during the first half of 2009. At the same time, a key central government anti-crisis measures package had been formulated and went into effect. Although the macroeconomic situation has improved since 2010, some serious negative features have remained. Such was especially the case of a high unemployment rate and stagnating wages. Above all else, the negative economic development also spread into worsening the public finance situation. Due to increasing budget deficits and public debt growth, combined with troubles in the Euro zone, urgent pressure has emerged for longer term fiscal consolidation.

There were no serious internal reasons leading to the expansion of the financial and economic crisis in Slovakia. For example, there were no serious problems with the banking sector that had been transformed a few years previously, and no signs of an extremely overheated real estate and property development market. The consequences of the economic crisis also mitigated many economic reforms completed earlier as well as the joining of the Euro zone in 2009 (although certain effects have been contradictory). The economic decline had been predominantly the result of global economic interdependency. The Slovak economy is small, but extremely open, depending on external economic environment development. It lost its growth dynamics during the last quarter of 2008, when GDP growth sharply

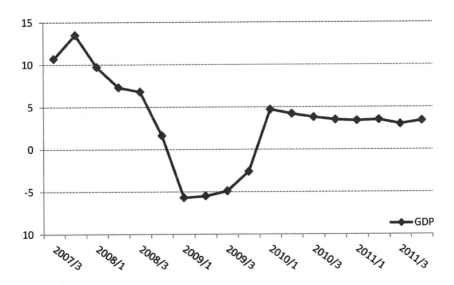

Figure 2.1   GDP development on a quarterly year-to-year basis in Slovakia
Source: Statistical Office of the Slovak Republic, 2012a.

decreased to a poor 1.6 per cent. The worst economic decline measured by annual GDP was in 2009 (-4.8 per cent). We can summarise, according to Buček (2010), that the largest decline had been the collapse in manufacturing (reflecting a large dependency on the car industry and electronics) and selected service branches. The crisis in the construction sector grew with a certain time lag. A more positive development returned in 2010 (4 per cent annual growth of GDP), but this was in comparison to the less productive 2009. The shift to more stable but still fragile economic growth was documented by a repeated GDP growth rate exceeding 3 per cent in all consecutive quarters of 2011 (3.3 per cent for 2011 annually, Statistical Office of the Slovak Republic 2012a). The positive economic development confirmed data about exports after 2009. While exports decreased 5.1 per cent in 2009 (compared to the previous year), they increased to 21.5 per cent in 2010 and 16.9 per cent in 2011 (Statistical Office of the Slovak Republic, 2012b).

Such negative economic development was naturally reflected in a worsened unemployment rate. Within a year, the registered unemployment rate increased from 7.5 per cent to 12 per cent (September 2008 to September 2009; UPSVAR, 2012). Even worse unemployment rate data was provided by a labour force survey (Figure 2.2). It culminated in a 15.1 per cent unemployment rate in 2010 (first quarter). Despite the signs of economic recovery since the beginning of 2010, this had not been converted into increased employment. The minor improvement seen in 2011 had been insufficient (unemployment rate 14 per cent in the last quarter of 2011, Statistical Office of the Slovak Republic, 2012c). The economy had focused on increasing its productivity and efficiency during the crisis (between 2006 to

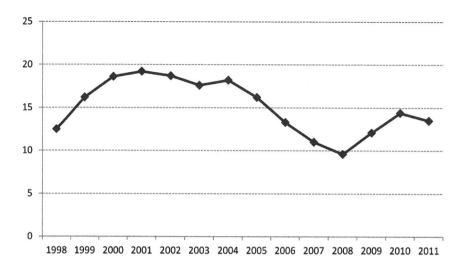

Figure 2.2   Unemployment rate development in Slovakia 1998–2011 (according to the labour force survey)

Source: Statistical Office of the Slovak Republic, 2012c.

2010 Slovakia moved became top of labour productivity per person employed in EU new member states – 81.3 per cent of the EU average according to Eurostat, 2012). It can be considered as a case of 'jobless recovery', when an economy is growing again but the unemployment rate remains high. The high unemployment rate also accompanied the loss of growth dynamics in wages. While in 2007 and 2008 nominal wages increased by more than 7 per cent, it was only 3 per cent in 2009, 3.2 per cent in 2010 and 2.2 per cent in 2011. This represented a decrease in real wages. In particular the tax base of public budgets was substantially eroded by this development.

Economic development had a deep impact on public finance. Any crisis usually means a decrease of tax incomes and the increase of public spending. The worsening of the financial situation was apparent at all levels of government. The most evident crisis indicator was the increase in the state budget deficits. While only 2.1 per cent in 2008, it increased to 8.0 per cent (2009) and 7.7 per cent (2010) of GDP. Reduction of the deficit to 4.8 per cent of GDP achieved in 2011 (Ministry of Finance, 2012) is an important improvement, but still insufficient. As a result, most public sector budget deficits during the crisis years were generated by the state budget. The share of local budgets of total public sector budget deficits was only 5.6 per cent in 2009 and 10.4 per cent in 2010, being in surplus in 2011. Another important indicator of public sector finance is the development of public debt. Total public sector debt was EUR 29.9 bln in 2011, compared to EUR 16.8 bln in 2006. While only 30.5 per cent of GDP in 2006, it jumped to 43.3 per cent in 2010. It is clear that after years of moderate growth of total public debt, it substantially increased during 2009 and 2010. Public debt had been lower thanks to positive economic development and a careful fiscal regime during previous years, prior to joining the Euro zone. Increased debt is primarily related to decreased budgets incomes related to the financial and economic crisis, and the absence of more extensive spending cuts in the public sector. The share of local self-governments of total public debt is also minor (5.2 per cent in 2010), although growth dynamics were higher in 2009 and 2010 compared to total public debt (Figure 2.3). A further increase should be reduced thanks to the adoption of 'debt brake' legislation (Constitutional Act No. 493/2011) in Slovakia, among the first countries in the European Union to do so.

The responses of central government to the crisis were aimed more at stimulating the economy, and less at reducing public spending. Explicit anti-crisis measures adopted especially during the first half of 2009 did not require huge resources. They were estimated at EUR 350–400 mln a year (for 2009 and 2010). Buček (2012) stressed that among the problems of anti-crisis measures adopted in Slovakia were their high number (about 60) and diversity. For various reasons, part of these resources was not spent (lack of interest, administratively demanding procedures). Among the more successful were contributions for new workplace creation, contributions to cover insurance payments of workplaces threatened by layoffs, support of local public workplaces and conditions for more flexible employment, as well as tax legislation concerning depreciation, or increased non-taxable income. Also popular were programmes focused on housing – credits for insulation, or subventions for solar panels and biomass heating. The central state also attempted to mobilise its investments (for

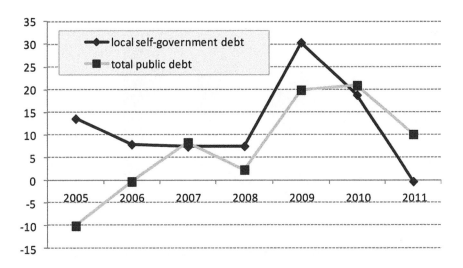

Figure 2.3   Year-to-year growth rate of public debt (in per cent)

Source: Ministry of Finance of the Slovak Republic, 2012.

example motorways) and support private sector investments (as in the energy sector). Longer term worse public finance development led to probably the most important intervention into the pre-existing public finance framework, with the increase of value added tax from 19 per cent to 20 per cent from 2011 (adopted in 2010). The decision to increase the central state share of personal income tax (PIT) from 6.2 per cent to 12.7 per cent from 2012 (adopted in 2011) had a similar background. It confirmed that central state reluctance to reduce public expenditures on the larger scale finally led to the search for additional resources on the revenue side of public budgets.

Local Self-government Finance Development

Slovak local self-governments were outside the direct influence of the financial and economic crisis. They were not involved in risky financial operations, and did not lose money in troubled banks. Due to the model of local taxation and revenue allocated to them, they were not so directly linked to the state of the local economy, but rather to the general situation in the economy and employment. Surprisingly, they did not face a reduction of revenues and expenditures in absolute terms in 2009 and 2010 (Figure 2.4). Nevertheless, they were confronted by significant changes in the composition of their revenues, and consequently were forced to react by adjusting their expenditures. The most serious have been the decrease

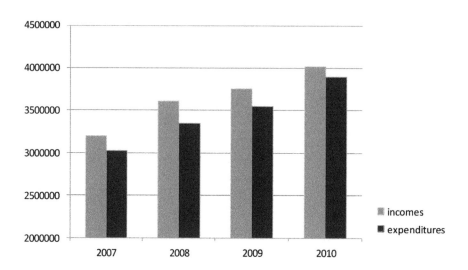

Figure 2.4   The development of local self-government incomes and expenditures (in thousand EUR)

Source: Ministry of Finance of the Slovak Republic, 2012.

in shared tax income (PIT), and increased dependency on state budget transfers and financial operations. The highest pressure on their expenditures was evident in 2010. One of the main issues that caused uncertainty in managing local finance had also been the unpredictability of future financial flows. Although the financial situation of local self-governments had not been so critical in general, they will still be under pressure in coming years.

We have to take into account the position of local self-government in Slovakia. It has developed into a well-respected level of government during the post-socialist period following 1989. The introductory phase of basic structures of local self-government building typified the first decade of post-socialist development. The next decade was accompanied by the strengthening of such structures by power decentralisation (for example in education, social services, planning, more delegated powers). The main reform period (2002–05) completed the fiscal reforms introduced from 2005. Since this year, we can observe the positive combination of more powerful and financially strengthened local self-governments and positive economic development in Slovakia. This was expressed by the expansion of local government activities, the completion of various development projects and increased financial capacity. These 'good times', mainly in 2007 and 2008, challenged the global economic crisis that intensively pervaded local self-government functioning from 2009.

The overall development of local finance confirms the less negative consequences of the crisis, if measured in terms of total incomes and expenditures. Even the more sluggish growth of incomes and expenditures during 2009 did not indicate substantial restrictions of their basic functioning. The first signs of the influence of the crisis could be seen in the changing basic composition of local finance structure (current, capital and financial operations). As far as incomes were concerned, the main shift occurred in the decrease of current incomes and the increase of incomes provided by financial operations. Current incomes decreased from a 76 per cent (2008) to a 66 per cent (2010) share of total incomes. In contrast, the share of financial operations of total incomes increased from 10 per cent (2008) to 18 per cent (2010). The basic structure of expenditure changed in favour of capital expenditures, accompanied by stagnation or minor growth in current expenditures and financial operation. This confirmed the priority of investments, more prudent behaviour and savings-oriented growth in the other two basic expenditure categories. The share of current expenditures decreased from 72 per cent (2008) to 66 per cent of total expenditures (2010), with a minor increase in absolute terms.

The decrease in shared tax yield can be considered as the most important influence of the crisis on local self-governments (Figure 2.5). Originally, local self-governments had been recipients of 70.3 per cent personal income tax (PIT) yield in Slovakia. It was transferred by state tax administration on a monthly basis reflecting set criteria (the main role being population number). The decrease in economic activity expressed in various forms such as reduced production, shorter working time, frozen salaries, no extra salaries and less employment meant a

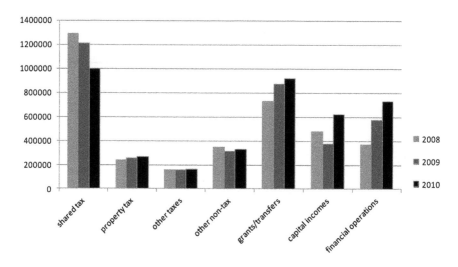

Figure 2.5   Main income items of local self-government (in thousand EUR)
Source: Ministry of Finance of the Slovak Republic, 2012.

decrease in this tax income. Increased non-deductible income introduced by the central state as an anti-crisis measure also had a negative influence. As a specific problem, the timing of the transfer of PIT yields to local self-governments emerged. Such had large disparities on a monthly basis, with the largest decline of transfers in May and June each year (see Figure 2.6). This was caused by tax legislation and related procedures such as tax declaration submission, tax payment postponement and so on. The huge decline in transfers during the mentioned months caused serious problems in the financial flow of many self-governments, peaking in 2010. Local self-governments intensively negotiated the problems with this important source of income with central government.

Local self-governments avoided any larger increase in local taxation within taxes under own administration during the first years of the crisis. Specific was the situation in real estate property tax collection, as one of the most stable and purely local taxes. Although we can observe an annually moderate increase of tax collection, a tax income increase in 2009 is clear compared to 2008 (7.3 per cent). However, this was not caused by a significant increase of taxation level (documented for example by Rohoška, 2012), but by a strong effort to collect property tax liabilities from previous years. It is important to mention that local self-governments in Slovakia directly administer this local tax, so it was quite a reasonable reaction to worsening financial flows during the first months of 2009 when the crisis peaked in the economy. It confirmed the immediate search for own ways to cope with the crisis. A minor increase of the income of local self-governments arose from other tax incomes (less important local taxes under direct administration).

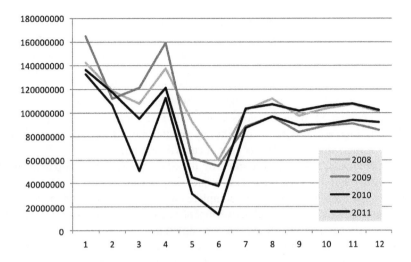

Figure 2.6   Personal income tax revenue of local self-governments according to months (in EUR)

Source: Financial Directorate of the Slovak Republic, 2012: own calculations.

The crisis influenced a decline in other non-tax incomes (for example local self-government entrepreneurial activities, yield from rented property) of about 10 per cent in 2009 compared to 2008. Even in 2010, despite a minor increase, this income was lower compared to 2008. The crisis had a similar short-term impact on capital revenues (Figure 2.5). This income had been only 79 per cent of 2008 income in 2009. It was caused primarily by the interim decline in interest in buying municipal property, caused by economic uncertainty and worse access to credit, for example for developers. However, this decline was compensated for in the next year: while this income was only EUR 376 mln in 2009, it increased to EUR 623 mln in 2010. A contrary trend concerns grants and transfers. Their increase at almost EUR 200 mln is quite significant (2008 to 2010, or 25 per cent). It confirms their stability despite the crisis, and it also already included compensation of the decline in PIT tax share decided by the central state. The largest increase within the local revenue system could be seen in financial operations. While it was only EUR 370 mln in 2008, it sharply increased to EUR 576 mln in 2009 and EUR 729 mln in 2010. This growth was based on borrowing and the use of own reserves from previous years.

Local self-government debt is a crucial indicator of the local self-government fiscal situation during the crisis. Its large growth is understandable, taking into account the abovementioned developments. It is important to know that it is a less influential section of total public debt growth. The local self-government share of total public debt was only 5.2 per cent in 2010. However, it had increased from 3.4 per cent in 2004. While the debt of local self-governments was EUR 720 mln in 2005, it was EUR 1390 mln in 2010. A major increase arose in the crisis years of 2009 and 2010. The growth dynamics in these years was even higher compared to total public sector debt (see Figure 2.3). Local self-governments in Slovakia had been criticised by representatives of the central state for such large-scale borrowing expansion, as opposed to the fiscal priorities of the public sector in general. Local self-government debt stabilised in 2011, when it slightly decreased compared to the previous year (EUR 1 386 mln, Ministry of Finance, 2012). The increase of debt in contributory organisations had been minor. Local self-government debt has in 90 per cent of cases a long-term nature (2010). Almost half of debts were resources provided by the State Housing Development Fund (Slov. Štátny Fond Rozvoja Bývania). Such large-scale expansion of debt was related to the borrowing needed to complete already started investment projects. On a significant scale, local self-government needed the necessary resources to co-finance already approved EU project completion.

Despite the already mentioned increase in expenditures, the crisis influenced the proportions of such increases across the various expenditure fields. This restructuring is more evident in 2010 and less so in 2009. It is partly the result of local budgets adopted even before the crisis, during the last months of 2008. Among expenditures that were under pressure we can mention personnel costs (salaries, insurance payments). The growth thereof decreased to 3 per cent in 2010, compared to 7 per cent in 2009. Local self-governments adjusted these costs with a certain delay in comparison to the general economic trend. Extensive cuts could be seen in the procurement of goods and services – at almost the same level as 2010 compared to 2009. Local self-governments also reduced rate payments. They used lower credit rates or renegotiated their credits. These items were behind the decrease of current expenditures share of total expenditures. The approaches in favour of greater efficiency were also documented by the data concerning capital expenditures. There was a huge shift in favour of new buildings and construction activity (almost 90 per cent of total capital expenditures). This meant a significant reduction in other investments or transactions. Construction activities in the education sector, infrastructure and housing played a substantial role in this development. This to a large extent was led by projects financed by EU funds and the State Fund for Housing Development loans. Local self-government concentrated on completing these advantageous investments for the long term, and reduced other capital expenditures. According to the COFOG structure (Figure 2.7), a stagnation or decrease of expenditures in environmental protection, transport (dominant in economic affairs) and social protection was evident.

Local Self-governments and Central State – Institutional Coordination, Cooperation and Conflict in Coping with Crisis

One of the key factors in the successful navigation of the crisis in public finance was the level of coordination and cooperation among sub-national governments

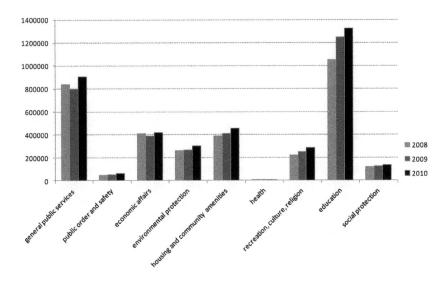

Figure 2.7   Expenditures according to selected COFOG categories in 2008–10 (in thousand EUR)

Source: Ministry of Finance of the Slovak Republic, 2012.

and central state institutions. In the case of Slovakia, the main players were central government (represented by the Prime Minister or the Ministry of Finance) and local self-governments (represented by their main associations). They negotiated various issues concerning the impact of the crisis at the local level, and the local self-government role in public finance consolidation. These relations developed across multiple phases with varying priorities and outcomes. Nevertheless, their coordinated effort guaranteed acceptable financial conditions for local self-government functioning and the delivery of services during the crisis.

It should be mentioned that at the beginning of the crisis there was a lack of significant debate focusing on the crisis' potential implications for local self-governments (latter half of 2008). It reflected the general social mood that Slovakia would not be seriously hit by the crisis. In the field of local finance, representatives of local self-governments paid greater attention to their standard agenda, even in December 2008. For example, they debated the financing of delegated powers and selected development programmes. Until the beginning of 2009, the crisis was not included in the main agenda of ZMOS's main bodies, although certain warnings had already emerged (Obecné Noviny, 2009a).

The crisis started to culminate within the Slovak economy at the end of January 2009. It stimulated the mobilisation of all institutions to search for anti-crisis measures. The central state initiated the first meeting of the national ad hoc body – the Economic Crisis Council (29th January), which included representatives of central government, employers, trade unions and banks, as well as ZMOS (this body had been active during the peak months of the crisis in the first half of 2009). Only a few days earlier, the first ZMOS working commission had been established by its Board to monitor the situation and consider necessary measures to address local finance in 2009 (Obecné Noviny, 2009b). The central government considered local self-governments as important partners – it had been aware that some measures could touch their financing and functioning. After the meeting on 6th February (Prime Minister, Minister of Finance and ZMOS Board), on 13 February 2009 the *Memorandum on cooperation in solving impacts of the financial and economic crisis on Slovak society between the Government of the Slovak Republic and the Association of towns and communities of Slovakia* was signed (in Slovak – *Memorandum o spolupráci pri riešení dopadov finančnej a hospodárskej krízy na slovenskú spoločnosť medzi Vládou SR a ZMOS; Association of Towns and Communities of Slovakia* – ZMOS, 2009). This memorandum provided the basic framework for adjustments concerning measures adopted against the crisis, and that involved local self-governments. It included the interim validity of certain measures adopted, stopped further transfers of powers to the local level and guaranteed certain compensations to local budgets related to anti-crisis measures adopted by the central level. Local self-governments promised to develop their own measures and willingness to adopt more prudent fiscal approaches. Among other initiatives, a specific declaration was prepared by the participants of the round table – *Economic crisis impact – challenges and solution for local self-government*, initiated by the mayor of Bratislava at the beginning of March 2009 (Obecné Noviny, 2009c). The real scope of crisis impact was not clear in March 2009, and representatives of local self-government were focusing on proposals to mitigate the crisis in general (for example addressing public finance and national economy). ZMOS prepared a 'package' of proposed measures to mitigate the crisis impact and sustain economic growth in April 2009 (Obecné Noviny, 2009d). It identified fields with the potential to generate employment at the local level (for example in anti-flood measures, energy savings, waste management, local roads, housing), possible sources of their financing (EU funds, special state funds) and mentioned the need to prepare new strategic development documents, as well as related legislative changes.

This framework preceded the adoption of new anti-crisis-oriented legislation – amendments concerning budgetary rules (Act No. 583/2004 as of Act No. 54/2009) and income taxes (as Act No. 60/2009). It released selected strict rules in local financing. For example, it allowed the use of capital income to cover current expenditures. Also allowed was more extensive spending without the obligation to have a budget in balance or surplus (in fact it meant more freedom in borrowing) until the end of 2010. The most damaging measure introduced by central government was increasing the tax deductible minimum for personal income tax (interim until the end of 2010). It generated a loss of available resources for local budgets, later multiplied by increased unemployment and salary freezes. During the first months of 2009, in many cases local self-government had adopted preventive measures to save some resources, but on a moderate scale (for example

3–5 per cent of current expenditures). However, as soon as May and June 2009 it was already clear that the negative effects of the crisis would be much deeper.

Despite the aforementioned central-local basic anti-crisis coordination as expressed for example in the *Memorandum on cooperatio*, local self-governments (as well as regional self-governments) were not directly involved in central state measures. Although quite a large number of central state measures were adopted, local self-governments did not participate in their direct implementation. For example, they were not involved in the extended public investments that remained under central state control. Aligned with the deepening of the crisis at the local level, the initial atmosphere of mutual understanding between central government and local self-governments was subsequently strained. As Buček (2010) pointed out, local self-governments were not satisfied with the strong restrictions they faced, while in contrast central government finances were increasing due to various measures and a lack of any notable spending cuts.

The rising tide of dissatisfaction had been expressed in various ways, especially after the sharp decrease of PIT yield transfer and adjusted forecast prepared by the Ministry of Finance concerning PIT tax income that appeared in summer 2009 (declared 17 per cent annual decrease in PIT income, or EUR 230 mln for 2009 and EUR 379 mln for 2010). Such development was considered unacceptable. Statements of disappointment were addressed to the Ministry of Finance by individual mayors, regional association of towns and communities (for example local self-governments from the Žilinský region in northern Slovakia), as well as the Union of Cities (for example Obecné Noviny, 2009e). Growing difficulties and pressure forced the Ministry of Finance to negotiate with representatives of ZMOS from July to October 2009 (including the formation of a joint working group). As compensation, ZMOS demanded EUR 130 mln for 2009 and EUR 200 mln for 2010. As a potential step in favour of such compensation, representatives of local self-governments proposed distributing 6.2 per cent state share of PIT to local and regional self-governments. This represented a change in PIT distribution formula to 75 per cent for local self-governments and 25 per cent to regional self-governments, and no share for the state budget (Obecné Noviny, 2009f). As a result, a special transfer to local budgets was negotiated in favour of local self-governments. As partial compensation for the income lost by lower PIT yield, they obtained EUR 100 mln for 2009 (in December 2009). These resources had to be obligatorily used for current expenditures, but not for salaries (Obecné Noviny, 2010a). A similar compensation package of EUR 72.5 mln was also announced for 2010, which was subsequently decreased to EUR 40 mln.

Central-local relations in the financial sphere were influenced by persisting lower yield from PIT, and calls for its compensation to local self-governments in 2010. In April local self-governments requested at least EUR 33 mln compensatory subvention, which was granted (Obecné Noviny, 2010b). Local self-governments pressed for subsequent compensation payments, especially after the repeated very low transfer of PIT yield during the spring and summer of 2010 (even compared to 2009). However, due to the parliamentary elections held in June 2010 and related changes in the government coalition, no important decisions were taken at the central level during this period. More symbolic and administrative was for example the decision to transfer the share of PIT tax yield one week earlier in July 2010 (Obecné Noviny, 2010c). The new central government considered local self-governments as a new opportunity for the negotiation of their need to mitigate the influence of the crisis. Besides financial compensation totalling EUR 141 mln, they emphasised the need to speed up the refunding of pre-financed expenditures spent on EU financed projects, as well as refunding new powers in social services. They also attempted to again open the issue of total PIT yield distribution only to self-governments (Obecné Noviny, 2010d). It should be mentioned that some interim changes ended in 2010 (such as the increased deductible tax minimum). The situation of local self-governments and their combined efforts also influenced the better economic outlook for 2011.

Local self-governments' tax revenues still suffered from the high unemployment rate and stagnating wages in 2011. A large oscillation also remained in the monthly transfers of PIT yield to local self-government (lower transfers in May and June). Nevertheless, the resources available to local self-government from PIT increased in comparison to the previous two years. Later in 2011 were the first proposals from the new central government concerning changes in the public finance system. Such also concerned local self-government. Among the most debated changes were proposals for the obligatory substantial increase of real estate property taxes (purely a local tax) at about 50 per cent, and the reduced share of local self-governments of PIT yield of a similar financial value. This was rejected by local self-governments. They also asked for a reasonable part (30–50 per cent) of the subvention provided to the Slovak Republic from the EU Solidarity Fund (Obecné Noviny, 2011a).

The central government proposal to change the main source of tax income for local self-governments initiated one of the largest mobilisations in the history of self-governments. The stable percentage share of PIT (since 2005) should have been replaced by a 'tax-mix' based on 9.72 per cent yield from the basket of main taxes (PIT, VAT, consumption taxes; National Council of the Slovak Republic 2011). This was refused by ZMOS as the main association of local self-governments, because they anticipated it would lead to lower income and financing difficulties for small self-governments (rural, small cities). The opposition was so strong that ZMOS called its first extraordinary congress in its twenty-plus-year history (Obecné Noviny, 2011b). Under such pressure, the legislative proposal that would have introduced this change was withdrawn before the second reading in the Slovak Parliament. Nevertheless, under the influence of the necessary fiscal consolidation, the share of local self-government of PIT yield decreased from 70.3 per cent to 65.4 per cent. This represented a compromise solution that guaranteed 7 per cent annual increase of total yield in financial terms for 2012. This was also balanced by the inclusion of local self-governments (as well as regional self-governments) into the constitutional act on budgetary responsibility (or colloquially 'debt brake act') and participation in public finance consolidation

(Trend, 2011). As a result, the debt of self-governments is not allowed to exceed 60 per cent of the previous year's current income (under the threat of penalty). The state does not guarantee the solvency of individual self-governments, and new powers cannot be transferred to self-governments without the related financial controls. Part of the new fiscal limits will be valid from 1 January 2015, providing time for adjustments in individual local self-governments.

From the previous paragraphs we can conclude that the debate between these two partners had more phases: initial and less intensive at the beginning of the crisis in the second half of 2008 (I); a deepening of the crisis leading to the intensification of the anti-crisis effort in spring 2009 (II) – however still with a less active role for local self-governments; facing stronger consequences of the crisis and following the publication of more realistic fiscal forecasts in the second half of 2009 (III), the pressure and activity of local self-governments to protect their financial interests increased; the next stage was negotiation within the 2010 state budget preparation in the second half of the year (IV); and the most intensive mobilisation caused the central government to plan, substantially changing the framework of local self-governmental finance during the second half of 2011 (V). While in the first phases it had been negotiation induced by the dynamics of the crisis, subsequently it followed the more general processes of public budgets preparation. The crisis became a longer term issue incorporated into standard processes of public finance management. Later developments were also influenced by longer periods of 'silence' and less activity caused by the change of central government, and a more positive macroeconomic development. In fact two points dominated these debates – taxes and central state compensations. Central-local relations in such a sensitive field and circumstances could not avoid short-term disruptions and mutual criticism. While local self-governments were criticised for increased borrowing and less cuts in spending, the central state was criticised by local self-governments for not responding sufficiently to their difficult financial situation. The delayed responses led to working less efficiently at local level. The local level also responded slowly, not calculating on such a deep escalation of the crisis into their budgets. Proposals from local self-governments were only heard in a minor scope (for example employment at the local level). Adopted measures were orchestrated predominantly by central government, as were their implementation.

Adaptation of Local Self-governments to the Crisis

Local self-governments had adapted quite successfully to the crisis in Slovakia. They were not so seriously hit, and avoided overly painful restrictions. Most could protect the standard and scope of services that they usually provided, and they prevented larger staff layoffs. Despite complications, they achieved acceptable progress in development as expressed in investments and own property value increased. In their responses, we can see measures that focused on revenues as well as expenditures. Such were reflected more in the internal restructuring of financial flows, and less in the significant decrease of financial options. While on the revenue side the search for the compensation of lost revenues dominated, on the expenditures side was the pressure for sustaining investments and cutbacks in current spending. The situation had been acceptable also thanks to the support of central state and access to EU funds. Despite focusing on own interests, local self-governments participated with understanding and solidarity in a social effort for public finance consolidation. They also avoided own measures that could have substantially increased the burden of the crisis on their citizens and local businesses.

We can highlight the most important adaptation techniques of Slovak local self-governments in the financial sphere that can be identified from aggregate data. Local self-governments avoided any radical measures that we could have expected under such conditions. Prevalent had been the search for compensation of declining revenues with other income sources. Extensive had been the use of returnable resources, mostly borrowing (as confirmed by debt growth) and the spending of own reserve funds. Local self-governments also carefully turned to the mobilisation of resources within their own local tax base (property tax and local taxes), but without any significant immediate increase of taxation (as well as no reduction of local taxation). They did not increase own local taxes, with the intention of limiting the burden of the crisis on local citizens and the business sector. Slowly evident was a progressive reduction in personnel costs, indicating the low increase of salaries and very limited increase (or even freeze) in staff numbers. Not surprisingly, we could observe standard short-term cuts in spending on goods and services, as the standard short-term method of reducing expenditures. Very reasonable can be perceived the prioritisation of investments into new buildings and public infrastructure, balanced by less investments into other assets.

The cohesive, clear and active representations of local self-governments by their associations against central state institutions was an important part of the success in preventing more devastating impacts of the crisis on their functioning. Nevertheless, local self-governments were less open, less flexible and less innovative in searching for measures to mitigate the crisis impact within central-local relations. Their approaches document the preference given to the preservation of the existing local finance framework that had been very beneficial for them already before the crisis. Such was expressed in strong efforts for the preservation or increase of PIT share, as the main source of their tax revenues. Very important is that the central state provided a stable basis with no cutbacks concerning standard transfers for local powers (for example in education). On the other hand, central government instability (parliamentary elections in 2010 and 2012) and internal diversity prevented the introduction of wider systemic changes in public finance, also in terms of local finance. It is questionable whether under a more compact central government coalition and longer term pressure for fiscal consolidation local self-governments would have been able to protect their current financial framework without making substantial changes.

The time aspects of local finance development during crisis are important issues from the perspective of institutional learning. The timing confirmed known experiences with a delay compared to the rest of the economy. Obstacles came later, thanks to procedures in tax collection and distribution. Although the first difficulties and serious financial scarcity emerged within the first 6–9 months after the crisis started, its impact and required adaptation culminated much later. If we consider October 2008 as the starting month of the crisis in Slovakia, it seems that a major impact in financial terms was observable within 18–24 months (approx. in 2010). This is confirmed especially by the decrease of PIT tax transfers to local budgets. While during the first months of the crisis local self-government functioned in accordance with planned budgets, they could use available reserves and so on, these possibilities subsequently became more limited. Mitigation of the crisis can be observed in 2011, when local finances were already closer to the standard situation. Although it seems that the situation in local finance has already improved, the crisis will continue to influence local self-government finance for years to come, especially due to the overall state of public finance in Slovakia.

The adaptation of local self-governments is also influenced by budgetary procedures and officially published public finance forecasts. Local budgets are also political documents that must be adopted by the Local (City) Council (as well as in the case of substantial changes) and its preparation requires a long period. Local budgets for 2009 were adopted before the crisis had started to strongly influence the real financial situation. Hence adaptation strategies were less deep in 2009, compared for example to 2010. Budgets for 2010 were already prepared within a different set of general expectations, and also keeping in mind the forecasts indicating the crisis' impact on the economy and public finance in Slovakia. Nevertheless, less precise public finance forecasts prepared under the supervision of the Ministry of Finance that are used in the drawing up of local budgets in coming years also contributed to insufficient responses. Such forecasts were mostly more optimistic than the actual development (for example tax revenues), and partially caused a larger gap between revenues and expenditures.

The Slovak local self-government financial system demonstrated quite a high level of robustness, as well as adaptation flexibility to mitigate the effects of the crisis. This has multiple reasons, which demonstrates that the current system has its advantages. As far as tax revenues are concerned, despite the decline in yields, the level of dependence on PIT share has been acceptable. Compared to other tax revenue options, PIT is a better choice as it is less sensitive and oscillating, for example compared to corporate taxes or VAT. As an analogy, quite suitable is the real estate property tax income framework. Due to the fact that Slovak local self-governments apply *non ad valorem* taxation (combining the size and location of real estate property), such tax generates more stable income compared to value based on real estate property taxation (with potential annual changes related to the devaluation of property), or unstable income from property transactions as applied in some countries (see for example Davey, 2011). Tradition and experience from the transition period can be considered to have played a role too. Most local self-governments used to have reserve funds available in times of (unexpected) scarcity. Due to the longer term regulation of local borrowing, they also had the capacity to borrow. Their access to required credits was not a problem thanks to the very limited effect of the crisis in the Slovak banking sector (municipal bonds are in fact not used). Current and new limits prevent too high local indebtedness in the future. Local self-governments avoided the sudden cuts and substantial financial restructuring that could be damaging. Of course, we should bear in mind the quite good situation in public finance in general. This allowed the central state to adopt a compensatory approach to local self-governments, compared to states with more urgent public finance scarcity. Besides the stable central state transfers, an important role is played by access to EU funds in protecting progress in local development (new investments). Part of the ability to adapt is related to the current division of powers, with the limited role of local self-government in crisis-sensitive fields of expenditures such as the financing of social welfare, housing and unemployment assistance.

Another issue is to which extent local self-governments contributed to the stabilisation and stimulation of the local and national economy, as well as public finance consolidation (despite their minor role from the macroeconomic perspective). Slovak local self-government did not substantially contribute to increased unemployment. According to the aggregate data, we consider that no substantial reduction in employment occurred. However, they were also unable to contribute to the creation of new workplaces. Miller and Svara (2009) see expanding or accelerating local capital projects as an option. The effort to sustain capital investments with reserves and borrowing has also had a positive and stimulating effect, also in the Slovak case. Their cutbacks in the procurement of goods and services were also mostly temporary. Local self-governments avoided any sharp increase in local taxes, user or administrative fees that could have harmed the business sector. After the criticism, local self-governments turned to more prudent financial behaviour that contributed more to the needed public finance consolidation, for example in reducing deficits and decreasing borrowing (at least in 2011).

We have to be aware that there are also large disparities in the financial situation between individual self-governments. This also means a wide range of responses compared to those outlined in local self-government adaptation to crisis. Such varied responses reflect diverse local conditions, local fiscal capacity, property situation, availability of reserve funds, access to credit links and so on. Numerous local self-governments were under fiscal pressure even before the crisis arrival. Unexpected and long term, this crisis caused difficulties especially to this group of local self-governments. There are documented cases of individual cities in Slovakia where such adopted measures were quite serious.

Conclusion

One of the key features of local self-governments functioning during the crisis was the less stable, less predictable and less autonomous financial environment. Such was not good news after the long-term effort for the stabilisation of basic frameworks and decentralisation of powers, which came into practice from the mid-2000s in Slovakia. It represents a reverse development, returning this level of government to a similarly unstable transitional period. Financial scarcity and dependency on transfers and grants provided by the central state or EU funds also reduces local fiscal autonomy. It is in fact against the longer term effort to increase the autonomy of local financing. It is against the priorities of the decentralisation process introduced one decade earlier that was considered a substantial part of the modernisation process of the post-socialist transition.

Experience has confirmed the importance of having well-functioning and responsible intergovernmental relations. Nevertheless, either central governments or local self-governments were unable to obtain support for their 'extreme' opinions in key tax issues (tax mix in the case of central state, as well as no PIT share for the state by local self-governments). This documents the moderate approaches that were possible. Finally, all government levels contributed to the fiscal consolidation processes in an acceptable manner. The situation of local self-governments positively influenced the efficient and active representation of local self-governments towards central government. But some strategic measures will be adopted during 2012 as a result of new central government activities, as well as the pressure of 'Fiscal Compact' initiated measures.

The situation of local government finance also indicated some opportunities that could be changed and which can act as 'first line' preventive measures against financial difficulties at the local level. Besides the limits already introduced within the 'fiscal brake' legislation, further options abound. If the gateway for the financial crisis to penetrate into local finance was largely dependent on PIT as shared tax and its oscillating yield, a certain emergency bottom limit of transfers can be introduced, for example on a monthly basis (to avoid sudden decreases with serious impacts). This is better and is efficiently manageable at the central level, and balanced within the framework of subsequent monthly transfers. The second option is the need to consider a shift toward more diverse and balanced local revenues. Reserve funds also appeared useful in preventing the escalation of the crisis at the local level. Rules, situations and obligatory limits for minimum reserve funds at the local level could be established. Among eventual measures could be the more efficient and preventive monitoring of the financial situation in individual self-governments (rating, automatic warning system), detecting fiscal stress (see for example Coe, 2008) with the more sophisticated use of information amassed by the Ministry of Finance. This should include regular information for their citizens regarding the financial situation by way of simple ratings. Nevertheless, financial planning and cash flow management should be improved. Local self-government can calculate for the already known annual cyclical nature of selected transfers (repeated decline in the spring). Public finance forecasting should be improved, and better fit the needs of local finance.

Acknowledgements

This contribution had been supported by VEGA Grant No. 1/0709/11 'Adaptability of spatial systems during the post-transformation period'.

References

Aalbers, M., 2009. 'Geographies of the financial crisis'. *Area*, 41, pp. 34–42.

Act No. 583/2004 on budgetary rules as amended by Act No. 54/2009.

Act 595/2003 Coll. on income tax as amended by Act No. 60/2009.

Association of Towns and Communities of Slovakia – ZMOS, 2009. Memorandum on co-operation in solving impacts of financial and economic crisis on the Slovak society between the Government of the Slovak Republic and the Association of Towns and Communities of Slovakia (in Slovak). Available at:<http>//ww.zmos.sk> [Accessed 23 March 2012].

Buček, J., 1993. 'Problémes de financement municipal en Slovaquie'. *Bulletin de la Societe Languedocienne de Geographie*, 116(3–4), pp. 335–45.

Buček, J., 2010. 'Municipal assets of the capital of the Slovak Republic Bratislava during global financial and economic crisis (in Slovak)'. *Geographia Cassoviensis*, 4(1), pp. 24–7.

Buček, J., 2010. 'The financial and economic crisis in Slovakia – its spatial aspects and policy responses'. In Gorzelak, G. and Goh, C. (eds), *Financial Crisis in Central and Eastern Europe: From Similarity to Diversity*, Warsaw: Wydawnictwo Naukowe Scholar, pp. 190–208.

Buček, J., 2012. 'Crisis in Slovakia 2009-2010: From saving the economy to saving public finance'. In Gorzelak, G., Goh C. and C. Fazekas, K. (eds), *Adaptality and Change – the Regional Dimensions in Central and Eastern Europe*, Warsaw: Wydawnictwo Naukowe Scholar, pp. 329–54.

Clarke, S.E. ed., 1989. *Urban Innovation and Autonomy – Policy Implications of Policy Change*, Newbury Park: SAGE.

Coe, C.K., 2008. 'Preventing Local Government Fiscal Crises: Emerging Best Practices'. *Public Administration Review*, 68(4), pp. 759–67.

Constitutional Act No. 493/2011 on Budgetary Responsibility.

Council of European Municipalities and Regions – CEMR, 2009. *The economic and financial crisis – Impact on regional and local authorities*. Brussels/Paris: CEMR

Davey, K. ed., 2011. Local government in critical times: Policies for Crisis, Recovery and a Sustainable Future – Council of Europe texts. Strasbourgh: Council of Europe Centre of Expertise for Local Government Reform.

Eurostat, 2012. Labour productivity per person employed. Available at: <http:// epp.eurostat.ec.europa.eu> [Accessed 6 April 2012].

Financial Directorate of the Slovak Republic, 2012. Personal income tax yield according to months. Available at: <http://www.drsr.sk/wps/portal> [Accessed 11 April 2012].

Gorzelak, G. and Goh, C. (eds), 2010. *Financial Crisis in Central and Eastern Europe: From Similarity to Diversity*, Warsaw: Wydawnictwo Naukowe Scholar.

Gorzelak, G., Goh C. and Fazekas, K. (eds), 2012. *Adaptality and Change – the Regional Dimensions in Central and Eastern Europe*, Warsaw: Wydawnictwo Naukowe Scholar.

Harvey D., 2011. 'Roepke Lecture in Economic Geography – Crises, Geographic Disruptions and the Uneven Development of Political Responses'. *Economic Geography*, 87(1), pp. 1–22.

Kling, J. and Nižňanský, V., 2004. 'Local Borrowing in Slovakia: From Deregulation to Regulation and Stabilization'. In P. Swianiewicz (ed.), *Local Government Borrowing: Risks and Rewards: A Report on Central and Eastern Europe*, Budapest: OSI/LGI, pp. 175–226.

Lobao, L.M. and Adua, L., 2011. 'State rescaling and local governments' austerity policies across the USA 2001–2008'. *Cambridge Journal of Regions, Economy and Society*, 4, pp. 419–35.

Martin, R., 2011. 'The local geographies of the financial crisis: from the housing bubble to economic recession and beyond'. *Journal of Economic Geography*, 11, pp. 587–618.

Miller, G.J. and Svara, J.H. eds, 2009. *Navigating the Fiscal Crisis: Tested Strategies for Local Leaders* (A White Paper prepared for ICMA by the Alliance for Innovation). Arizona State University.

Ministry of Finance of the Slovak Republic, 2012. *Final Account of the Slovak Republic 2008–2011.*

National Council of the Slovak Republic, 2011. Governmental proposal of Act on allocation of tax yield to self-government No. 503. Available at: http://www. nrsr.sk [Accessed 10 August 2012].

Obecné Noviny, 2009a. 'Financial crisis will not threat good quality of self-government work in 2009 (in Slovak)'. *Obecné Noviny*, 19(1–2), p. 3.

Obecné Noviny, 2009b. '10th meeting of ZMOS Board – Communique (in Slovak)'. *Obecné Noviny*, 19(7), p. 3.

Obecné Noviny, 2009c. 'First round table meeting in Bratislava (in Slovak)'. *Obecné Noviny*, 19(11), pp. 12–13.

Obecné Noviny, 2009d. 'Proposal of ZMOS measures to mitigate financial crisis impact and sustaining economic growth in the Slovak Republic (in Slovak)'. *Obecné Noviny*, 19(15), pp. 3–4.

Obecné Noviny, 2009e. 'According to mayors cities are facing collapse (in Slovak)'. *Obecné Noviny*, 19(30), p. 3.

Obecné Noviny, 2009f. 'ZMOS Board resolution, Bratislava August 5th, 2009 (in Slovak)'. *Obecné Noviny*, 19(33–4), p. 3.

Obecné Noviny, 2010a. 'Calculation and purpose of use (in Slovak)'. *Obecné Noviny*, 20(5), p. 3.

Obecné Noviny, 2010b. 'Ministry of Finance has EUR 33 mln at disposal for contribution to the local budgets (in Slovak)'. *Obecné Noviny*, 20(17), p. 3.

Obecné Noviny, 2010c. 'Finance for cities and villages one week earlier (in Slovak)'. *Obecné Noviny*, 20(27), p. 3.

Obecné Noviny, 2010d. 'The resolution of ZMOS concerning actual financial situation of local self-governments and PIT yield forecasts'. *Obecné Noviny*, 20(29), p. 3.

Obecné Noviny, 2011a. 'The 2nd meeting of new ZMOS Board – Communique (in Slovak)'. *Obecné Noviny*, 21(18), p. 3.

Obecné Noviny, 2011b. 'Self-government principally disagree with change of its financing and calls for extraordinary congress of ZMOS (in Slovak)'. *Obecné Noviny*, 20(39), pp. 1–2.

Pailais, T., 2009. *Local Governments and the Financial Crisis: An Analysis*, Washington: Cities Alliance.

Rohoška, R., 2012. *Real Estate Property Taxation in Slovak Cities: Factors of Differentiation* (in Slovak). Unpublished MSc Thesis. Bratislava: Comenius University, Department of Human Geography and Demography.

Sedmihradska, L., Bobcheva, N. and Lados, M., 2011. *Local government finance in times of crisis – An early assessment*, Bratislava: NISPAcee.

Smith, A. and Swain, A., 2010. 'The Global Economic Crisis, Eastern Europe, and the Former Soviet Union: Models of Development and the Contradictions of Internationalization'. *Eurasian Geography and Economics,* 51(1), pp. 1–34.

Staehr, K., 2010. 'The global financial crisis and public finances in nthe new EU countries in Central and Eastern Europe: Development and challenges'. *Public Finance and Management*, 10(4), pp. 671–712.

Statistical Ofice of the Slovak Republic, 2012a. Macroeconmic statistics. Available at: <http://www.statistics sk> [Accessed 4 April 2012].

Statistical Office of the Slovak Republic, 2012b. Foreign Trade Statistics. Available at: <http://www.statistics sk> [Accessed 10 September 2012].

Statistical Office of the Slovak Republic, 2012c. Unemployment statistics according to labour force survey. Available at: <http://www.statistics sk> [Accessed 4 April 2012].

Trend, 2011. State will limit local budgets (in Slovak). 1 December. Available at: <http://ekonomika.etrend.sk> [Accessed 7 August 2012].

UPSVAR 2012. Monthly unemployment statistics. Available at: <http://www.upsvar.sk> [Accessed 4 April 2012].

Chapter 3

The Economic Adjustment Program Impact on Local Government Reform in Portugal

Carlos Nunes Silva

Introduction

The XIX Government program includes as one of its main objectives the reform of local government (Governo de Portugal, 2011). This has been in the political agenda almost since the first revision of the democratic Constitution in 1976 but this time the constraints determined by the economic adjustment program seem to have created the conditions for the implementation of some of the most controversial of these proposals.

The chapter addresses the following research question: to what extent did the economic adjustment program (2011–14) determine the content and the method adopted in the current local government reform in Portugal? For that, the chapter examines and discusses the adjustment program, in particular its proposals in the field of local government, and argues that the nature and the extent of some of the 'local state' reforms have been in part required and/or facilitated by this program. Nonetheless, the analysis also shows that part of it, as is the case of the reduction of the number of parishes, had been tried or initiated by previous governments, supported by a different political majority in Parliament. The chapter describes the main options and the rationale behind some of these political options and describes measures related to local government or with a direct impact on this sub-national tier of public administration.

In what follows, the chapter is organized into 3 main parts. In the first – Local Government Reforms in Portugal – the chapter offers an overview of local government reforms implemented in the last decades. The second part examines and discusses the structure and content of the economic adjustment program (EC/ECB/IMF, 2011) and how it impacts on local government. The third part analyses each of the four components of the local government reform proposed by the XIX Constitutional Government. The chapter ends with some concluding remarks on the implementation of the proposed reform and on the need to monitor its impacts.

Local Government Reforms in Portugal

The political regime overthrown in 1974 was characterized by a highly centralized administrative organization. The two sub-national tiers of public administration, the municipality and the parish, were part of the state administration (administrative deconcentration) and not forms of local self-government (administrative decentralization). The competences, the financial capacity and the human resources were very limited.

It was against this background that the new democratic regime adopted, in the political Constitution approved in 1976, a model of local self-government with three tiers, comprising the region, the municipality and the parish (Amaral, 2008; Canotilho and Moreira, 1993; Miranda, 2007). While for the municipality and parish were adopted the existing maps (304 municipalities and 4,025 parishes) for the region the decision was postponed and has never been implemented. Its creation suffered a severe setback in 1998 when its implementation was rejected in a national referendum (Silva, 2000a). Despite all the institutional changes introduced since then, Portugal continues to be one of the most centralized countries in Europe.

This part of the Constitution related to the local government system was, to a certain point, a compromise between perspectives that favoured forms of direct democracy and those that were in favour of representative democracy. The first local elections took place in December 1976 and since then several changes have been introduced in the local government system. The structure and competences of municipalities and parishes were first defined in 1977, and the first local government finance system in 1979. In the first years of the democratic regime, different perspectives on local self-government emerged and to some extent the reforms proposed and implemented in the last three decades can be described as the result of the continuous confront between contrasting perspectives (representative democracy/direct democracy; proportional/majority representation; mono party executive board/proportional representation in the executive; finance system based on local taxes/based mainly on transfers and so on).

The successive reforms of the 1976 Constitution introduced changes or led indirectly to changes in the local government system. The first major attempt was made in 1982 by the Social-Democrat Party and the Christian Democrat/Popular Party (the two parties that support the current XIX Government) following the first revision of the Constitution in that same year (Silva, 1995). Although not implemented, due to changes in the political circumstances, the proposal touched almost all the key aspects of the system. To a certain point, some of the principles that support the current reform were already present in this first attempt. The second Constitutional revision, in 1989, eliminated from the system forms of citizen participation still closely linked with the principles of direct democracy, introduced in the 1976 Constitution as part of the political compromise reached after the Revolution.

All the following political majorities introduced changes of one sort or another in the local government system. The coalition between the Socialist Party and the Social-Democratic Party was responsible for the 1984 reform, which included the approval of the second local government finance law. The following political majority (a single party majority – Social Democrat Party) introduced important changes in the competences, in the municipal organization and association and in the local finance system, among other aspects. Important changes were also introduced by the two socialist governments that followed, separated in a short period by a coalition government between the Social Democrat Party and the Popular Party (Silva, 2009).

If the previous local government reforms have been an attempt to correct aspects of the original local government system that the practice proved to be no longer appropriate, or to be unacceptable from the point of view of one of the two main political majorities that have rotated in power in the last three decades, the reform proposed by the XIX Government, a coalition between the Social Democrat Party and the Popular Party, in 2011, in the context of the economic adjustment program, although retaining some of the previous political arguments and proposals of these two political parties, seems to be much more determined than previous ones by the need to reduce public expenditures, within a much broader rationale, even if only unsatisfactorily defined, reform of the state. This is what the following sections of this chapter aim to examine and discuss.

The Economic Adjustment Program (2011–14)[1] and its Impact on Local Government Reform

In 2010, the general government deficit was 10 per cent of GDP and expenditure was 51 per cent of GDP. In the first two years (2011–12) of the economic adjustment

---

1 Portugal: Memorandum of Understanding on specific economic policy conditionality, 3 May 2011: 'With regard to Council Regulation (EU) no 407/2010 of 11 May 2010 establishing a European Financial Stabilisation Mechanism, and in particular Article 3(5) thereof, this Memorandum of Understanding details the general economic policy conditions as embedded in Council Implementing Decision [...] of [...] on granting Union financial assistance to Portugal. The quarterly disbursement of financial assistance from the European Financial Stabilisation Mechanism (EFSM) will be subject to quarterly reviews of conditionality for the duration of the programme. The first review will be carried out in the third quarter of 2011, and the 12-th and last review in the second quarter of 2014. Release of the instalments will be based on observance of quantitative performance criteria, respect for EU Council Decisions and Recommendations in the context of the excessive deficit procedure, and a positive evaluation of progress made with respect to policy criteria in the Memorandum of Economic and Financial Policies (MEFP) and in this Memorandum of Understanding on specific economic policy conditionality (MoU), which specifies the detailed criteria that will be assessed for the successive reviews up to the end of the programme. The review taking place in any given quarter will assess compliance

program the deficit was cut in half and expenditures reduced to 45 per cent of GDP. Further fiscal adjustment is planned for 2013–14 (EC/ECB/IMF, 2011).

Although the size of the state, and for that matter also that of the local state, and its functions, are a matter of political choice, in the current economic and financial circumstances the reforms proposed seem to have been driven more by the financial requirements of the adjustment program than by an autonomous national political decision. The changes underway will affect the size of the local state (for example, number of local governments units; local public service provision, in particular universal access and so on), and the local finance system. The discussion of the functions of the state, within the scope of the Constitution, will certainly have a direct impact on local government expenditure levels and in policy outcomes. As the economic adjustment program seeks to achieve by 2014 a considerable permanent annual expenditure reduction, the reforms proposed in this context by national government aims, among other aspects, to enhance efficiency in the provision of goods and services to the population, which, combined with the need to reduce the public debt, requires significant public spending reduction.

The Memorandum of Understanding (MoU) on Specific Economic Policy Conditionality

The Memorandum of Understanding (MoU) is organized into 7 main sections (EC/ECB/IMF, 2011): i) Fiscal policy (subdivided in specific fiscal policy objectives and measures for each of the three years, 2012–14); ii) financial sector regulation and supervision; iii) fiscal-structural measures (public finance management framework; budgetary framework; public private partnerships; state-owned enterprises; privatization; revenue administration; public administration; health care system); iv) labour market and education (labour market; education and training); v) goods and services markets (energy markets; telecommunications and postal services; transport; others); vi) housing market; vii) framework conditions (judicial system; competition, public procurement and business environment).

---

with the conditions to be met by the end of the previous quarter. If targets are missed or expected to be missed, additional action will be taken. The authorities commit to consult with the European Commission, the ECB and the IMF on the adoption of policies that are not consistent with this Memorandum. They will also provide the European Commission, the ECB and the IMF with all information requested that is available to monitor progress during programme implementation and to track the economic and financial situation. Prior to the release of the installments, the authorities shall provide a compliance report on the fulfilment of the conditionality' (EC/ECB/IMF, 2011, p. 1).

'On 8 April 2011, Eurogroup and ECOFIN Ministers issued a statement clarifying that EU (European Financial Stabilisation Mechanism) and euro-area (European Financial Stability Facility) financial support would be provided on the basis of a policy programme supported by strict conditionality and negotiated with the Portuguese authorities, duly involving the main political parties, by the Commission in liaison with the ECB, and the IMF' (MoU, p. 1)

In the first section of the MoU on fiscal policy, the document states that the main objective is to reduce the government deficit up to a balanced budgetary position in the medium term by adopting measures on both expenditure and revenue side (for example public administration deficit 5.9 per cent of GDP in 2011, 4.5 per cent of GDP in 2012, and 3.0 per cent of GDP in 2013). In order to achieve that, a number of measures have been adopted specifically for local government, identifying which ones should be followed in each year (for example, 2012 to 2014): reorganization of local government and the provision of central administration services at the local level; promotion of staff mobility in central, regional and local administrations; introduction of limits to staff admissions in public administration aiming to achieve annual decreases in 2012–14 of 2 per cent in local and regional administration; freezing of wages in the government sector in nominal terms in 2012 and 2013 and limitation of promotions; reduction of transfers to local and regional authorities with a view to having this sub-sector contributing to fiscal consolidation; introduction of changes in property taxation to raise revenue by reducing substantially the temporary exemptions for owner-occupied dwellings; introduction of changes in the transfers from central to local governments to ensure that the additional revenues are fully used for fiscal consolidation (EC/ECB/IMF, 2011). This is addressed by the third axis ('Municipal and Inter-municipal management and financing') of the local government reform proposed by the national government in its Green Book of Local Administration Reform presented in September 2011 (Governo de Portugal, 2011a).

In the third section – the fiscal structural measures – the MoU includes several proposals directly relevant for the current local government reform. The MoU explicitly refers the need to adapt the local and regional financial legal frameworks to the overall reform, namely the recently revised Budgetary Framework Law, by including all relevant public entities in the perimeter of local and regional government. In the case of the municipal enterprises, the MoU requires an evaluation of this sector and the application of new and more restrictive limits on the debt of municipal enterprises, as well as the need for a new legal framework regarding its creation, functioning, including stronger control powers by central government, and the suspension of the creation of this sort of organization until the new framework is adopted (EC/ECB/IMF, 2011).

In the field of property taxation, the measures adopted in the MoU have a clear impact in local government. 'The Government will review the framework for the valuation of the housing stock and for tax purposes and present measures to (i) ensure that by the end of 2012 the taxable value of all property is close to the market value and (ii) property valuation is updated regularly (every year for commercial real estate and once every three years for residential real estate as foreseen in the law)' (EC/ECB/IMF, 2011). All these issues are addressed in the first axis ('Municipal enterprises') of the local government reform proposed by the national government in its Green Book of Local Administration Reform.

The privatization proposed in the MoU requires 'an inventory of assets, including real estate, owned by municipalities and regional governments, examining the scope for privatization' (EC/ECB/IMF, 2011). Besides these actions, other structural measures included, for instance, proposals to increase the efficiency and cost effectiveness of public administration, through reductions in management jobs and in the number of administrative units, not only in central government but also in local and regional administration. Each municipality should present a plan to attain job reductions and cuts in the number of administrative units. This process includes also public and quasi-public entities, including foundations, associations and other bodies, which after due cost-benefit evaluation should be eventually closed, not only those related with central government but also with regional and local government. This is addressed by the third axis ('Municipal and Inter-municipal management and financing') of the Green Book of Local Administration Reform.

The MoU is clear about the need to reorganize local government administration. According to the MoU: 'central government should develop until July 2012 a consolidation plan for the reorganization and significant reduction of the number of municipalities and parishes, in articulation with EC and IMF staff. This reform, which will come into effect by the beginning of the next local election cycle, is expected to enhance service delivery, improve efficiency, and reduce costs'. This issue is addressed by the second and fourth axis ('territorial organization' and 'local democracy') of the Green Book of Local Administration Reform.

The MoU also requires the identification and correction of potential duplication of activities and other inefficiencies between central administration and local government, and between this and locally based central administration services. Human resources in local government should also be reduced by the introduction of a limit in staff admissions to achieve annual decreases in 2012–14 of 2 per cent in the total number of local administration employees.

In the field of 'Administrative burden', the MoU requires maintenance of the de-bureaucratization efforts implemented by previous governments. Besides other measures, the 'Zero authorization' project should also be applied in local government (for example, to abolish authorizations/licensing and to substitute them with a declaration to the Points of Single Contact for the wholesale and retail sector and restaurants and bars). The last recommendation in the MoU is related to this issue and proposes a reduction of administrative burdens, to be achieved through the application of the Simplex Program to the municipalities.

Rethinking the State: Selected Expenditure Reform Options

The idea that a 're-foundation of the State', in the sense that a deep reform of the social functions of the state is necessary, is a fundamental issue in the political rhetoric of the current government. As part of that process, the International Monetary Fund (IMF) released, in January 2013, the report 'Portugal. Rethinking the state – selected expenditure reform options' prepared in response to the request for technical assistance made by the Portuguese government (IMF, 2013). The aim of this report is to complement the analysis made by the national government on spending cuts as well as the discussion of the functions of the state. Even though different in its nature and objectives from the MoU, it is important to bring this document into consideration in the analysis of local government reform as some of its proposals may well be responsible for some of the options that will be taken and implemented in this field.

Although the main areas for spending reduction identified by the IMF in this report are two of the major budgets items – the government wage bill and pension spending (24 per cent of GDP and 58 per cent of non-interest government spending) – this will inevitably have direct consequences on local government budgets and also in its actual functions, namely if the reform in the education sector includes not only an overall reduction in employment in the sector, but also a transfer of new competences to local government in this sector, as has been considered on several occasions before. Besides permanent employment reduction, other reforms have also been considered in the report in the field of public employment (for example, compensation schemes to attract talent and labour mobility) which will also have an impact on local government. The second targeted area – pensions (for example, transition to a new system and changes in entitlements) – will impact local government indirectly, as it is expected that it will increase the demand for different forms of social support confronting municipalities and parishes.

In addition to these changes in public employment spending and pensions, the report recommends changes in other social spending programs (for example, family benefits, unemployment insurance and minimum income guarantee), as well as in the education and health systems, in both cases with a stronger emphasis on cost recovery, although not at the expense of universal access to quality services, which will inevitably impact on local government.

A number of conclusions and recommendations included in the report created a wave of negative responses, in different parts of the political spectrum, including large sections within the parties that support the government. In sum, the report discusses expenditure reform options in Portugal by reference to the debate on the size and functions of the state, as well as the reform experiences of other countries.

For the IMF, 'the focus of expenditure reform should be on improving equity and efficiency in the process of achieving certain outcomes. Better equity (e.g., through improved targeting) and better efficiency (e.g., through reduced spending) can often go hand-in-hand, and, together, they lay the foundations for achieving a more robust economic growth, sound public finances, and an exit from the crisis' (IMF, 2013).

Although focused mainly on central government functions and competences, some of the issues identified in the report and the proposals or recommendations made may have a direct impact in local government. For example, in the reform options suggested for fine-tuning non-pension social benefits, to promote effectiveness and equity, the IMF recommends the reform of programs that serve similar purposes including those given out by local governments. For example, 'the mean-testing for housing benefits given at the local level should be brought in line with the minimum income program (RSI)' (IMF, 2013: 51). The report supports the purpose of central government to put in place a system to monitor the total benefits received by households, which will (should) include the range of benefits being provided by central government (for example, RSI and family benefits) and by local governments (for example, housing support and other discretionary allowances).

The Local Government Reform: The Green Book Proposal

The local government reform proposed by the XIX Government (2011–), seen as a key instrument of its strategy to 'Change Portugal' ('Mudar Portugal'), is closely related with the MoU, despite the fact that most of these issues have already been considered by previous governments (for example, territorial reorganization of parishes; reform of the municipal enterprise sector). The reform proposed in the Green Book addresses four main areas: i) local government enterprises; ii) the organization of the territory; iii) municipal and inter-municipal management and local government finance; and iv) local democracy. It has two main objectives: to provide financial sustainability to the local government system; and to introduce a new paradigm of municipal management (Governo de Portugal, 2011a). In order to achieve these two objectives a number of policy options were identified: zero budget basis; scale economies in municipal management in both current expenditures and in capital investment; more transparent municipal government; simplified organizational structures; territorial cohesion; and reduction in local public expenditure.

Although some of these policy options have been in the political discourse of the current political majority for many years (Silva, 1995; 1996; 2000, 2004), its importance within the program of the XIX Government was reinforced by the political compromise taken by the Portuguese government in the context of the Economic Adjustment Program (EC/ECB/IMF, 2011), as in this document the Portuguese government agreed to reorganize local government until June 2012. This direct connection with the adjustment program meant that the main driver (and argument) in the proposed local government reform became unequivocally the reduction of costs through efficiency increases and improvements in public service provision. This required, among other changes, the reform of the local government finance system.

The proposed reform has four main axes: i) local government enterprises; ii) the organization of the territory; iii) municipal and inter-municipal management and local government finance; and iv) local democracy (Governo de Portugal, 2011a). Although all these issues are directly addressed in the MoU, they have also been in the political agenda before. The MoU seems to have been a catalyst for this process by offering the arguments for a speedy and comprehensive reform of local government in Portugal.

The way the reform was prepared and the importance of the changes included in the proposed reform of local government, which may even require revision of the Constitution, as the decision of the Constitutional Court on the Inter-municipal Communities prove (Tribunal Constitucional, 2013), places a number of uncertainties on the implementation of the reform. An administrative reform with this importance requires a larger political consensus than that of the political majority that voted it in Parliament. In the case of the territorial reorganization proposed, the debate should have considered other dimensions, namely issues of identity and the provision of local public services, which are certainly very important in rural parishes, as well as alternatives to the merger of parishes as is the use of different administrative regimes for different categories of local government units. The need to speed up the whole process in order to meet the timetable of the economic adjustment program seems to explain some of these deficiencies, which ultimately may be responsible for the failure of some of its key components.

Local Government Enterprises

In the first axis of the proposed reform – local government enterprises – the main goal is to reduce the number of entities and to adapt the sector to its strategic mission according to the local context and specific needs. This required the adoption of a new legal framework.[2] This reduction of the number of enterprises will be achieved through extinction or fusion. Municipal enterprises with negative results in three consecutive years and those in which more than 50 per cent of its income come from transfers from the municipality budget should be closed. The Memorandum of Understanding states that the Portuguese government will carry out an evaluation of the sector, will apply new and more restrictive debt limits, will increase national government control and will adopt a new legal framework for the creation and functioning of these enterprises, suspending temporarily the creation of new entities.

The Organization of the Territory

In the second axis – the organization of the territory – the main goal is the reduction of the actual number of parishes (4259), the lower tier of local self-government just below the municipality, although the reduction of municipalities is also considered.[3] A similar requirement exists in the MoU signed with Greece, initially in 2010[4] and

---

2 Law 52/2012, 31.08.2012, replaced the previous legal framework defined in Law 53-F/2006. The previous government, the XVIII Constitutional Government, launched the process for the reform of municipal and inter-municipal enterprises. A research study was commissioned to the UTL (ISEG, 2011) and a Commission (CALBSEL, 2011), whose aim was to produce recommendations based on that research report, was created. The information collected and the work of this commission was later incorporated by the new government in its proposal for the reform of the local enterprise sector.

3 The previous Government (XVIII Constitutional Government) announced, in March 2011, a series of debates to discuss the territorial reorganization of parishes (Oliveira, 2011).

4 Memorandum of Understanding between the European Commission acting on behalf of the Euro Area Members States, and the Hellenic Republic (EC, 2010a).

subsequently revised and amended, while in the case of Ireland, signed in 2010,[5] there is no such requirement for the reduction of local government units. The new parishes will be implemented in the next local elections that will take place in the second half of 2013. The reform aims to increase scale and size to allow the decentralization of more competences to this tier. This reform in the parish map will be complemented by a revision in the regime of competences of both parishes and municipalities. Contrary to the parishes, in the case of municipalities the aim is to provide incentives for a voluntary merger of municipalities, although a new legal framework for the compulsory territorial reorganization of municipalities is not ruled out by the national government as a next step in this reform process.

This component of the reform – local government territorial organization – was regulated in May 2012 (Law no. 22/2012) and the final outcome of this complex and controversial process was approved in January 2013.[6] Besides a detailed regulation of the reorganization of the territory at the lower tier of local government (parish/*freguesia*), this new legal framework also allowed the reduction of municipalities by voluntary fusion, providing financial incentives for that, although in practice municipalities did not adhere to these two possibilities and for that reason the municipal map remains the same as before. Law 22/2012 also allowed the transfer of parts of the territory from one municipality to another.[7] The entire process has been controversial[8] and, at the time of writing, a number of uncertainties about the result of the legal dispute make this an open process. In order to smooth the process, the law established a financial incentive for the cases in which the aggregation resulted from a voluntary agreement.[9] The political opposition voted against the new legal regime. In numerous municipalities all over the country even local councillors, members of the ruling parties, have opposed some aspects of this new legal regime. While there is an overall agreement that in some cases it is reasonable and beneficial to merge very small parishes in urban areas, and therefore punctual changes in the number and limits of parishes do make sense, disagreement seems to be the mark of this relatively blind reduction

---

5   Memorandum of Understanding between the European Commission and Ireland (EC, 2010b).

6   The new legal framework Law 22/2012 and Law 11-A/2013 replaced the previous legal framework (Law 11/82 and Law 8/93, on the creation of parishes). For a critical overview of this new legal framework see, among others, Batalhão (2012), Cruz and Silva (2012), Carneiro (2012), A.C. Oliveira (2011), F.P. Oliveira (2012), Alexandrino (2012).

7   One parish moved from one municipality (Santarém) to another (Golegã).

8   For example, it is worth to mention the reaction in Algarve. The proposal pointed for a reduction of around 18 parishes in the entire region of Algarve, which has 84 parishes; while a single municipality (Barcelos) in the Northern part of the country has 89 parishes.

9   In all new parishes the transfer from the state budget is equal to the sum of the transfer of the pre-existing parishes. In the new parishes resulting from a voluntary agreement there is a 15 per cent increase in the state transfer during the first four years. A similar incentive existed already in the Local Finance Law (Law 2/2007, article 33). In this case, an increase of 10 per cent for the new parish.

of parishes, in particular in rural areas. This reduction in the number of parishes, the largest ever done in Portugal since it became a sub-national administrative tier in the nineteenth century, will represent a major change in the local government structure. The merger of such a large number of parishes, announced several times but never completed, seems to have been possible mainly due to the conditions created by the MoU.

Municipal and Inter-municipal Management and Local Government Finance

In the third axis of the reform – municipal and inter-municipal management and local government finance – the goal is to rationalize the different forms of inter-municipal cooperation (for example, Inter-municipal Communities; Metropolitan Areas of Lisbon and Porto) avoiding repetition and functional redundancy between these upper tiers and the constituting municipalities and to cut down the management structures in the municipalities. Another goal is the differentiation and a better coordination of the competences of parishes, municipalities and the different forms of inter-municipal cooperation (Inter-municipal communities; Metropolitan Areas and so on), improving the democratic control and legitimacy of the metropolitan areas. Inter-municipal cooperation will also be addressed in order to avoid redundancies and to improve the quality of these organizations. The local finance system was treated separately from the other issues included initially in this third vector.

This issue – inter-municipal cooperation and metropolitan government – has been the target of several reforms in the past (Moreira, 2007; Silva, 2002; 2006; Silva and Syrett, 2005; 2006) and the need for a new one was being considered before the MoU (Amorim, 2009, 2009a; Lopes, 2009; Oliveira, 2009). For that reason, the assistance program is clearly not the driver of the ongoing reform although the context and the conditions set up by the program can be seen as a facilitator of what was proposed in the Green Book. A different issue is the nature of the supra-municipal entities that the government proposed, declared unconstitutional in a decision taken by the Constitutional Court in May 2013 (Tribunal Constitucional, 2013). In fact, the proposed reform, if implemented, would produce a dilution of the third tier of sub-national self-government, the administrative region, making its future implementation irrelevant. This and other similar court decisions on other reforms adopted by central government are sources of a profound uncertainty with the corresponding negative impact in the functioning of the system. In order to prepare the reform of competences and the transfer of new competences from the state to the municipalities and to the different forms of inter-municipal cooperation a pilot study was carried out in two inter-municipal communities, one predominantly rural and the other urban (DGAL, 2012). The proposed reform in the internal organization of municipalities also seeks the reduction of jobs, by determining a maximum according to the demographic size of the municipality.

Although not explicitly addressed in the Green Book for local administration reform, the regional organization of central government, the so-called CCDR (5

NUT-II regional boards), is a key variable in the way local and central government coordinate their policies, and for that reason should have been directly considered in the proposed local government reform. Having experienced several reforms in the past, since it was first created in 1969, it is now an institution more open to the participation of different local interests (Oliveira, 2008). Closely related with this issue, although not considered in the Green Book or in the MoU, is the long due implementation of the regional self-government tier established in the Constitution but which has never been implemented (Caupers, 2009), in clear opposition to what is written in the Constitution and against the widely accepted view on this issue, in particular within international organizations of which Portugal is a member, as is the case of the Council of Europe and its Congress of Local and Regional Authorities, or the Assembly of the European Regions.[10]

The reform of the local finance system, a key piece of the new architecture of local government in Portugal, is not yet concluded, although the basic structure of the new law is already known.[11] The revision of the previous local finance law, approved in 2007, is clearly required by the MoU, in particular due to the need to adapt to the new national budget rules, and is also considered in the Green Book of Local Administration Reform, in particular the need to reduce the dependency of municipal finance in relation to the real estate market (MoU, 2011; Rocha, 2011). Besides that, over the years the application of the 2007 law recommended the change or improvements of some aspects of the law which were also considered on this occasion[12] (Carvalho, 2009). A few basic principles structure this reform: i) a new paradigm for local government finance, adapted to the present circumstances; ii) transparency and accountability in all spheres of local government action; and iii) effective coordination between central and local government, budgetary control in order to avoid financial disequilibrium in municipal budgets. A number of new rules were introduced to guarantee balanced budgets, limited municipal debts, consolidated budgets and external audits of municipal accounts.

Local Democracy

The fourth axis of the proposed reform – local democracy – was intended to include a reform of the local electoral law, a new bill for local councillors, new rules for the constitution as well as the competences of the executive and deliberative boards

---

10   European Parliament (1988). Community Charter for Regionalization, 18.11.1988. Council of Europe (1985). European Charter of Local Self-Government, 15.10.1985. CLRA (2008). Draft European Charter of Regional Democracy – Recommendation 240 (2008) of the Congress of Local and Regional Authorities of the Council of Europe.

11   PL 609/2012, 2012.12.27 – proposal for a new local government law submitted to the Parliament (approved by the two parties that support the government – PSD and CDS; waits final discussion and approval by the Parliament).

12   RCM no. 18/2012, 13 February: create a technical commission to prepare a proposal for the new law.

of local government (municipalities and parishes). Changes in the supporting staff of the elected councillors are also part of the objectives of this reform. This reduction affects the number of elected members in both the executive board and in the assembly, as well in the number of staff directors due to the reduction in the number of board members. Besides the goal of cost reduction, the national government intends to introduce the following changes: i) a model of politically homogeneous executive boards in the municipality subjected to the control of the Municipal Assembly, which will receive more powers and competences; ii) the mayor is the number one of the wining list for the assembly being the other members of the executive chosen by the mayor among members of the municipal assembly;[13] and iii) reduction of the members of the executive board, based on the number of electors (in the municipalities of Lisbon and Porto: 12 and 10 councillors (*vereadores*), respectively; 6 full time in Lisbon; 5 full time in Porto; in municipalities with 100,000 or more electors: 8 councillors, of which 4 full time; municipalities with more than 50,000 and less than 100,000 electors: 6 councillors, of which 3 full time; municipalities with more than 10,000 and less than 50,000 electors: 4 councillors, of which 2 full time; municipalities with 10,000 or less: 2 councillors, of which 1 full time). At the same time, the Green Books proposes a reduction in the number of the municipal assembly members and stronger control powers for the municipal assembly over the executive board, reforming in favour of the assembly the present balance of powers between the two boards.[14]

Conclusion

In conclusion, the evidence reveals that some of the components of the local government reform were put in practice due to the political and social environment created by the economic adjustment program. However, despite this 'encouraging environment', the evidence also confirms, first, that the reform program is in practice shorter than what was included in the political program of this parliamentary majority and, secondly, that it has been unevenly implemented until now. In fact, if it is certain that the reform of local enterprises progressed, in part due to the fact that it was started by the previous government, even before the MoU established it as one of its goals, in the second vector of the reform – the territorial reorganization – the actual practice is much less than what was initially

---

13 This proposal has not been implemented yet, at the time of writing, as the two coalition parties have not reached agreement on this issue (Oliveira, 2012).

14 In May 2012 was adopted, by a group of local councillors, the Mirandela Declaration on Municipal Assemblies with a number of recommendations regarding the functioning of this board (Declaração de Mirandela sobre as Assembleias Municipais, 26.05.2012). The legal framework that rules the relation between the municipal assembly and the municipal executive board, both directly elected, is due to be changed as claimed in different occasions in the past. For a recent overview of this debate, see Amorim (2009), Oliveira (2009, 2012).

admitted, and faces strong opposition in numerous municipalities and parishes, some of which contested the law approved. In addition, the evidence available so far does suggest that there will be no significant reduction in public expenditures as a result of this territorial reform which makes it irrelevant for the objectives of the MoU.

It was confined to the lower tier of local government, the parishes, whose number has been significantly reduced, mainly through aggregation of previous units, and there are no prospects for a reduction of the number of municipalities as initially admitted by the political program of the XIX Government and by the MoU. This was a highly controversial process and it is still far from being completed as it has been contested in the courts by different stakeholders with some of these claims still waiting a court decision. In addition to this uncertainty, a reversal of the proposed new administrative map or of part of it cannot be completely ruled out since a number of these legal norms have been questioned by legal experts and political parties, as well as by citizens directly affected by the merger reform.

In part related with the territorial reform as well as with the management of municipal activities is the reform of inter-municipal cooperation and metropolitan governments. Some of the norms included in this legal framework were contested by different institutional stakeholders and were declared unconstitutional by the Constitutional Court, in May 2013. For that reason, the prospects for the inter-municipal cooperation model proposed are still uncertain at the time of writing.

Finally, the proposed reform of key elements of the local democracy is also far from completed and some of its key objectives, as is the case of electoral system for the municipal boards, which did not get the agreement of the parties in the coalition that supports the XIX Government, seem to have been abandoned.

The fact that the reform approved has only partially been implemented and the legal uncertainty about some of its key aspects recommends further research. It is also crucial to follow up the impacts of what has been approved and implemented in the various domains of this reform: merger reforms and the organization of the territory; local government enterprises; municipal management; inter-municipal cooperation; local government finance; and the different dimensions of local democracy touched by this reform.

References

Alexandrino, José Melo, 2012. 'A administração local autónoma: situação actual e propostas de reforma apresentadas na sequência do Memorando da Troika'. *Direito Regional e Local*, 18: 5–13.

Amaral, Diogo Freitas, 2008. *Curso de Direito Administrativo*. Coimbra: Almedina.

Amorim, Carlos de Abreu, 2009. 'Algumas notas sobre o regime jurídico das assembleias municipais portuguesas'. *Direito Regional e Local*, 7: 37–43.

Amorim, João Pacheco, 2009a. 'Breves reflexões sobre os novos regimes das Associações de Municípios e das Áreas Metropolitanas de Lisboa e Porto'. *Revista de Direito Público e Regulação*, 2: 73–102.

Batalhão, Carlos José, 2012. 'Algumas dúvidas jurídico-constitucionais sobre a reforma territorial das freguesias (um olhar sobre a Lei no. 22/2012, de 30 de maio)'. *Direito Regional e Local*, 20: 15–25.

CALBSEL, 2011. Livro Branco do Sector Empresarial Local. Comissão de Acompanhamento da Elaboração do Livro Branco do Sector Empresarial Local. November 2011.

Canotilho, J. Gomes and Moreira, Vital, 1993. *Constituição da República Portuguesa Anotada*, Coimbra: Almedina (3ª ed.).

Carneiro, José Luís, 2012. 'A proposta de reforma da administração local – "O estado do debate"'. *Direito Regional e Local*, 17: 30–38.

Carvalho, João Batista da Costa, 2009. 'Os Municípios Portugueses: análise financeira e cumprimentos da Lei das Finanças Locais'. *Direito Regional e Local*, 6: 17–26.

Caupers, João, 2009. 'Divisão administrativa e órgãos regionais'. *Direito Regional e Local*, 8: 3–8.

CLRA, 2008. *Draft European Charter of Regional Democracy* – Recommendation 240 (2008) of the Congress of Local and Regional Authorities of the Council of Europe.

Council of Europe, 1985. European Charter of Local Self-Government, 15.10.1985.

Cruz e Silva, Pedro, 2012. 'Notas sobre a Proposta de Lei no. 44/XII do Governo para a reorganização administrativa territorial autárquica'. *Direito Regional e Local*, 17: 39–48.

Declaração de Mirandela sobre as Assembleias Municipais, 26 de maio de 2012.

DGAL, 2012. Estudo-Piloto Comunidades Intermunicipais: Modelos de Competências, de Financiamento, de Governação, de Gestão e de Transferência de Recursos. Relatório Final. Lisbon: Direcção-Geral das Autarquias Locais.

EC, 2010a. Memorandum of Understanding between the European Commission, acting on behalf of the Euro Area Members States, and the Hellenic Republic.

EC, 2010b. Memorandum of Understanding between the European Commission and Ireland.

EC/ECB/IMF, 2011. Portugal: Memorandum of Understanding on specific economic policy conditionality, 3 May 2011 (34 pp.).

European Parliament, 1988. *Community Charter for Regionalization*, 18.11.198.

Governo de Portugal, 2001. *Programa do XIX Governo Constitucional*. Lisbon: Presidência do Conselho de Ministros.

Governo de Portugal, 2011a. *Documento Verde da Reforma da Administração Local. Uma Reforma de Gestão, uma Reforma de Território e uma Reforma Política (2 volumes)*. Lisbon: Governo de Portugal, Gabinete do Ministro Adjunto e dos Assuntos Parlamentares.

IMF, 2013. *Portugal. Rethinking the state – selected expenditure reform options*. Washington: International Monetary Fund.

ISEG, 2011. *Consultoria Técnica para elaboração do livro branco do sector empresarial local. Relatório final*. Novembro 2011. Lisbon: Instituto Superior de Economia e Gestão, Universidade Técnica de Lisboa.

Lopes, Licínio, 2009. 'O regime das Comunidades Intermunicipais: mais um caso exemplar de degradação da autonomia municipal'. *Revista de Direito Público e Regulação*, 2: 9–18.

Miranda, Jorge, 2007. *Constituição Portuguesa Anotada*. Coimbra: Coimbra Editora.

Moreira, Vital, 2007. 'Associações intermunicipais e áreas metropolitanas'. *Direito Regional e Local*, 00: 5–19.

Oliveira, António Cândido, 2008. '40 anos de desconcentração territorial regional em Portugal'. *Direito Regional e Local*, 1: 5–13.

Oliveira, António Cândido, 2009. 'O funcionamento das assembleias municipais em Portugal'. *Direito Regional e Local*, 7: 29–35.

Oliveira, António Cândido, 2011. 'É necessária uma reforma territorial das freguesias?' *Direito Regional e Local*, 13: 5–9.

Oliveira, António Cândido, 2012. 'As assembleias das autarquias locais e o bom funcionamento da administração pública'. *Direito Regional e Local*, 19: 5–11.

Oliveira, António Cândido, 2012. 'As assembleias das autarquias locais e o bom funcionamento da administração pública'. *Direito Regional e Local*, 19: 5–11.

Oliveira, Fernanda Paula, 2012a. 'A proposta de Lei no. 104/XII: uma perspetiva geral'. *Direito Regional e Local*, 20: 5–14.

Rocha, Joaquim Freitas, 2011. 'Finanças públicas restritivas – o impacto das medidas da Troika nas regiões autónomas e nas autarquias locais'. *Direito Regional e Local*, 15: 5–14.

Silva, Carlos Nunes and Syrett, S., 2005. 'Metropolitan Governance and Regionalism: the Case of Lisbon'. In Iwona Sagan and Halkier, Henrik (eds), *Regionalism Contested. Institution, Society and Territorial Governance*, Aldershot: Ashgate, pp. 247–64.

Silva, Carlos Nunes and Syrett, S., 2006. 'Governing Lisbon: evolving forms of city governance'. *International Journal of Urban and Regional Research*, vol. 30(1): 98–119.

Silva, Carlos Nunes, 1995. *Poder Local e Território. Análise geográfica das políticas municipais, 1974–94*. Dissertação de doutoramento em Geografia, Universidade de Lisboa, 489 p.

Silva, Carlos Nunes, 1996. 'O financiamento dos municípios'. In César Oliveira (Coord.), *História dos Municípios e do Poder Local. Dos finais da Idade Média à União Europeia*, Lisbon: Círculo de Leitores, pp. 433–62.

Silva, Carlos Nunes, 2000. 'Local government growth and retrenchment in Portugal: politicization, neo-liberalism and new forms of governance'. In Hoggart, Keith, Clark, Terry Nichols (eds), *Citizen Responsive Government*, New York: JAI Press, pp. 223–41.

Silva, Carlos Nunes, 2000a. 'A 'Região' em Portugal: do reforço da descentralização à fragmentação do Estado'. *Treballs de la Societat Catalana de Geografia*, Barcelona, vol. XV (49): 231–50.

Silva, Carlos Nunes, 2002. 'Gestão de Áreas Metropolitanas: o "Modelo GAM-ComUrb"'. *Cadernos Municipais – Revista de Acção Regional e Local*, XVI (81): 42–63.

Silva, Carlos Nunes, 2004. *Portugal: Sistema de Govern Local*. Barcelona: Institut de Ciències Politiques i Socials, Universitat Autónoma de Barcelona & Diputació de Barcelona.

Silva, Carlos Nunes, 2006. 'Decentralisation and Regional Governance in Portugal: Self-government or Inter-municipal Co-operation?' In Salet, Williem (ed.), *Synergy in Urban Networks?* The Hague: Sdu Publishers, pp. 204–26.

Silva, Carlos Nunes, 2009. 'Local Political Leadership in Portugal: Excepcionalism or Convergence Towards a "Mayoral Model"?' *Lex Localis – Journal of Local Self-Government*, 7(3), July 2009: 243–56.

Tribunal Constitucional, 2013. Acórdão No. 296/2013, 28 Maio de 2013 (sobre normas do Decreto no. 132/XII – Comunidades Intermunicipais).

Chapter 4

Public Services in European Countries: Between Public/Municipal and Private Sector Provision – and Reverse?

Hellmut Wollmann

Introduction[1]

Public services generally encompass water supply, sewage, waste management, public transport and energy provision. In Anglo-Saxon terminology they are usually called public utilities, while they are labelled *services publics industriels* in French, *servizi pubblici* or *servizi di pubblica utilità* in Italian and *Daseinsvorsorge* (services for the public) in German. In European Union (EU) policy the term *services of general economic interest* has been introduced (see Wollmann/Marcou, 2010b).

For analysing and discussing the delivery of public services two conceptual axes will be employed in this chapter: its *organizational* form and its *operational* logic:

> a) The organizational form ranges between public (state/municipal) sector and private sector.

If carried out by the public (state/municipal) sector the public service may be rendered either *directly* by state/municipal administration and its personnel (*in house, en régie*) or *indirectly* through units which, while remaining in state/ municipal ownership, stand organizationally (and often also financially) separate from the core administration. In the latter variant one also speaks of *formally* or *organizationally* privatized (or *corporatised*) organization (see Grossi et al., 2010; Kuhlmann/Fedele, 2010: 40). Of this, in Germany the so called *Stadtwerke* (city/ muncipal works) and in Italy the so called *municipalizzate* are exemplary.

As they often carry out more than one function and service they take the organizational form of multi-utilities.

Functional privatization means the transfer (delegation, outsourcing) of the delivery of public services to an outside actor who, as a rule, is a private sector provider, typically by way of a time-limited contract (concession).

---

1   For other references see also Wollmann (2011) and Wollmann/Marcou (2010c).

Material (or *asset*) privatization signifies that the ownership of the facility concerned changes, as rule by way of sale, from public (state/municipal) to private ownership, be it completely or only partially. In the latter variant *mixed* (or *hybrid*) companies or, in recently prevalent terminology, *public private partnerships* (PPP) are formed in which public and private financial and other resources are combined. In fact, in some countries such mixed companies have a long tradition in the delivery of public services.

Against this background the term *remunicipalization* (or recommunalization) refers to the reverse process when functionally privatized (outsourced) functions and services are turned back into public/municipal operation or materially (asset) privatized facilities are purchased back and return to public/municipal ownership, be it entirely or partially (see Röber, 2009; Wollmann/Marcou, 2010c; Wollmann, 2011; Kuhlmann/Wollmann, 2014).

> b) Regarding the *operational principle or logic* which guides the process, performance and output of service delivery a significant distinction can be made between an *economic* logic or rationale and a *political* one.

The *economic* logic and rationale is (ideally typically) directed primarily at economic efficiency in terms of maximising economic benefits/profit and of minimising costs (by possibly externalising social, ecological, and so on, costs). The economic logic is typical of the private sector actor whose prime leitmotif is profit-seeking and private-regarding and whose spatial frame of reference is the (as it were, borderless) capitalist market.

By contrast, the *political* logic pertains (ideal-typically) to a wide range of goals and effects among which political, social, ecological, and so on, objectives (welfare effects, Mühlenkamp, 2012: 22; 2013: 3) are prone, in the case of goal conflicts, to be given priority over (strictly) economic ones. Such *political* logic and rationale is characteristically adopted by politically elected and accountable decision-makers in national parliaments or local councils who ideally are public-regarding and geared to the common good and best interest of, say, the local community.

In its comparative intent the chapter pursues a threefold dimension:

> a) In a *cross-country* perspective it addresses (four) European countries: the UK:England, Germany, France and Italy.
> b) In a *cross-policy* view it focuses on energy and water provision as two network (grid)-based public utilities.
> c) In a *historical* (*longitudinal, over time*) perspective different phases are discerned of which it is assumed that each of them has specifically shaped the organizational form and operational logic of service delivery in order. For the purpose of this chapter five such stages are (hypothetically) identified, that is, first, the emergence of local government (based in the nineteenth century), second, the public sector-centred delivery of the advanced welfare state (until the 1970s), third, the neo-liberal policy/New

Public Mangement (NPM) driven promotion of private sector delivery (since the late 1970s), fourth, a post-neo-liberal/post-NPM comeback of public/municipal delivery (since the late 1990s) and fifth, a new privatization push in the wake of recent budgetary (sovereign debt) crisis (for the concept of different historical phases see Millward, 2005; Röber, 2009; Wollmann/Marcou, 2010b, 2010c; Clifton et al., 2011).

While the development of the organizational form and operational logic of service delivery will be regarded, methodologically speaking, as dependent variables, the explanatory scheme will be significantly inspired by the (neo-)institutionalist debate (see Peters, 1995; Wollmann/Marcou, 2010b).

In line with the historical (over time) perspective, the *historical* variant of institutionalism will be writ large which highlights the structural impact that institutional, political as well as cultural traditions, through ensuing path-dependencies(see Pierson, 2000), may have on the further course of institution building and institutional choice.

By contrast the *actor-centred* variant (see Scharpf, 1997) emphasises the voluntarist influence which the decisions and interests, political will and skill of the relevant political and economic actors may exercise on the future institutional course. Under certain conditions (particularly in the case of regime shifts or government shifts), this may amount to a deviation and rupture from a path-dependently staked-out trajectory.

Moreover, *discursive* institutionalism (see V. Schmidt, 2008) accentuates the (political, ideological, and so on) discourses whose constitutive beliefs and concepts set the stage for shaping and legitimising decision-making in the national as well as international policy arenas.

The guiding question of the following comparative account and analysis will be whether (and why) the development of the organizational and the operational logic of public service delivery have shown convergence or divergence. Due to the limited space of this chapter the arguments are bound to remain quite sketchy, if not fragmentary, where the complex subject matter would call for more substantiated treatment.

First Stage: Nineteenth Century – the Emergence of Local Government Based Public Service Provision

In the course of the nineteenth century, during a period of rampant industrialisation and urbanisation in which Britain was a European front-runner and Germany followed suit in Continental Europe, the provision of public utilities (water, sewage, waste, public transport, energy) in its initial basic form was deemed mainly a responsibility of the local authorities. After the early engagement of private sector entrepreneurs, which largely ended in bankruptcy, local authorities saw themselves compelled to take over their facilities. For the provision of public services the local authorities often created municipal companies (called *Stadtwerke* in Germany and *municipalizzate* in Italy), which often rendered more than one service, operated as multi-utilities. A sort of (embryonic) local welfare state took shape which, while derided by contemporary conservatives and Manchester liberals as municipal socialism (see Wollmann, 2011), responded to a broad range of socio-economic needs and interests of the respective local community and its stakeholders. Being embedded in local level decision-making the operational logic of this early regime of local government-based service delivery may be interpreted as reflecting political rationality.

Second Stage: Public Service Provision Under the Advancing and Climaxing of the Welfare State

With the expansion of the national welfare state which unfolded in the early twentieth century and climaxed during the 1960s and early 1970s, the provision of public utilities was regarded as a key responsibility of the public sector. This development was rooted in the (as it were social democratic) belief that the conduct of the public services in the best interest of the citizens was ensured by having them rendered by the public sector, be it state or municipal, and its public personnel directly. Hence, in its *organizational form* the provision of public services was marked by a quasi-monopoly of the public sector, while, in its *operational* logic, it was shaped by a political rationality which, being embedded in political decision-making and political control, would be, geared, first of all, to the general good and in the best public interest.

In the following the development will be sketched in singling out the energy and water sectors as cases in point.

After 1945, under the incoming Labour Government, the UK epitomized the public sector-centred (post-war) welfare state. In 1946 the energy sector which historically was largely in the hands of the local authorities was nationalized by turning the existing local companies over to public authorities under the control of the central government (see McEldowney, 2007). The local authorities were left with some all but minor functions (district heating). In 1973, the water sector which was historically operated by a thousand local water undertakings was nationalized as well by establishing ten public (central government-controlled) Regional Water Authorities (see McEldowney/McEldowney, 2010).

Similarly in post-war France in April 1947 the energy sector was nationalized by incorporating the existing private energy companies into two state-owned (monopolist) energy corporations, *Electricité de France* (EdF) and *Gaz de France* (GdF). Although the municipalities retained the ownership of the local grids, only 5 per cent of them chose to operate the grids themselves (*en régie*), while, in line with the century-old practice of the countrys municipalities of functionally privatizing or contracting out (*gestion déléguée*) service provision, most of them outsourced energy provision by way of long-term *concession* contracts to EdF and GdF. Only a minority of some 230 small municipal energy corporations (*enterprises locales de distribution d'électricité*, ELD) were exempted from nationalisation and continued their local operations, particularly in hydro-powered generation of electricity (see Allemand, 2007: 31).Thus, the state-owned companies came to dominate the local markets and were poised to become national, if not international champions in the energy sector.

In the water sector, too, following the traditional practice of *gestion déléguée*, most municipalities delegated (outsourced) the water services to private water companies (see Bordonneau et al., 2010: 134)[2]. As a result, France's water sector is now dominated by the big three water companies (Veolia, Suez and SAUR) that serve some 70 per cent of the households[3] and have become national champions and even global players in the water sector.

In Italy, too, in 1962 the energy sector was largely nationalized by integrating most of the existing (some 1,270) regional and local energy companies in state-owned company ENEL (*Ente nazionale per l'energia elettrica*). Only a small number of municipal corporations (*municipalizzate*) were exempted from nationalization and have continued in small-scale generation and distribution of electricity (see Prontera and Citroni, 2007).

Italy's water sector was traditionally serviced by small municipal water companies whose great number reflected the high degree of territorial fragmentation of the country's municipalities.

In post-war (West) Germany, in stark contrast with the UK, France and Italy, the energy sector did not undergo any nationalization since the country's post-war reconstruction was directed by a conservative-bourgeois coalition government which rejected nationalization as a socialist measure (with the – Socialist – German Democratic Republic, at the other side of the Iron Curtain, perceived as an political and ideological deterrent) and, instead, embarked upon an ambitious privatization programme, including the state-owned Volkswagen factory.

Against this background, (the West) Germany's post-war energy sector showed an asymmetrical duality of energy providers. On the one hand, it was dominated by a handful of major (regional) energy companies which, operating as private law listed stock companies, were owned by a spectrum of private investors and, to a minor degree,[4] also by municipalities. On the other hand, municipalities

---

2   With the exception, for instance, of the Cities of Paris and Grenoble where the water services continued to be provided *en régie* or through municipal companies.

3   *Veolia Environnement* (known officially as *Compagnie Générale des Eaux* in France) provided drinking water to 24.6 million people and waste-water services to 16.7 million people in partnership with more than 8,000 municipalities including Lyon.

Suez (known as *Compagnie Lyonnaise des Eaux* in France) provided 12 million people with water services in 5,000 municipalities and 9 million with waste-water services in 2,600 municipalities.

SAUR provided water and sanitation services to 5.5 million people in more than 6,700 municipalities and municipal associations, mainly in rural and peri-urban areas.

4   Such as RWE.

held a significant position in the energy sector, particularly in the transmission, distribution and (to minor degree also) generation of electricity, mainly in the traditional organizational form of the multi-utility *Stadtwerke* (city/municipal work). Being legally restricted to their respective local territory the *Stadtwerke* has often tended to establish protected local markets, if not local monopolies (see Ude, 2006). The operational logic of the municipalities and of their *Stadtwerke* in their engagement in the local energy provision can be interpreted as mirroring a political rationality as, embedded in local political decision-making and control, their activities are prone to respond to specific local (social, ecological and so on) needs and interests of the local community, possibly at the detriment of (strictly) economic criteria, as mandated by economic rationality. A case in point is using profits made in energy provision to cross-subsidize deficit-ridden local services, such as public transport. Another important example of non-economic.

Germany's water sector has as well been traditionally characterized by a myriad of small municipal water companies in the organizational form of multi-utility city works (*Stadtwerke*).

Third Stage: The Neo-liberal Shift – From Public Sector-based to Private Sector-based Service Provision

Since the 1980s, the public sector-centred organizational form and the *political* rather than *economic* operational logic of public service provision have encountered mounting criticism.

For one, the public sector-centred service organizational form of public service provision in the advanced (social democratic) welfare state has been attacked by the advocates of neo-liberal beliefs and New Public Management maxims for being basically and structurally inefficient. Remedy for this alleged public sector failure was seen in dismantling the (quasi-monopolist) public sector by way of privatizing the provision of services – be it by functional privatization (that is outsourcing) to outside (first of all private sector) providers, or by material (asset) privatization, that is, transfer to private ownership (see Grossi et al., 2010).

Another thrust of criticism was directed at the prevalence of an operational logic which, in a political rationality, tends to give priority to social, ecological, and so on, goals, while neglecting or putting last economic efficiency, that is, economic rationality. Redress was seen in the marketization (market liberalization, compulsory/obligatory tendering) of service provision.

The neo-liberal shift received its initial powerful political and discursive thrust in the UK after 1979 under Margaret Thatcher's conservative regime whence it spread first to other Anglophone and subsequently to Continental European countries. Since the mid-1980s it has been further propelled by the European Union's market liberalization drive to create a single European market by 1992 for goods, services and capital. Market liberalization has been targeted, not least at the provision of public utilities which in EU terminology has been labelled services of general economic interest (see Wollmann and Marcou, 2010b). As, in the past, such services were typically rendered in *territorially* defined and often somewhat protected national and local markets coming close to a virtual national or local monopolies, they were bound to become a prime target of EU's market liberalisation drive which aims at breaking up such territorially and locally secluded and protected markets and at paving the ground for single market-wide, in a way de-territorialized, competition.

In the following the energy and water sectors will again be singled out as cases in point in order to identify the impacts of this neo-liberal policy shift.

Energy Sector

In the UK, in anticipating (and, in fact, serving as model for) the EU's market liberalization intervention in the energy sector, the Conservative government under Margaret Thatcher proceeded, through the Electricity Act of 1989, to privatize the country's electricity sector which had been nationalized in 1949. At first 14 regional private sector companies were established. Later on their number was reduced to five as a result of mergers. International energy companies, such as France's EdF and Germany's RWE and E.on, entered the British energy market by becoming (minority) shareholders of the British private companies (see Drews, 2008: 51). Along with the privatization legislation the government revolutionized energy service provision by creating a national grid company to operate the transmission grids and by establishing a governmental regulatory agency to serve in a watchdog function.

At the local level, on an all but marginal scale, local government-related companies continued to operate heat- and power-combining facilities mostly in connection with district heating. They were restricted to cater only to local consumption needs but could sell and feed electricity into the national grid.

The EU has started, since the early 1990s, to intervene in the electricity sector by issuing *directives* which, in the EU's norm setting hierarchy, oblige the EU member states to translate (transpose) them into binding national legislation. After the (first) Directive 92/92 of 19 December 1996 largely failed to deregulate the electricity market, the EU followed up with the so-called Acceleration Directive (2003/54 of June 26th 2003) which introduced two particular instruments. For one, in distinguishing between generation, transmission and distribution/supply as three key functions of energy provision, the EU Directive aimed at organizationally unbundling these three functions. The basic idea was that, in order to ensure price competition in the interest of the consumer, non-discriminatory access to the transmission grid/network should be guaranteed to all providers. Second, the directive obliged each member state to put in place a national regulatory agency in a watchdog function.

In France, during the 1990s the national government at first showed little inclination to implement the EU's market liberalisation drive, probably because such implementation would have impaired the market-dominating quasi-monopolist position of state-owned EdF. In fact, in pursuing a distinctly protectionist industrial policy the government promoted EdF as a national champion to expand into international markets (see Beckmann, 2008: 246). Furthermore, nuclear power generated electricity makes up to 75 per cent of France's entire electricity production which resulted in comparatively low energy prices so that there was little need in the public discussion to call for privatization as an incentive of price competition. Consequently, there has been little incentive in France to evoke a public discussion on the need of having more price competition.

Finally in 2004, in responding to the EU Acceleration Directive of 2003, France moved to *formally* privatise EdF by transforming it into a private law stock company to be listed on the stock market. However, private (institutional or individual) ownership has been legally limited to 30 per cent of shares of EdF. Consequently, as of 2010 up to 84.8 per cent of shares of EdF are still held by the French state. However, in reaction to the unbundling, EdF has meanwhile set up an organizationally independent grid company (see Marcou, 2007, 21 f.).

In the shadow of the quasi-monopolist position of the still largely state-owned EdF the marginal role the some 230 municipal energy companies that were exempted from nationalisation in 1946 has not been noticeably boosted; they continue to provide just 5 per cent of the country's entire energy supply.

In Italy, in reaction to the EU Directive 96/92 the Italian government at first, in 1999, *formally* privatized the (quasi-monopolist) state-owned energy company ENEL by transforming it into a private law stock market-listed company. Subsequently ENEL was obliged to sell significant shares of its stocks to private (institutional and individual) investors, including Italian as well as foreign competitors (such as France's EdF and Germany's RWE and E.on). As a result, state ownership in ENEL has been reduced to some 30 per cent. Furthermore, in 1999, the EU's debundling imperative was put into practice by legally obliging ENEL to set up independent grid companies and to sell some of them to the municipal companies (*municipalizzate*) of major cities. Moreover in 1997 an independent watchdog regulatory agency (*autorità per l'energía elettrica ed il gas*) was created.

At the same time, the municipal companies (*municipalizzate*) that had been exempted from nationalisation in 1962 continued to play a noticeable role particularly in the generation of renewable energy (see Prontera and Citroni, 2007).

In this context it should be added that in a reaction to Chernobyl nuclear catastrophe of 26 April 1986, the construction of nuclear power plants in Italy was overwhelmingly rejected by a country-wide referendum held on 8 November 1987.[5]

In Germany, as a reaction to the EU Directive 96/92/EC, the Federal Energy Act of 1998 was adopted which aimed at liberalising Germany's energy market. In the first phase, the legislation had the somewhat paradoxical effect of triggering a downright wave of mergers (Deckwirth, 2008: 82) which resulted in the emergence of E.on, RWE, EnBW and (Sweden's State-owned) Vattenfall as the big four

---

5   The ban on nuclear power stations was confirmed by the national referendum held on 13 June 2011.

dominant players on Germany's energy market. At the same time, faced with the competitive pressure by the big four and with a mounting budgetary plight, many municipalities saw themselves compelled to sell local grids and shares of their *Stadtwerke* to the big four. In a development which, by some, was seen as foreboding the demise of the *Stadtwerke* (*Stadtwerkesterben*) (see Wollmann, 2002; Wollmann and Baldersheim et al., 2010).

Water Sector

Different from the energy sector, with regard to the water sector the EU does not have the competence to intervene by way of sector-specific deregulation. However, it has influenced the provision of drinking water and waste-water treatment by directives concerning the respective water quality.[6] Insofar as in some countries national legislation has regulated water provision, they fell in line with the general neo-liberal policy trend without explicit EU obligation.

In the UK, in further pursuing its neo-liberal policy drive the Conservative government, in 1989, effected the (*material/asset*) *privatization* of the country's water sector by selling the (ten) public regional water authorities to private sector water companies. At the same time a regulatory agency (OFWAT) was created following the model of the infrastructure regulatory agency set up in other sectors such as telecommunications and energy. As a result some 25 private sector water companies emerged which formed regional monopolies. Subsequently most of them have been taken over by private-equity funds, half of them foreign (see Bakker, 2003: 369 ff; Hall and Lobina, 2077: 23 ff.), which turned out highly profitable for them (Drews, 2008: 53).

In Scotland and Northern Ireland, water supply has not been (asset) privatised and is still operated in public ownership. In England and Wales, under the privatised regime, the water tariffs for private households are double compared to those in Scotland's public regime (see Hall and Lobina, 2001: 22).

In France where, during the 1970s, water provision has been increasingly dominated by the big three private sector water companies (Veolia, Suez and SAUR)[7] (see Bondonneau et al., 2010: 134), an additional privatization impulse came in the wake of the municipal elections of 1983 when right-wing council majorities and neo-liberal-minded mayors were elected who pushed for outsourcing (functional privatization) of water provision (to one of the big three). Conspicuous privatization cases were the cities of Paris and Grenoble which until then had retained municipal operation (*en régie*) (see Hall and Lobina, 2001b).

In Italy, well into the 1990s, water provision was operated by some 9,000 small municipally owned facilities (Armeni, 2008). Because of the small size and the

---

6   This applies particularly to the Urban Waste Water Treatment Directive (91/271/EEC) of 21 May 1991 and the Drinking Water Directive (98/83/EC) of 3 November 1998 concerning potable water quality.

7   See above footnote 3.

lack of adequate capital investment, water provision has been costly with wide-spread leakage in the pipe systems aggravating the waste of water. In 1994 the Law Galli aimed at significantly reorganizing the country's water services by reducing the existing organizational fragmentation. A new institutional inter-municipal structure called *Ambiti territoriali ottimali*, ATO,[8] was introduced which was designed to introduce competition into local water provision and to possibly involve also private sector companies, including foreign ones, in the water services (for details see Ascquer, 2013).

Subsequently, in 2009, the *Ronchi Decree*[9] was adopted in 2009 under the right-wing Berlusconi government. It was destined to break the legal ground for the further privatization of the water services, particularly with the provision that the share in water companies held by the municipalities themselves must not exceed 30 per cent while making 70 per cent available for private investors. However, the implementation of this legislation has been halted, due to the outcome of the national referendum held on 8 June 2011 that ruled out the privatization of water.

In Germany, while the water services have been traditionally operated mostly by the municipalities themselves (in house) or by (about 7,000) *Stadtwerke* (see Citroni, 2007; VKU, 2010: 13), private sector water companies have entered the water market since the 1980s and 1990s by acquiring minority share positions in *Stadtwerke*. This applies to almost half of the country's 109 largest cities (see Deckwirth, 2008: 85). Among these private water companies, the French service giants Veolia and Suez and their German counterparts RWE and E.on feature most prominently. In the perhaps most conspicuous case, Veolia and RWE, in 1999, acquired a total of 49.9 per cent of the shares of Berlin's Water Works, Germany's largest water company[10].

Fourth Stage: A post-neo-liberal/post-NPM Comeback of Public/Municipal Delivery (Since the Late 1990s)

Since the late 1990s the conceptual and political context has, internationally, nationally and locally, moved into a post-neo-liberal and post-NPM direction that fosters a comeback of the public/municipal sector as a provider of public services. Is the pendulum swinging back to public/municipal sector-based service provision?

Since the late 1990s it has become more and more evident that the (high-flying) neo-liberal promises that (material or functional) privatization would usher in better quality of services at lower prices has not materialized. On the contrary, private service providers have often made use of the next possible opportunity to

---

8   Translated: Optimal Territorial Areas.

9   Named after Andrea Ronchi who was minister in the recent right wing Berlusconi government.

10   For the example of the city of Stuttgart, see Libbe et al. (2011b: 9).

raise prices and tariffs while at the same time deteriorating the working conditions of their employees. This conceptual and political disillusionment observable on the local level ties in with a corresponding shift in the national and international discourse in which, in the wake of the worldwide finance crisis that was triggered by the bankruptcy of Lehman Brothers on 15 September 2008, the relation between the state and the private sector has been critically reappraised and the crucial role of the state to redress private sector failures and market failures has been rediscovered (to the point of private businesses, not least banks, conspicuously for being bailed out) and has politically, ideologically and institutionally brought the state back in.

The disenchantment with private sector service provision has come strikingly to the fore in a survey which was conducted in 2010 by the Association for Public Service Excellence (APSE)[11] among 140 local authorities in England, Scotland and Wales. While 60 per cent of the responding local authorities indicated that they have begun or were preparing or planning to take previously outsourced services back (insource) into their own operation (see APSE, 2011: 11), in their responses, 'a need to improve efficiency and reduce service costs was the most cited reason for insourcing' (see APSE, 2011: 11). The assessment that in providing public utilities public enterprises are, as a rule (at least), on a par with private sector providers comes out in most available studies (see the broad overview in Mühlenkamp, 2013: 18)[12]. The balance sheet becomes even more favourable for public/municipal provision if the transaction costs of the outsourcing of services (costs of monitoring, contract management and so on) are taken into account,[13] not to speak of the negative welfare effects of privatized service provision and the positive ones (social, ecological and so on) of public/municipal provision (see Florio, 2004: 341[14]; see also Mühlenkamp, 2012: 42; 2013:18).

Renewed Self-confidence and Action Orientation of Local Government

Hence, not surprisingly, the local authorities, for one, have rediscovered the provision of public utilities under their own responsibility and in their own operation as a strategy to generate revenues (that is profit) instead of leaving this to private sector providers. (In a recent survey conducted among German municipalities 74

---

11 See APSE's website www.apse.org.uk.

12 See Mühlenkamp, 2013: 18: 'Research does not support the conclusion that privately owned firms are more efficient than otherwise-comparable state-owned firms'. See also Bel et al., 2010, who, on the basis of numerous studies on water and waste services, summarize that 'our analysis provides empirical evidence that private production of local services is not systematically less costly than that of public'. See also Bel and Warner, 2008: 1341.

13 On this see also APSE, 2011: 11.

14 Florio, 2004: 341: 'The main conclusion of my study is that privatization had more modest effects on efficiency than the theory or property rights and other orthodox privatization theories may have expected. On the other hand, privatization did have substantive regressive effects on the distribution of incomes and wealth in the United Kingdom'.

per cent of the respondents indicated that a prime reason for remunicipalization was to achieve additional revenues, see Lenk et al., 2011; Reichard/Röber, 2012). Moreover, they seek and use this opportunity to regain political control over the quality and price-setting of service provision and to pursue social, ecological, and so on, objectives (welfare effects), for instance by way of cross-subsidizing structurally and chronically deficient service sectors (such as public transport). In doing so, they act upon and play out a political rationality which (ideally) is oriented on the common good and best interest of the local community.

Value Change in the Political Culture and Popular Perception

This reassessment of the merits of public sector-based service provision is also reflected and supported in a growing popular perception and sentiment which tends to value public sector service provision higher than private sector provision. This trend is evidenced by a growing number of local referendums in which the privatization of public services and facilities is rejected or their remunicipalization is demanded (for German examples see Mehr Demokratie, 2012: 42 ff.; Kuhlmann and Wollmann, 2014). On the national level a striking pertinent event was the national referendum held in Italy on 8 June 2011 in which the privatization of water provision was overwhelmingly rejected. The international if not global dimension and perspective of this development shows in the emergence and actions of social and political movements of which *Attac*[15] is exemplary.

Reassessment of the Local Government Level in the Intergovernmental Setting

The readiness and motivation of local authorities to engage themselves and their municipal companies in the provision of public utilities has recently been fostered by remarkable changes in their intergovernmental setting.

For one, in the EU, and concomitantly in the national contexts, the status and function of the local government level has recently been strengthened as in the Treaty of Lisbon of December 2009 where local government has been explicitly recognized for the first time ever in EU constitutional law.[16] Furthermore, and particularly relevant for the delivery of services of general economic interest, in a protocol to the Treaty of Lisbon (which has the same legal status as the Treaty itself) it has been stipulated that regarding these services of general interest the EU explicitly recognizes 'the essential role and the wide discretion of national, regional and local authorities in providing, commissioning and organizing services of general economic interest as closely as possible to the needs of the

---

15   http://www.attac.org/node/3727.

16   Article 3a section 2 of the Treaty of Lisbon: 'The Union shall respect the equality of Member States before the Treaties as well as their national identities, inherent in their fundamental structures, political and constitutional, inclusive of regional and **local self-government'** (bold letters added, H.W.).

users' as well as 'the diversity between various services of general economic interest and the differences in the needs and preferences of users that may result from different geographical, social or cultural situations'. This means that the EU has significantly mitigated its programmatic single market mandate and claim by virtually allowing local exceptions and possibly even local markets.

Furthermore, in certain policy fields, the local government level has been recognised as an important actor both by the EU and by the national governments. This applies prominently to environmental protection and energy saving. So, at their summit held in March 2007 the European heads of state agreed on an Energy Policy for Europe which called for a 20 per cent increase in energy efficiency, a 20 per cent reduction of greenhouse gas (GHG) emissions and a 20 per cent share of renewable energy sources in overall EU energy consumption by 2020 (see Praetorius and Bolay, 2009). For achieving these energy and climate preserving policies the local authorities have been recognized as crucial actors.

Grid-specific Window of Opportunity

Finally, as in the field of grid-based services, such as energy and water, the municipalities in most countries have the right to grant (time-limited) concessions to the enterprises that want to establish and use such grids, and as currently many of these concessions contracts expire, a window of opportunity is opening for the municipalities to renegotiate the concessions contracts and to possibly remunicipalize the services.

On this backdrop it will be briefly discussed in the following whether and why such remunicipalization has taken place. Hereby the energy and water sectors will again be singled out as cases in point.

Energy Sector

In the UK, since the (asset) privatization of the energy sector in 1989, the country's energy market has been dominated by private energy companies, while the local authorities were left with an all but marginal role, for instance in the operation of district heating services (see McEldowny, 2007). However in a recent conspicuous policy turn, the conservative-liberal coalition government has explicitly encouraged the local authorities to resume a responsibility in the energy sector particularly by engaging in the generation and utilisation of energy saving and renewable energy generation technologies.[17] The national goal has been set to supply 15 per cent of the country's energy consumption from renewable energy

---

17 On 28 August 2010, Chris Huhne, Secretary of State for Energy and Climate Change, wrote in a letter to all local authorities that 'for too long, Whitehall's dogmatic reliance on "big" energy has stood in the way of the vast potential role of local authorities in the UK's green energy revolution' http://www.decc.gov.uk/publications/basket. aspx?FilePath=News%2f376-unlocking-local-power-huhne-letter.pdf&filetype=4#basket.

by 2020. Enabling legislation has followed suit. In the meantime a considerable number of local authorities have initiated local projects, particularly pertaining to power and heat coupling (in conjunction with district heating) and in solar energy. Sheffield, Leeds and Bradford are leading the UK in renewable energy installations[18] (see McEldowney, 2013). However, the local level initiatives appear to have recently slackened. 'The climate change work has narrowed, is very weak or absent in 65 percent of local authorities' (Scott, 2011).

In France, the electricity market continues to be dominated by EdF which is still in 80 per cent state ownership, generates 75 per cent of the country's energy production from its 24 nuclear power stations and is encouraged by government policy to be a champion on the national as well as international energy markets.

Some 230 municipal energy companies which were exempted in 1946 from nationalisation continue to provide energy services to not more than 5 per cent of the households. Their generation of electricity is, to a considerable degree, based on renewable (particularly hydro) sources. So far, notwithstanding their potential in renewable energy, the role of the municipal companies has apparently remained limited also because they continue to be legally restrained to only serve their respective local market (see Allemand, 2007: 40).

While ENEL (which is in 30 per cent state ownership) and other institutional and individual (largely private sector) companies currently play a major role in Italy's energy market, the municipal energy companies (*muncipalizzate*) which, in 1962, were exempted from the nationalisation continue to hold a fairly strong position in the energy sector (see Prontera and Citroni, 2007). This applies particularly to big cities. In 2008 the municipal companies of Milano (1.2 million inhabitants) and Brecia (190,000 inhabitants) merged to form a consortium-type stock company called *A2A* which is listed on the stock market and generates 3.9 per cent of the country's electricity, while a multitude of other small municipal companies generates another 10 per cent (see AEEG, 2011: 51). As Italy has politically and legally committed itself to do without nuclear power, the municipal energy companies whose power generation traditionally has a strong alternative and renewable (hydro) energy component (see AEEG, 2001: 52) appear to be poised for an expanding role in the country's energy sector (see Prontera, 2013).

Whereas, well unto the late 1990s, the big four private sector energy companies made significant advances on Germany's energy market, recently the *Stadtwerke* have significantly regained ground for a number of reasons (see Wollmann and Baldersheim et al., 2010; Libbe et al., 2011b: 6 ff.).

For one, as the EC Acceleration Directive 2003/54 exempted energy companies with less than 100,000 consumer households from applying the unbundling

---

18   http://www.energyefficiencynews.com/i/4462/, For an updated list ('league table') of the UK's local authorities most active in renewable energy generation see http://www. aeat.com/cms/assets/MediaRelease/2011-press-releases/Microgeneration-Index-Press-Release-11th-March-2011.pdf.

requirement, most *Stadtwerke* do not fall under the unbundling requirement. It should be noted that the exemption was written into the directive upon demands made by the German federal government explicitly on behalf of the German municipalities which claimed that the unlimited application of the unbundling mandate would jeopardise the operational and economic survival of their *Stadtwerke*.

Moreover, since the *Stadtwerke* have traditionally focused on energy-saving technologies (such as heat and power coupling, HPC), they have become crucial local actors in the eyes of the federal government all the more as the latter, in a dramatic policy turnaround in reaction to the nuclear disaster in Fukushima, decided, in June 2011, to terminate the country's nuclear power generation by 2022. At the same time, the European Commission, in recognizing the competitive potential that the local energy companies have in the local and regional energy markets, proceeded to strengthen their competitive muscle by exerting pressure on the big four (E.on, RWE, EnBW, Vattenfall) to sell local grids and give up previously acquired minority shares in *Stadtwerke*.

Furthermore, the *Stadtwerke* have learned how to cope with the new competitive environment by improving their entrepreneurial skills and their operational base (for instance by promoting inter-municipal cooperation, by involving private investors and so on).

Moreover, the municipalities have (re-)discovered the potential of their *Stadtwerke* to achieve much needed local revenue and to satisfy specific (social, and so on) needs and interests of the local community, and to thus practice political rationality, for instance by cross-subsidizing deficit-ridden local public transport services.

Finally, this recent push coincided with the expiration of an increasing number of concession contracts on local grids.[19]

Hence, many municipalities have turned to repurchase local grids and shares of the *Stadtwerke*. The dynamics of this development is evidenced also by a growing number of newly founded *Stadtwerke*.[20] A conspicuous recent example is Thüga, a subsidiary of E.on, which was purchased in the summer 2009 by a consortium of some 100 *Stadtwerke* for the amount of €3 billion;[21] it now holds about 6 per cent of the country's electricity market.

As of 2010, 700 *Stadtwerke* out of a total of 1,372 municipal companies[22] are engaged in the energy sector, with one-third of them in power generation. Of the locally generated electricity, 84 per cent stems from heating and power coupling

---

19   Between 2000 and 2001 some 3,000 out of a total of 20,000 concession contracts, see Libbe et al., 2011b: 6.

20   See Libbe et al., 2011b: 8 for an (incomplete) list of some 30 newly founded *Stadtwerke*.

21   See for instance Euroforum, 28 October 1998, '*Stadtwerke* and municipalities reconquer the energy market', http://www.blogspan.net/presse/stadtwerke-und-kommunen-erobern-energieversorgung-zuruck/mitteilung/122972/.

22   With 241,535 employees which is about one-tenth of the entire local government personnel – see VKU, 2010: 9.

(HPC) and 16 per cent from other, particularly renewable, energy sources. The locally generated electricity amounts to 10.4 per cent of Germany's entire power generation (see VKU, 2009).

Water Sector

Although the privatized water services in England and Wales have been severely criticized (not least for high tariffs and high operating profits),[23] a politically relevant discussion about turning the water services back to public (state or local) operation has so far not materialized.

While in France, well into the early 1990s, the privatisation of water services by the traditional modality of outsourcing (*gestion déléguée*, to one of the big three) has further advanced a process of remunicipalizing water services has gained momentum since the late 1990s. First of all steep price and tariff hikes have increasingly discredited the privatization of water provision. When left-wing council majorities and mayors regained power, they sought to undo the privatisation effected by their right-wing predecessors and to make use of the expiration of concession contracts in order to remunicipalize water services. The pertinent decisions made in Grenoble and in Paris (in 1989 and in 2000 respectively) are cases in point (see Let Strat, 2010 for these and other examples).[24, 25]

It should be kept in mind, however, that the pace of remunicipalisation has remained hampered by the high compensation payments liable to be made to private investors and by the lack of skilled local government personnel (see Bordonneau et al., 2010: 136). Moreover, experience shows that the three large private water companies find themselves in a powerful negotiation position which often amounts to what has been critically labelled a regulatory capture of the municipalities (see Varin, 2010). Thus, about 90 per cent of contracts tend to be renewed with the same concessionaires. On the top of it, many municipalities, including large ones, do not have the capacity to monitor and control the concession contracts, particularly regarding increases of water tariffs (see Cour de Comptes, 2003).

In Italy, the large-scale privatisation of Italy's water sector at which the Ronchi Decree of 2009 was targeted was conspicuously stopped by the national referendum held on 11 June 2011 in which the Ronchi Decree was rejected by a 96 per cent majority. The political mobilisation against water privatisation was largely carried by the (left-leaning) *Forum Italiano dei Movimenti per l'Acqua*[26]

---

23   The tariffs increased by 46 per cent in real terms between 1990–2000, while the operating profits rose by 142 per cent in eight years, according to Hall and Lobina, 2001.

24   As a result, the percentage of water services rendered by the municipalities themselves rose from some 18 per cent of the country's population in 1970 to 28 per cent in 2008 (see Table 1 in Bordonneau et al., 2010: 134).

25   In the case of Grenoble the mayor was convicted of corruption and sentenced to prison. The concession contract concerned was cancelled, see Hall and Labina, 2001.

26   Translated: Italian Forum of Water Movement.

which was founded in 2006 and was composed of some 150 municipalities and political organizations.[27]

While in Germany, well into the early 2000s, private water companies, including major players such as Veolia, Suez, RWE and E.on, made significant advances in the (still municipally dominated) water sector, recently a counter-trend has apparently set, as municipalities make use of upcoming expiration of concession contracts to renegotiate the contracts and to regain control over the local water services. This development has been prompted not least by demands of the local citizens, as expressed in a growing number of binding local referendums. Thus, in the city of Stuttgart where, in 2003, water provision was completely sold to a large German provider (EnBW), the city council, in responding to a pertinent local referendum, decided in June 2010 to repurchase the water work, once the concession contract expires in 2013[28] (for other examples see Kuhlmann and Wollmann, 2013).

Remunicipalization in a Wider Country and Sector Perspective?

Varying in rate and intensity processes of remunicipalization can be also observed in other service sectors, such as waste management, public transport, as well as in other countries (see Hall, 2012; Dreyfus et al., 2010). An intriguing example of the dynamics of a local multi-utilities operation is offered by the German city of Bergkamen (50,000 inhabitants) which, under the innovative leadership of a committed mayor, has become a pilot in remunicipalizing public services in a broad multi-utility mix that includes energy, waste management and public transport (see Schäfer, 2008; for other examples see Kuhlmann and Wollmann, 2014).

Fifth Stage: A New Privatization Push in the Wake of Recent Budgetary (Sovereign Debt) Crisis

New Wave of Privatization Triggered by the Recent Budgetary Crisis?

In the most recent development there are indications that again the pendulum may be swinging back again towards stepped up privatization in the public utilities sector.

For one, this may pertain to the EU countries in general as the European Commission has, in late 2012, proposed a directive on the award of concessions contracts which would pertain to all types of services of general economic interest and thus also including water services. It would mean that whenever a concession on these grid-based services elapses and comes up for prolongation the

---

27   http://www.fame2012.org/index.php?id=52.

28   http://www.wasser-in-buergerhand.de/nachrichten/2010/stgt_fuer_rekommunalisierung_wasser.htm.

municipalities would be obliged to put it out to tender. On 29 January 2013 the draft directive was approved by the respective Committee of the European Parliament. The draft directive has evoked great alarm and concern particularly among the German municipalities and their *Stadtwerke*. They perceived and rejected the draft directive as contradicting and virtually nullifying the wide discretion that the Lisbon Treaty of December 2009 recognized and accorded to the local authorities in their decision on how to locally organize service provision.[29] At the time of writing, the issue of the draft directive is still pending as it still needs to be finally adopted and, if adopted, to be transposed into national legislation.

However, a new wave of (large-scale) privatization in the public services sector (and beyond) appears to be triggered in the budgetary crisis-ridden South European countries which face increasing demands by the European Commission, the European Central Bank and the International Monetary Fund, embodied in the so called Troika, to sell public assets, including not least municipal public service providing facilities and companies in order to reduce the public (sovereign) debts[30].

Conclusion

In the conclusion of the chapter we will resume the initially formulated guiding question of whether and why the organizational form (*public/municipal* or *private*) of public service delivery as well as its operational logic (*political* or *economic*) shows convergence or divergence over time in the countries and service sectors under consideration.

Our analysis and account suggest that the each of the five developmental phases that were hypothetically discerned shows common as well as varied features. The explanation of such commonality as well as variance may be, in drawing on the aforementioned conceptual variants of institutionalism, sought, first of all, in path-dependent structures, political (and so on) decisions and discourses.

A pronounced, organizationally convergent development can be detected in the historical origins of local level service provision since the second half of the nineteenth century. The local authorities were engaged in the provision of (then still elementary) public services in what conservative and Manchester liberal opponents of the time mockingly called municipal socialism. Thus, for some services and some countries an all but path-dependent tradition of local government-based delivery, be it in house or through municipal companies (such as *Stadtwerke* in Germany), has caught roots. An early deviation from this pattern emerged in France where the municipalities tended to outsource service provision

---

29   See for instance, http://www.right2water.eu/de/news/how-concessions-directive-new-piece-longer-struggle-privatise-water-and-make-money-out-water.

30   Regarding the pressure of the European Union on Greece, Portugal and Spain to privatize water see http://www.tni.org/pressrelease/eu-commission-forces-crisis-hit-countries-privatise-water.

to outside (mostly private sector) providers which has become a France-specific path-dependent feature of service provision and has turned out the launching pad for private sector service companies to come to dominate the national and international markets.

Reflecting the political/ideological disposition of the advancing and advanced (national) welfare state to rely on public sector-centred service provision, it was after 1945, in a largely convergent development, politically decided in the UK (under the incoming Labour Party with a socialist connotation), in France (under DeGaulle with a modernist connotation) and later in Italy, to nationalize the energy sector, that is, to turn it over to state-owned companies (in France: EdF; in Italy: ENEL) or agencies. By contrast, in (West) Germany the energy sector continued to be left to the existing plurality of (largely) private sector companies as any nationalization was politically and ideologically alien to the conservative (post-war) federal government. The hitherto existing local energy companies were more or less marginalized.

With regard to water provision (and to other public services), the local authorities, in line with their path-dependent tradition, continued to render such services, in Germany and Italy particularly through municipal companies (*Stadtwerke, municipalizzate*), and in France in the traditional form of outsourcing (*gestion déléguée*). As an exception, in the UK the water sector was also nationalized which added to making the UK appear the epitomy of the post-war (social democratic) advanced public sector-centred welfare state.

Under the impact of the neo-liberal policy shift (and later of the EU's market liberalization drive) the UK was first, and went the furthest, in entirely (asset) privatizing the hitherto state-owned energy sector, as well as, subsequently, the publicly operated water sector. Italy and France followed suit in privatizing ENEL and EdF, respectively: however, in Italy the state retained 30 per cent and in France as many as 80 per cent of the shares – the latter hinting at France's determined protectionist industrial policy. In Germany, the deregulation of the energy sector led, in a seeming paradox, to mergers and market concentration of the big four private sector providers. The municipally owned energy companies (*Stadtwerke*) seemed doomed to be squeezed out (*Stadtwerkesterben*).

Since the late 1990s, as the neo-liberal policy and discourse dominance has faded and given way to the perception of the shortcomings and drawbacks of private sector-based service provision along with the reappraisal of the capacity and potential of the public/municipal sector, in the field of energy provision the municipalities and their companies have returned to or have stepped up their activities particularly, herein encouraged by national and EU policies, in renewable energy and energy saving measures – with the German *Stadtwerke* figuring prominently In water provision, too, the municipalities and their companies have begun to regain ground which they recently lost to private sector providers. Thus the pendulum that, under the neo-liberal shibboleth, swung towards private sector predominance has started to oscillate back to public, particularly municipal sector provision. In a historical long-term perspective the organizational form appears to have run full cycle, from local government to local government provision.

Most recently, however, in the budgetary (sovereign debt) crisis-ridden South European countries, under external international pressure, embodied by the so-called Troika, a new wave of privatization has been unleashed which is targeted, through the sale of public, not least municipal, assets to reduce and relieve the public indebtedness.

Regarding the *operational logic* of public service provision, in the historical long-term perspective the local government based delivery in the early nineteenth-century phase which can be seen as guided by a political rationality in the sense of taking a wide range of local (social, infrastructural and so on) needs and interests of the local community into account, possibly at the detriment of strictly economic goals. In the further development of the advancing and advanced national welfare state and its public sector dominance of service provision, again political rationality can be interpreted as giving priority to the wide spectrum of social, ecological, and so on, goals (welfare effects), but at the risk of neglecting or putting last narrowly understood economic concerns. In reaction to this alleged disregard of economic efficiency the neo-liberal market-liberalization phase gave prime importance to economic rationality at the possible price of ignoring non-economic (social, ecological, welfare and so on) concerns.

At last, the remunicipalization of service delivery arguably holds the promise and harbours the potential of combining the political and the economic rationalities. Being politically embedded in the local community, its demands and accountability, the provision of public services is prone to respond to and heed the gamut of needs and interests in what is captured in the term and concept of political rationality. At the same time, however, facing the challenges by private sector competitors, the municipalities and their companies have been compelled and have learned to adopt and pursue economic rationality as well. Putting it somewhat pointedly and ideally, the remunicipalization of public services has the potential to combine and achieve the best of the two worlds.

References

AEEG (Autorità per l'Energia Elettrica ed il Gas) (2001). Annual Report on State of Services.

Allemand, Rosalyn, 2007. 'Les distribiteurs non-nationalisés d'electricité face à l'ouverture de la concurrence'. In *Annuaire 2007 des Collectivités Locales*, CNRS. Paris, pp. 31–42.

Armeni, Chiara, 2008. 'The right to water in Italy', http://www.ielrc.org/content/f0801.pdf.

Ascquer, Alberto, 2013. *Explaining partial privatization of public service provision: the emergence of mixed ownership water firms in Italy (1994–2009)*, unpubl. Ms.

Beckmann, Jens, 2008. 'Die Entkernung des Service Public in Frankreich'. In Bieling, Hans-Jürgen et al. (eds), *Liberalisierung und Privatisierung in Europa*, Verlag Westfälisches Dampfboot, pp. 125–51.

Bel, G., Fegeda, X. and Warner, M.E., 2010. 'Is private production of public services cheaper than public production? A meta-regression analysis of solid waste and water services'. *Journal of Policy Analysis and Management*, 29(3), pp. 553–77.

Bolay, Sebastian, 2009. *Einführung von Energiemanagement und erneuerbaren Energien. Untersuchung von Erfolgsfaktoren in deutschen Kommuinen*, Diss. Uni Potsdam.

Bordonneau, Marie-Agnès, Canneva, Guillem, Orange, Gerard and Gambier, Dominique, 2010. 'Le changement de mode de gestion des services d'eau'. In *Droit et Gestion des Collectivités Territoriales*, Annunaire 2010, Editions le Moniteur, Paris, pp. 131–47.

Citroni, Giulio, 2010. 'Neither state nor market: municipalities, corporations and municipal corporatization in water services: Germany, France and Italy compared'. In Wollmann, Hellmut and Marcou, Gérard (eds), *The Provision of Public Services in Europe. Between State, Local Government and Market*, Edward Elgar, pp. 191–216.

Clifton, Judith, Lanthier, Pierre and Schröter, Harm, 2011. 'Regulating and deregulating the public utilities, 1830–2010'. *Business History*, 53(5), pp. 659–72.

Cour des Comptes, 2003. La gestion des services publics d'eau et d'assainissement (rapport au président de la République suivi des réponses des administrations et organismes intéressés).http://www.cace.fr/jurisprudence/ccomptes/cour/cdc2003.html

Denkwirth, Christina, 2008. 'Der Erfolg der Global Players. Liberalisierung und Privatisierung in der Bundesrepublik Deutschland'. In Bieling, Hans-Jürgen et al., (eds), *Liberalisierung und Privatisierung in Europa*, Verlag Westfälisches Dampfboot, pp. 64–94.

Drews, Kathrin, 2008. 'Großbritannien: „TINA" oder Paradigma einer gescheiterten Reorganization?' In Bieling, Hans-Jürgen et al. (eds), *Liberalisierung und Privatisierung in Europa*, Verlag Westfälisches Dampfboot, pp. 34–63.

Dreyfus, Magali, Töller, Annette Elisabeth, Iannello, Carlo and McEldowney, John, 2010. 'Comparative study of a local service: waste management in France, Germany, Italy and the UK'. In Wollmann, Hellmut and Marcou, Gérard (eds), *The Provision of Public Services in Europe. Between State, Local Government and Market*, Edward Elgar, pp. 146–66.

Florio, Massimo, 2004. *The Great Divesture – Evaluating the Welfare Impact of the British Privatization 1979–1997*. Cambridge, MA and London.

Grossi, Giuseppe, Marcou, Gérard and Reichard, Christoph, 2010. 'Comparative aspects of institutional variants of public service provision'. In Wollmann, Hellmut and Marcou, Gérard (eds), *The Provision of Public Services in Europe. Between State, Local Government and Market*, Edward Elgar, pp. 217–39.

Hall, David and Lobina, Emanuele, 2001. *UK – water privatisation – a briefing*. London: PSIRU report.

Hall, David and Lobina, Emanuele, 2001b. Private to Public: International lessons of water remunicipalisation in Grenoble, France (PSIRU, web www.psiru.org).

Hefetz, A. and Warner, M., 2004. 'Privatization and its reverse. Explaining the dynamics of the government contracting process'. *Journal of Public Administration Review and Theory*, 14, pp. 171–90.

Kuhlmann, Sabine and Fedele, Paolo, 2010. 'New public management in continental Europe'. In Wollmann, Hellmut and Marcou, Gérard (eds), *The Provision of Public Services in Europe. Between State, Local Government and Market*, Edward Elgar, pp. 49–69.

Kuhlmann, Sabine and Wollmann, Hellmut, 2014. Public Administration and Administrative Reforms in Europe. An Introduction into Comparative Public Administration, Edward Elgar: Cheltenham (forthcoming).

Le Strat, Anne, 2010. Paris: An example of how local authorities can regain control of water management. Available at: http://www.waterjustice.org/?mi=1&res_id=280.

Libbe, Jens and Hanke, Stefanie, 2011. 'Rekommunalisierung – neue alte Wege der öffentlichen Daseinsvorsorge'. *Der Gemeindehaushalt*, 5, S. pp. 108–116.

Libbe, Jens, Hanke, Stefanie and Verbücheln, Maic, 2011. *Rekommunalisierujng. Eine Bestandsaufnahme*, Difu Papers August 2011.

Lorrain, Dominque, 1995. 'Le changement silencieux'. In Lorrain, Dominique and Stoker, Gerry (eds), *La privatisation des services urbains en Europe*, Paris: La Découverte, pp. 105–25.

Marcou, Gérard, 2007. 'Le cadre juridique communautaire et national et l'ouverture à la concurrence: Contraintes et opportunités pour les collectivités territoriales'. In *Annuaire 2007 des Collectivités Locales*, Paris: CNRS, pp. 9–28.

McEldowney, John, 2007. 'La fourniture d'énergie et l'administration locale: Une étude de cas du Royaume Uni'. In *Annuaire 2007 des Collectivités Locales*, Paris: CNRS edition, pp 121–9.

McEldowney, John and McEldowney, Sharron, 2010. 'L'eau: Réguler une ressource naturelle dans un climat économique changeant. Le cas de l'Angleterre'. In *Droit et Gestion des Collectivités Territoriales, Annuaire 2010, Les enjeux de la gestion locale de l'eau*, Paris: Le Moniteur, pp. 259–75.

Mehr Demokratie e.V., 2012. Bürgerbegehrensbericht 2012. http://www.mehr-demokratie.de/fileadmin/pdf/2012-09-04_BB-Bericht2012.pdf.

Millward, R., 2005. *Public and private enterprise in Europe: Energy, telecommunication and transport 1830–1990*. Cambridge: Cambridge University Press.

Mühlenkamp, Holger, 2012. 'Zur relativen (In-)Effizienz öffentlicher (und privater) Unternehmen- Unternehmensziele, Effizienzmaßstäbe und empirische Befunde'. In Schaefer, Ch./ Theuvsen (Hrsg), Renaissance öffentlichen Wirtschaftens, Nomos: Baden-Baden, pp. 21–47.

Mühlenkamp, Holger, 2013, From State to Market Revisited. Empirical Evidence on the Efficiency of Public (and Privately-owned) Enterprises, MPRA paper http://mpra.ub.uni-muenchen.de/47570/.

Peters, Guy B., 1995. 'Political institutions: old and new'. In Goodin, Robert and Klingemann, Hans-Dieter (eds), *A New Handbook of Political Science*, Oxford: Oxford University Press.

Pierson, Paul, 2000. 'Increasing returns. Path dependence and the study of politics'. *American Political Science Review*, vol. 94, pp. 251–67.

Praetorius, Barbara and Bolay, Sebastian, 2009. 'Implementing energy efficiency innovations: The strategic role of local utilities'. Available at: http://cleanenergysolutions.org/node/1445.

Prontera, Andrea and Citroni, Giulio, 2007. 'Energie et administrations locales en Italie: Dénationalisation, libéralisation et concurrence'. In *Annuaire 2007 des Collectivités Locales*. Paris: CNRS, pp. 191–208.

Reichard, Christoph and Röber, Manfred, 2012. *Remunicipalization in Germany Trends and Interpretations*, unpubl. Paper.

Reidenbach, Michael, 1995. 'L'Allemagne: L'adaptation graduelle'. In Lorrain, Dominique and Stoker, Gerry (eds), *La privatisation des services urbains en Europe*, Paris, pp. 81–104.

Röber, Manfred, 2009. 'Privatisierung ade? Rekommunalisierung öffentlicher Diensteleistungen im Lichte des Public Managements'. *Verwaltung und Management*, vol. 15, no. 5, pp. 227–40.

Schaefer, Ch. and Theuvsen, L., (eds) (2012), *Renaissance öffentlicher Wirtschaft*, Nomos. Baden-Baden, S. 21–48.

Schäfer, Roland, 2008. 'Privat vor Staat hat ausgedient. Rekommunalisierung: Modetrend oder neues Politikphänomen?' In *Öffentliche Finanzen, Sonderbeilage*, 19.6.2008, S. 3.

Scharpf, Fritz W., 2000. *Interaktionsformen. Akteurzentrierter Institutionalismus in der Politikforschung*, Opladen: Westdeitscher Verlag.

Schmidt, Vivien A., 2008. 'Discursive institutionalism. The explanatory power of ideas and discourses'. *Annual Review of Political Science*, vol. 11 http://papers.ssrn.com/sol3/papers.cfm?abstract_id=1141448.

Scott, Faye, 2011. *Is localism delivering for climate change? Emerging responses from local authorities, local enterprise partnerships and neighborhood plans*. Executive summary. Available at: http://www.green-alliance.org.uk/grea_p.aspx?id=6100.

Ude, Christian, 2006. 'Stadtwerke – Eckpfeiler kommunaler Selbstverwaltung'. *„der städtetag"*, no. 3, S. 21–5.

Varin, Katherine, 2010. Le service public de l'eau en France. Available at: http://www.globenet.org/aitec/chantiers/sp/eau/SPeauFrance.html.

Verbücheln, Maic, 2009. *Rückübertragung operativer Dienstleistungen durch Kommunen auf Beispiel der Abfallwirtschaft*, Difu Papers January 2009.

VKU (Verband kommunaler Unternehmen) (2010). Kompakt 2010, Kommunale Versorgungs- und Entsorgungsunternehmen in Zahlen. Available at: http://www.vku.de/presse/publikationen/kompakt-2010.html

Wollmann, H., 2007a. 'L'engagement des collectivités locales (les communes) dans la fourniture d'énergie (l'électricité), une perspective internationale'. In *Annuaire 2007 des Collectivités Locales*, Paris: CNRS édition, pp. 111–9.

Wollmann, H., 2007b. La fourniture d'énergie, l'administration locale et le marché: le cas de l'Allemagne'. In *Annuaire 2007 des Collectivités Locales*, CNRS édition Paris, pp. 161–71.

Wollmann, H. and Marcou, G., 2010. 'From public sector-based to privatized service provision. Is the pendulum swinging back again? Comparative summary'. In Wollmann, H. and Marcou, G. (eds). Elgar: Cheltenham, pp. 240–260.

Wollmann, Hellmut, 2002. 'Will traditional German local government survive in the face of Europeanization and New Public Management reforms?' *German Journal of Urban Studies*, no. 1. Available at: http://www.difu.de/index.shtml?/publikationen/dfk/en/.

Wollmann, Hellmut, 2007a. 'L'engagement des collectivités locales (les communes) dans la fourniture d'énergie (l'électricité), une perspective internationale'. In *Annuaire 2007 des Collectivités Locales*, Paris: CNRS, pp. 111–9.

Wollmann, Hellmut, 2007b. 'La fourniture d'énergie, l'administration locale et le marché- le cas d'Allemagne'. In *Annuaire 2007 des Collectivités Locales*, Paris: CNRS, pp. 161–71.

Wollmann, Hellmut, 2008. *Reformen in Kommunalpolitik und –verwaltung. England, Schweden, Frankreich und Deutschland im Vergleich*, VS Verlag: Wiesbaden.

Wollmann, Hellmut, 2011. 'From Public/Municipal to Private and Reverse?' *Croatian and Comparative Public Administration*, vol. 11, no 4, pp. 889–910. Available at: http://en.iju.hr/ccpa/ccpa/downloads_files/001-Wollmann.pdf.

Wollmann, Hellmut, 2013. 'Comeback of the local authorities and their companies in energy policy in European comparison' (in French translation). In *Droit et Gestion des Collectivités Territoriales, Annuaire 2013*, Paris: Le Moniteur (forthcoming).

Wollmann, Hellmut and Marcou, Gérard (eds), 2010a. *The Provision of Public Services in Europe. Between State, Local Government and Market*, Edward Elgar: Cheltenham.

Wollmann, Hellmut and Marcou, Gérard, 2010b. 'Introduction'. In Wollmann, Hellmut and Marcou, Gérard (eds), 2010a. *The Provision of Public Services in Europe. Between State, Local Government and Market*, Edward Elgar: Cheltenham, pp 1–14.

Wollmann, Hellmut and Marcou, Gérard, 2010c. From public sector –based to privatized service provision. Is the pendulum swinging back? In Wollmann, Hellmut and Marcou, Gérard (eds), *The Provision of Public Services in Europe. Between State, Local Government and Market*, Edward Elgar: Cheltenham, pp. 168–82.

Wollmann, Hellmut, Baldersheim, Harald, Citroni, Guilio, Marcou, Gérard and McEldowney, John, 2010. From public service to commodity: the demunicipalizatin (or remunicipalization?) of energy provision in Germany, Italy, France, the UK and Norway. In Wollmann, Hellmut and Marcou, Gérard (eds), *The Provision of Public Services in Europe. Between State, Local Government and Market*, Edward Elgar: Cheltenham.

PART II

Chapter 5
The Role of Local Governance in Strengthening Cross-border Cooperation

Milan Bufon

Introduction

Intensified diplomatic activities of sub-national administrative units and the development of new interstate economic and political interactions are undoubtedly indicators of in-depth changes related to the status and functions of state systems. The traditional exclusive and state-centered Westphalian order has been thus seriously challenged by the growing number of cross-border initiatives and connections that have also addressed the institutional issues related to: (1) the very objectives of cross-border cooperation; (2) cross-border frameworks or systems; and (3) dynamics of the cooperation itself within the context of the integration processes on the European continent.

The intensification of cross-border cooperation is usually associated with the process of increasing economic globalization and social co-dependence, with cross-border cooperation being expected to contribute to the elimination of actual or potential conflicts in borderlands. In view of that, the so-called cross-border regionalism is envisaged to become a constituent part of a complex, multilevel system of governance incorporating not only national, but also local and regional agents. From the normative point of view, such transfer of power would demand that all parties involved reach a higher level of international cooperation, eventually leading to new forms of regional governance carried out above or below the existing or prevailing national practices.

However we should also consider that European cross-border regionalism is not a uniform development, but rather a mosaic of very different initiatives and situations. According to Scott (1999), cross-border regionalism is a system of regional forms of cross-border cooperation characterized by very heterogeneous institutional strategies as it is constituted through multilateral agreements relevant to not only individual national governments but also local administration and civil society; a system that may be based upon the European regional policy whose most noticeable forms of manifestation are the Interreg programme and the Association of European Border Regions (AEBR).

These European policies undoubtedly resulted from positive outcomes of cross-border entities such as Benelux, a union operating at wider regional level, or Euregio, an association operating at a lower regional level along the German-Dutch border. Within this context, cross-border cooperation envisages the formation of special planning commissions usually composed of institutional administrators of the parties involved, as well as representatives of different professional bodies, in particular local universities and other non-government social organizations mostly from the economic and cultural fields. Cross-border regionalism thus proves to be not only a system of government, but also a system of integration of different interests and development visions that may have a more long-term and sustainable bases, thus de facto (but not necessarily de jure) facilitating the (re)integration of borderlands, or that may be only a manifestation of short-term opportunism when it comes to obtaining European funding and to patching up local budgets.

In the case of Interreg, its major objectives are indeed economic cooperation, development of cross-border infrastructure and cooperation in the environmental field, yet the programme also takes into account social and cultural aspects of cross-border cooperation. Naturally, in different borderland situations emphases fall differently: along the new internal borders between former Western and Eastern Europe, the emphasis is undoubtedly placed on harsh cross-border infrastructural measures, the aim of which is, first and foremost, to resurrect cross-border communication; while along old internal borders within the EU 15 area substantial funding is mostly allocated to soft integration at information and social levels and to better coordination of development planning and integration of functional measures (Marks and Hooghe, 2001). Even if joint cross-border social and spatial planning has recorded several notable achievements, such as the establishment of nature reserves and protected areas and the development of cross-border transport infrastructure and cooperation between universities, it still remains underdeveloped as it is impeded by various administrative and decision-making procedures on both sides of the border on the one hand, and by different forms of local patriotism springing from historical conflict-burdened motives or merely from pre-election calculations of local politicians on the other hand.

The situation is radically different in the North American area where cross-border cooperation is integrated in the system of interstate economic collaboration and has no far-reaching goals of social (re)integration. Cross-border economic cooperation started with the first free-trade agreement between Canada and the USA (CUFTA), signed in 1989, and in 1994 superseded by the North American Free Trade Agreement (NAFTA) in order to include Mexico as well. The North American area is characterized by bigger systemic and social differences, while the local cross-border-related element is of a relatively low importance since there are only two border lines in North America, extremely distant from one another (Anderson and Gerber, 2008). The main objective of the bloc is therefore the liberalization of economic and trade exchange, even if the partner states also try to achieve results in the fields of not only joint management of water and energy resources and pollution, but also collaboration between universities and other public institutions where the most active agents are not federal or national bodies but local communities directly interested in such collaboration (that is federal states and their administrative structures).

With the latter being much bigger than their counterparts in Europe, the notion of cross-border cooperation, particularly in the case of sparsely populated areas in North America, covers a much larger territory than in the EU. In comparison with the situation in Europe, American local communities (at least in the case of the USA) boast, as a rule, much greater autonomy so that from the point of view of functional cross-border cooperation federal states could play a much more important role than the majority of regions in Europe. The main obstacle is state restrictions in the field of free movement of people, resulting from the fear of illegal immigration and new security measures introduced after the September 2001 events, owing to which the internal borders within the NAFTA system are even more protected than the external borders of the EU system. Such restrictions not only pose a great hindrance to cross-border communication, but also impede the disentanglement of other concrete functional cross-border problems.

The EU would like to solve such problems at its external borders through the use of instruments such as the Interreg program or the European Neighborhood Policy whose implementation has mostly been entrusted to local governments. In the North American area, the majority of functional cross-border problems is, by contrast, solved by federal agencies that joined forces in the tripartite Commission for Environmental Cooperation (CEC) or in the bilateral (American-Mexican) Border Environment Cooperation Commission (BECC) on the one hand and by a number of NGOs dealing with individual aspects and problems of cross-border co-existence at local level on the other. Arizona-Sonora is the only association that could be regarded as a North American Euroregion if one ignores the facts that it operates in a mostly sparsely populated desert area and that its two centres are as many as 355 miles apart (Gonzales, 2004).

The comparison of European and American cross-border policies reveals that it is only in the European case that the issues related to cross-border integration and cooperation are increasingly addressed at the institutional level and therefore primarily a manifestation of de facto integration and cooperation of local and regional authorities financially supported by the joint transnational institution, that is, the EU. Similar incentives cannot be observed in the North American area where informal and non-government organizations and associations play a slightly more influential role and foster more flexible forms of cross-border cooperation. Both cases, however, do not exhibit more sustainable, in-depth and comprehensive forms of vertical (sectoral) and horizontal (spatial) (re)integration (Blatter, 2004). The EU does foster a myriad of cross-border incentives that, however, may be quite non-transparent and chaotic since in certain areas various Euroregions tend to compose real matryoshkas and that only rarely exhibit real coordination between not only the neighbours but also public and private interests within individual borderlands. Regional cross-border policies thus remain mostly administrative and bureaucratic in character, addressing real life and real needs of the borderland population only to a small extent.

This chapter will explore the changing role of local governance in strengthening cross-border cooperation. It will first explore some basic European instruments for cross-border policies as an element of both subsidiarity and regionalization. It will also approach the complex issue related to the management of EUs external borders and the creation of new potential insides and outsides. Finally, it will discuss the functioning of Euroregions as new sub-state actors of cross-border policies, functional integration and the new European multilevel governance. It represents the open character of the European social and planning principle and a real challenge of (re)integration of previously politically divided regions, but it has to cope with a persistent closed state organization and nationalism.

European Instruments for Cross-border and Neighbourhood Policies

Both cross-border and neighbourhood policies can be regarded as one of the most visible elements of contemporary European re-territorialization and multilevel governance composing an unprecedented network of co-dependence between transnational macro-regional institutions, states, regions and local communities (Scott, 2002). Since the mid-1980s, individual national politics in Europe have had to respond to the challenge of gradual Europeanization enabling regional and local communities to get in direct contact with transnational authorities in Brussels. The so-called subsidiarity became the guiding principle of reforms carried out since 1988 in accordance with the European structural policy.

The principle of subsidiarity not only calls for a process of vertical coordination between individual decision-making levels, but also introduces non-government agents into the decision-making process itself. Thus it somehow breaks up traditional hierarchical relations within individual national systems and encourages the regionalization of social and spatial processes both at the top-down and bottom-up levels, which naturally may give rise to new potential conflicts. After 1989, these developments were further complicated by in-depth geopolitical transformations on the European map that on the one hand gave new momentum to tendencies for horizontal (re)integration of the continent, and on the other slowed down the process of vertical integration or federalization of the European political system owing to not only a great number of new national players (which, however, were mostly centralized in character) and increasing economic globalization (giving rise to global crises), but also unexpected internal conflicts such as the one in the territory of former Yugoslavia. The EU did not manage to provide a unanimous response to all these new challenges since its major members more and more explicitly promoted their own political and economic interests within joint bodies.

Europe has thus not managed to shape a more harmonized spatial and social policy even if the issue has recently been discussed by competent European bodies and addressed by numerous expert studies. The latter mostly focus on urban systems, urban vs rural relations, accessibility of development systems or structures and natural and cultural heritage protection in the context of sustainable environment protection and the unity-in-diversity paradigm. Such views are no longer based on the principles of Christallers hierarchical spatial organization. They tend to be based on the idea of polycentric networks of urban regions, which no longer regard state borders as its supreme limit. In 1999, this joint development effort resulted in the adoption of the European Spatial Development Perspective (ESDP), which consolidated the vision of the so-called trans-European freight corridors. The ESDP also promoted the establishment of the so-called virtual regions ranging from Euroregions to larger regional integrations such as the Baltic region, the Atlantic Arc and the EUROMED region.

The EGTC and the Functional Cross-border Cooperation between Local Communities

All these regional cross-border entities received increased thematic and financial support in the last EU financial period (2007–13) within the framework of the so-called Objective 3 dedicated to European territorial cooperation. The EU contribution to this Objective amounts to nearly €8 billion allocated to as many as 53 cross-border cooperation programmes (which accounts for 74 per cent of the entire funding) and to 13 areas of transnational and interregional cooperation (26 per cent of the entire funding). The most important cohesion programme is most probably the European Observation Network for Territorial Development and Cohesion (ESPON). With cross-border integration often being hindered by national legislations and other administrative impediments, in 2006 the European Commission introduced a new legal instrument – European Grouping for Territorial Cooperation (EGTC) – enabling the establishment of a cross-border legal entity in order to carry out cross-border programmes and projects. The EGTC is allowed to form its own structure, to manage its own resources and to employ its own personnel. Potential EGTC members sign a convention and adopt a statute in line with the principle of the European legal order, while relevant national bodies have to approve their convention on cooperation, if appropriate, within three months. The EGTCs established so far provide common public services on the basis of already established Euroregions or are re-established with the aim of building cross-border infrastructure, carrying out cross-border transport services and other social services, launching joint agencies in the fields of energy and environmental protection, developing bilingual information systems in borderlands, collaborating in the field of research and education and so on (Hobbing, 2005). The majority of EGTCs have established administrative bodies, the members of which are not only their founding parties, but also other stakeholders and NGOs.

The EGTC instrument is envisaged to facilitate the operation and establishment of new Euroregions – entities that have proved to be the most efficient means for the promotion and implementation of European integration processes and policies in the field. In addition, it is an expression of broader efforts to create a common (European) system of multilevel governance in the fields of spatial planning and regional development practices, the aims of which are to assure solidarity and integration on the one hand and growth and competitiveness on the other.

Designed as open, such a system places emphasis on the production of spatial or organizational concepts, yet is not that well defined when it comes to concrete instructions and guidelines. Fairly undefined relations between society, economy and the environment are reflected in development visions that concomitantly stress the importance of dense economic networks, the sense of cultural heritage and European identity and innovation capability. The system of European spatial planning thus remains largely symbolic and constantly vacillates between functionality of development practices and situations in the most innovative parts of the EU 15, in particular the European centre delimited by the London-Paris-Milano-Munich-Hamburg pentagon which the rest of Europe should simply follow (or even submit itself to), and polycentricity of various subsystems that should co-create the European area and society in an equal (yet divided) manner (Faludi, 2000; Richardson and Jensen, 2000).

This development dilemma is undoubtedly a representative reflection on broader wavering between the federal and confederate concepts of how to organize the EU: the former presupposes a more integrated, as well as more hierarchical and centralized order with the free market regulating social and spatial development potentials in an open and competitive European system, while the latter gives precedence to diversity and the possibility of fairly large interventions of state regulators in the planning and implementation of development policies. It is the latter that seems more in favour of cross-border policies since they are a result of complex multilevel regulation and channelling to which the very presence of the state border as the principal element of social and spatial discontinuity gives its proper sense and motivation, whereas in an open system the internal borders would be bereft of their importance. As a result, cross-border cooperation and integration management, regulated by the Interreg programme and the EGTC instrument, is largely bureaucratic in character and does not satisfy actual expectations of numerous Euroregions and local communities, especially when Euroregions and cross-border programmes are established only at formal level and with the aim of assuring part of the European funding to individual administration units in borderlands or even to central state-directed apparatuses supervising them (Bufon, 2011).

The European Neighbourhood Policy: Creating New Insides and Outsides?

Another relatively complex issue is the management of EU external borders as addressed by the European Neighbourhood Policy (ENP). The aim of the ENP is to connect the tendency to reaffirm the traditional function of the external border, that is, the separation of the EU system from the rest of the world even if only in the socio-political sphere, and the concomitant tendency to overcome them and to establish cross-border regions of socio-economic cooperation and integration. This troublesome relationship deteriorated after the 2004–07 EU enlargement when candidate states – located in the in-between or border central and eastern European areas that during the transition period functioned as a spatial and social filter between the EU and the rest of the world – finally joined the system and had to completely rearrange their control systems at their new external borders. The threat of a Fortress Europe, which would cut off all cross-border ties at the EU external borders, gave rise to many protests by the local population, in particular along the Polish-Ukrainian, Slovak-Ukrainian and Hungarian-Ukrainian borders (Dimitrovova, 2010). The reasons for complaining were not only trivial calculations of numerous minor and major traffickers and smugglers who emerged after the liberalization of border regimes within the former Eastern Bloc, but also the deeper motives of those who had not expected that the deliverance from the undemocratic Communist regime would subject them to the new democratic discrimination between true and untrue Europeans. Such division would become even more absurd in many multicultural borderlands where the identification with the same nation or with the prevailing ethnic and linguistic group in the neighbouring country enabled members of the national minority to obtain double citizenship. Inequality in terms of possible cross-border movement would therefore create even greater disproportion between the potentials of ethnos and demos and lead to further political instrumentation and conflicts (Bufon, 2006a).

The European Commission responded to this issue at the end of 2006 by adopting not only the general principle Everything but Institutions applying to neighbouring states that are not envisaged to join the EU (even if the EU itself never clearly declared what its final size was supposed to be), but also a new regulation according to which the EU external borders would be allowed to introduce special border regimes allowing the borderland population easier cross-border movement, naturally on the condition that such a regime would be approved by the neighbouring state and defined by an adequate bilateral agreement. Concomitantly, the European Commission embarked on talks with EU neighbouring states in order to reach necessary agreements related to the return of illegal immigrants.

In what regards the closer neighbours of the EU, such agreements were reached with Ukraine and Moldova; some member states reached special ad hoc bilateral agreements, as in the case of Italy and Libya, even if officially the EU did not recognize Libya as a state with sufficient level of democracy to entrust it with the procedure of returning illegal migrants (allegedly, Gaddafis Libya subjects them to forced labor); whereas certain transition states, such as Morocco, do not intend to sign an agreement as they believe that such a procedure would incur huge expense. Slow development has also been characteristic of the vision of an enlarged free zone market, which would economically tie the EU with its close neighbourhood states in the areas of Eastern Europe and the Mediterranean, thus compensating for their full membership in the EU. Many in the EU would implement such a regime in the case of Turkey as well, a long-standing candidate for EU membership and as such an important player in the European free zone market. In practice, the former buffer zone composed of candidate states from central and Eastern Europe would now be relocated to the ENP area (Apap and Tchorbadjiyska, 2004).

Such selective or Eurocentric practices spurred many authors (Weaver, 1997; Zielonka, 2006) to ponder over new (western) European imperialism, interested in its external marginal areas only if they could bring it economic profit or pose it a safety threat even if, owing to its internal split, the EU is not able to provide a unanimous and efficient response to it, as was the case in former Yugoslavia where the conflicts were somehow mitigated only under external American constraint. Such an imperialist stance, if present, is apparently based on economic rather than military and strategic grounds and is supposed to count on comparative economic advantages arising from a large discrepancy in the development stage between the centre and the periphery within the system conceived in such a way. However, contemporary authors also highlight that in the long run the maintenance of diversity costs more than its abolishment (Marchetti, 2006), and so the EU has launched an assistance programme (ENPI with a budget of € 15 billion for the 2007–13 period) within the ENP programme, which is in many ways modelled upon the regional policies developed within the EU.

The European Regional and Integration Policies and the Role of Local Governance

The combination of internal and external regional policies, as discussed in the previous section, creates a complex system of concentric circles based on a bigger or smaller spatial distance from European development centers and on higher or lower degree of integration in the EU system built upon not only the free market, but also the monetary union and the Schengen area. Owing to the special decision-making system based on the power and importance of individual member states, differentiation can also be observed within the EU system itself, for example between the EU 15 states and the new members and even between the EU 15 group itself (that is between the real engine of the integration – the German-French connection, including the in-between Benelux – and the other EU 15 states). The enlargement and deepening of the EU therefore also entails the spread and deepening of ideas and incentives launched and developed in the centre of this integration and then adopted by other members. From such a point of view, European imperialism is multifaceted, operating according to the system of soft spread and implementation of certain values and mechanisms of co-dependence.

Internal and external co-dependence, however, changes the nature and function of political borders, transforming them from separators of social spaces into their integrators. European cross-border policies have thus expanded the classic, closed linear concept of political border to an open, dynamic geographical area of cooperation and integration within which the standard enforcement of visa regime and strict border control would undoubtedly function as a highly disturbing element. What actually arises here is the old discussion on which typology of border regime contributes more to the elimination of potential cross-border conflicts: is it the open border or the closed border? By preventing communication between the populations on both sides, the latter automatically eliminates potential conflicts, while the former brings together potentially quarrelsome sides and, by encouraging their co-dependence, turns them from enemies into friends.

Naturally, the process of European integration should spur all stakeholders in the field of cross-border policies to choose the open option, with the EUs attitude towards its external borders being relatively softer than the USAs attitude towards its external borders within the NAFTA association even if some EU members would prefer to employ American methods owing to their calculations in the field of domestic policy, especially when it comes to the limitation of the invasion of foreigners, that is the threat that has proven to be such an efficient generator of various populist stances in the old and new Europe (Kepka and Murphy, 2002).

Political interests of individual states in the preservation of the old Westphalian (closed or state-centric) concepts are therefore not always in complete accordance with (open or integration-oriented) the visions and policies of the EU or its joint bodies. Within such a context, the reality of European cross-border policies and practices along internal and external borders is inevitably fairly labile and contradictory, reflecting perpetual vacillation between not so much the abstract federal and confederate concepts of European organization as the real tendency to preserve and emphasize separate ethnic and national identities and positions on the one hand and the search for possible common European demos, as well as between historical memories and concrete needs of the present on the other. These dilemmas and development splits are also related to the question of how to regard and manage different territorial and social dimensions recently addressed by several authors (for example Anderson, 1996; Beck, 2007; Brenner, 1999) who pointed out the contradictory intertwining of various co-existing forms of territoriality and the changing relation between internal and external spaces in Europe.

Euroregions as New Actors of Cross-border Policies

In any case, it can be argued that the European practices have recently made real progress as far as the development of cross-border policies is concerned, making them an integral part of the European integration system. Cross-border cooperation, for which the abbreviation CBC is generally used, was born and developed in the area of Benelux and western German borders as early as the 1950s and 1960s. The area also coined the term Euroregion, generally used today for institutionalized cross-border cooperation of borderland municipalities or administrative units managed by special joint bodies such as a wider assembly and a narrower presidency, composed of elected representatives and local units, a secretariat for the execution of regular duties and special working bodies addressing common issues. The assembly and working bodies may also be composed of other stakeholders such as economic, professional and non-government organizations, as well as individuals who can contribute to the attainment of shared objectives (Bufon, 2011).

Such a practice proved to be fairly innovative as all policies with a cross-border dimension had traditionally been directed by the central authorities either on a unilateral or on a bi- or multilateral basis (in the case of special international agreements with other countries). It was only the initiative of the Council of Europe that gave a new, international dimension to local communities and peripheral national authorities: by launching the Interreg programme, the EU somehow incorporated such a dimension into its regional policy.

In practice, the initiative proved difficult to realize at legal level since legislations of individual countries did not make it possible, and so the majority of Euroregions operated on the basis of agreements with a different level of formality. In most cases, two or more associations of local communities integrated on the basis of internal legislative rules. Local communities obtained new options to formalize cross-border cooperation in 1980 when the Council of Europe launched the Madrid Convention; the new instruments were first used by Euroregions in Benelux and in the area between Benelux and Germany. In the course of time, there appeared the differentiation between real Euroregions, which incorporate all the abovementioned elements for actual institutional cross-border cooperation and which had been officially established on the basis of the Madrid Convention, and instrumental Euroregions, which operate only to the extent necessary for obtaining and using funding from the Interreg programme. In the latter, the most active agents are usually various public and private agencies operating separately on both sides of the border and specializing in lobbying and technical preparation of projects through which they finance their own operation. As a rule, instrumental Euroregions boast no permanent joint bodies of cross-border management characteristic of the real Euroregion (Bufon, 2006b).

Another element of differentiation between both types of Euroregions is territorial size as real Euroregions usually cover a historical or functional territory within which there develops functional cross-border co-dependence and real need for solving common issues, while instrumental Euroregions are artificially composed of NUTS 3 units that are, according to EU criteria, entitled to Interreg funding. In short: the former operate mostly in accordance with the bottom up approach, the main aim of which is to solve a shared problem; the latter mostly employ the top-down approach, the main aim of which is to obtain European funding. Another difference lies in the fact that in instrumental Euroregions local communities, for which the Interreg programme has been designed, have no say in decision-making processes as decisions are mostly made on their behalf by provincial or regional authorities within whose territory Euroregions are located or even by central national apparatuses that take care of the allocation of funding among individual regional authorities and individual project teams via political (and anything but transparent) channels, that is via ad hoc established joint management committees (Perkmann, 1999). Naturally, this contamination of the process of CBC with Eurocracy and state bureaucracy, if not even with pronouncedly partial party-related interests, has harmed genuine cross-border initiatives and needs arising at local level in many ways and in many places has even prevented real Euroregions from being established or submitted them to interests of instrumental Euroregions, which often rely upon the increasing political and economic power of regional authorities.

In view of that, the time of establishment of a certain Euroregion plays a fairly important role in its functioning, as has been proved where the Interreg programme helps old Euroregions, on the basis of which the entire system of the implementation of cross-border policies described above was actually created, in order to preserve their role in the complex multilevel system of management, while younger Euroregions find it very difficult to adopt a fairly discernible or independent role or may not even be established at all. Another important factor is the management structure in individual countries: for example, in Germany, states are usually too big to be the main agent of cross-border integration, and so Euroregions tend to be fairly efficient as they are not rivalled by other administrative units; moreover, as a federal republic, Germany is much more decentralized than neighbouring France where CBC is under greater control of the central authorities, and so Euroregions along the German-French border are less developed than their counterparts along the German border with Benelux. Another question posed by Perkmann is related to the very objectives and results of CBC. In his opinion, they can be divided into the following three groups: (1) spread and implementation of European policies; (2) establishment of territorial coalitions that are otherwise unstable; (3) creation of conditions for the emergence of new players in borderlands.

Borderlands between Convergence and Divergence Potentials

As mentioned above, borderlands have been witnessing the development of new forms of horizontal and vertical co-dependence and co-management involving both European institutions and central or peripheral authorities and other stakeholders from two or more countries, which can entrust the management of cross-border policies to special joint bodies or Euroregions in order to make it as efficient as possible. In short, Euroregions are a very good manifestation of a new, multilevel European regional and integration policy within which, however, different relationships between co-dependence and co-management are anything but determined and stable, which naturally crucially affects the level of success of the Euroregions themselves and the multilevel management approach taken in order to strengthen cross-border territorial entities and their functions. If the realization of European policies goes hand in hand with their regionalization, such developments may be regarded as a more or less conscious attempt to lessen the influence of the state since the state still remains the main and most influential agent in the process of social and spatial planning. Even in the EU, the state remains the main bearer of spatial and social identity of the population (Paasi, 2002). Cultural diversity is most probably the most distinctive characteristic of our continent, with the prevalence of nation-states in this part of the world indicating that political representativeness in the region is mostly based on ethnic and linguistic differentiation of the European population. Inasmuch as the element of representativeness is present in the process of the regionalization of the European area, regions can take over from the state the function of new ideological containers of the identity represented in a certain regional environment, which in turn takes over the status of dominant social group through regional political autonomy or self-government (Bufon, 2004).

Cross-border policies are probably the most discernible manifestation of the new system of governance and planning gradually developed within the EU system. This process of Europeanization of spatial and development policies has led to the emergence of new institutional structures and ties that transcend state borders and annul traditional hierarchy in the decision-making process. According to some authors (for example Castells, 1998), such developments bring about the formation of a new, postmodern socio-political network structure or authority manifested in the system of the so-called multilevel governance involving not only inter- and supra- but also sub-state dimensions. The first dimension is somehow personified by the European Council, the second by the European Commission and the European Parliament and the third by different Euroregions and cross-border associations of regions. Within such a context, the Interreg programme functions as an actual possibility of implementing multilevel, network governance, and can be regarded as a success story of European integration policies in the field. This project-oriented cross-border cooperation and integration is also a reflection of a typical European practice that on the one hand brought about the boom of different pragmatic Eurocratic agencies and committees, and on the other the realization of new and unimagined development scenarios and visions for the future. The latter are mostly a subject of the ESDP, which however has to constantly cope with various development and spatial regulations since the perspective of the open European social and planning area is still divided into closed national (state) systems that get their meaning in the very European principle of subsidiarity.

In any case, changes in the function and status of different territorial units and levels lead to changes in the function and status of their borders, which in todays Europe mostly move in the continuum between socio-cultural divergence and socio-economic integration. It is this relationship that gives rise to major problems with cross-border cooperation as in many places there arise a big discrepancy between expectations and needs of the local population and the practice of cross-border policies. The two communities meeting the other one along the border are both spatially close and socially apart: spatial closeness is mostly dependent on the typology of the border regime, which can pose major or minor obstacles to cross-border movement, while social distance depends on the level of socio-cultural homogeneity and better or worse functional integration of the borderland population and area. The term cross-border cooperation itself presupposes that there exists a certain obstacle, that is the border, that has to be overcome, while the term social and spatial (re)integration calls for complete removal of the obstacle (Houtum and Struever, 2002). In such a context, analysts of border situations and potentials of cross-border co-dependence have to consider both the symbolic and functional nature of this obstacle since it can be established that it is precisely because internal borders no longer function as obstacles in the EU that they increasingly assume the role of symbolic, mental borders, which can be a new real obstacle to actual (re)integration of the border area and society. Borders therefore everywhere produce environments of simultaneous potential opportunity or threat, coexistence or conflict, cooperation or competition, convergence or divergence. The feasibility of prevalence of one or the other option depends on time and place, while in some cases even both options can be observed in one and the same area (Anderson and ODowd, 1999).

Another problem, characteristic of Europe in particular, springs from the genesis of the border line itself since one and the same political border can be regarded as an object of historic victory by one side and as an object of historic defeat by the other; in addition, this perception may differ in state centres and the borderlands themselves where the very presence of national minorities can generate the existence of two contradictory views of the past that often have a crucial impact on the feasibility of cross-border communication and even social and spatial (re)integration in the present.

When discussing the level of cross-border co-dependence or integration measurable with several indicators (Bufon, 2008b), it would make sense to compare this level with those related to the co-dependence or integration between the borderland in question and nearby areas within the same state system, as well as to observe changes in these various spatial and social forms of integration through time. In such a manner one can test the hypothesis that traditionally connected historical regions split by the political border resulting from the formation of nation-states tend to be better connected or more co-dependent than traditionally separated borderlands. That is especially the case in various historically multicultural regions in Central and Eastern Europe exhibiting not only a great capacity for functional (re)integration, but also a relatively high degree of potential conflicts owing to divergent historical memory and, consequently, underdeveloped forms of institutional cross-border integration. Underdeveloped forms of institutional, that is to say social and political cross-border integration, can also be met in a number of old borderlands in Western Europe due to a centralized form of state organization; such borderlands usually also foster underdeveloped ties of functional cross-border cooperation, whose existence is otherwise facilitated by social and cultural affinities on the one hand and social and economic disparities on the other (Bufon, 2011). With the latter diminishing, social and cultural affinities along EU internal borders play an increasingly important role in the EU. Along external borders, the main drive of cross-border interactions is usually social and economic disparities as is evident especially in the case of the American-Mexican border.

Conclusion

In this chapter, we have discussed both challenges and problems emerging from an intensified cross-border integration which, particularly in Europe, creates a sort of cross-border regionalism. The latter might be sought as a new constituent part of a complex, multilevel system of governance, which could be quite bureaucratic and limited to the creation of artificial Euroregions seeking only to attract European funds, but may also represent a system of grass-rooted social and spatial (re) integration efforts within politically divided borderlands and thus re-acting local societal and territorial co-dependence. Local cross-border cooperation is therefore not only concerning the future reorganization of functional economic, social and administrative units, but also the question of a possible reorganization of national and cultural areas, still constrained in the classic nation-state model. In this context, the role of local and regional communities is emerging both in regard to the preservation of their original settlement area (the *cultural landscape*), and the (re)creation of cross-border and trans-community co-dependence in an integrated region or *functional space*.

The issues of borders and cross-border (re)integration are therefore closely related to the question of changing territoriality, which is characterized by the tendency to preserve social control within state property on the one hand, and by the tendency to (re)activate suppressed social and spatial co-dependence at regional level on the other. Changes in the function of political borders and the (re)activation of old and new forms of territorial co-dependence are a result of the simultaneous processes of de-territorialization and re-territorialization allegedly caused by globalization which is believed to weaken the traditionally exclusivist or closed nature of state systems and to intensify cross-border as well as wider international co-dependence (Berezin and Schain, 2003). Globalization therefore exhibits the tendency not only to do away with political or any other borders and to shape a new, completely open social space, in which both history and geography would make no sense as such processes can be partly monitored only in the economic field, but also to reconstruct the existing social spaces where along traditional horizontal political borders there also exist other, vertical levels of social and spatial organization that can be integrated only through a new, multilevel system of governance. Classic interstate relations are therefore integrated into macro-regional systems, while deconcentration of political and economic relations facilitates the formation of inter-regional and cross-border ties primarily based on existing local potentials, yet not immune to broader geopolitical and geostrategic influences.

Certain authors (Anderson, 1996) saw in this deconstruction of the European state-centric system, resulting from supra- and sub-state challenges, the threat of regression to the pre-modern, feudal era, with the fragmentation of unitary and federal states creating a new Europe of region. In such a neo-feudal system, borders would make no sense at all owing to the prevailing complex system of various authorities whose areas of competence would intertwine and overlap, while classic one-dimensional identity would be replaced by multiple identities, with people identifying themselves not only with national, but also regional and macro-regional or global territorial and social dimensions. This potential of multiple, discreet identity is, naturally, related above all to functional organization of society and space, that is to demos rather than ethnos since in the course of time the latter exhibits much greater stability and regenerative capacity (Bufon, 2008a). The Europe of states is thus challenged and strengthened at the same time by both the Europe of regions and the Europe of nations since they both would like to assert themselves and develop by following the unitary state model, even though it differs from the classic model in its greater international integration and functional co-dependence. Last but not least, both visions have their starting point and their goal in borders no matter how we understand them since it is through borders that they define their exclusivity and assert their network character in the international arena.

However, the European integration process has deeply challenged the Westphalian system as an organization of the world into territorially exclusive, sovereign nation-states. In fact, integration is becoming embedded in a wide discourse on globalization and regionalization. The debate has been centered on two questions: first, does the EU still represent only an intergovernmental institution dominated by the executives of the member states, or has it evolved beyond such a state-centered system. This is particularly the case of borderlands and cross-border regions, the front-lines of territorially demarcated, closed modern states. On the contrary, these areas, thanks to the increasing international role of local governance, are now shaped by intensive socio-economic and socio-cultural inter-dependencies and are providing not only new perspectives for a concrete (re) integration of neighbouring border areas and societies, but also in removing the problem of the other within the EUs political and planning system. It seems that it is on the very competence to channel integration processes in borderlands that both the current and future forms of our society and its development perspective will depend.

References

Anderson, J., 1996. The shifting stage of politics – new medieval and post-modern territorialities. *Environment and Planning*, 14(2), pp. 134–55.

Anderson, J. and ODowd, L., 1999. Borders, border regions and territoriality – contradictory meanings, changing significance. *Regional Studies*, 33(7), pp. 593–604.

Anderson, J.B. and Gerber, J., 2008. *Fifty Years of Change on the U.S.-Mexico Border – Growth, Development, and Quality of Life*. Austin: University of Texas Press.

Apap, J. and Tchorbadjiyska, A., 2004. *The Impact of Schengen along the EUs External Borders*. CEPS Working Document 210. Brussels: Centre for European Policy Studies.

Beck, U., 2007. Reinventing Europe – a cosmopolitan vision. In Rumford, C. (ed.), *Cosmopolitanism and Europe*. Liverpool: Liverpool University Press, pp. 39–50.

Berezin, M. and Schain (eds), M., 2003. *Europe without Borders – Remapping Territory, Citizenship and Identity in a Transnational Age*. Baltimore: The Johns Hopkins University Press.

Blatter, J.K., 2004. From "spaces of place" to "spaces of flows"? Territorial and functional governance in cross-border regions in Europe and North America. *International Journal of Urban and Regional Research*, 28(3), pp. 535–55.

Brenner, N., 1999. Beyond state-centrism? Space, territoriality, and geographical scale in globalisation studies. *Theory and Society*, 28(1), pp. 39–78.

Bufon, M., 2004. *Between Territoriality and Globality – Current Issues of Areas of Social and Cultural Contact* (Med teritorialnostjo in globalnostjo – sodobni problemi območij družbenega in kulturnega stika). Koper: Annales.

Bufon, M., 2006a. Between social and spatial convergence and divergence: an exploration into the political geography of European contact areas. *GeoJournal*, 66(4), pp. 341–52.

Bufon, M., 2006b. Geography of border landscapes, borderlands and euroregions in the enlarged EU. *Rivista Geografica Italiana*, 113(1), pp. 47–72.

Bufon, M., 2008a. Inter-cultural Dialogue and European Areas of Social and Cultural Contact (Medkulturni dialog in evropska območja družbenega in kulturnega stika). *Annales*, 18(1), pp. 79–88.

Bufon, M., 2008b. *On the Margin or in the Centre? – Border Areas and the Challenge of European Integration* (*Na obrobju ali v osredju? Obmejna območja pred izzivi evropskega povezovanja*). Koper: Annales.

Bufon, M., 2011. *No More Shall Foes, But Neighbours Be – Management of Integration Processes in Border Regions*. Koper: Annales.

Castells, M., 1998. *The Information Age – Economy, Society and Culture*, vol. III: End Of Millenium. Oxford: Blackwell.

Dimitrovova, B., 2010. *Remaking Europes borders through the European Neighbourhood Policy*. CEPS Working Document 327. Brussels: Centre for European Policy Studies.

Faludi, A., 2000. The European Spatial Development Perspective – what next? *European Planning Studies*, 8, pp. 237–50.

Gonzales, P.W., 2004. Conflict and accommodation in the Arizona-Sonora region. In Pavlakovich-Kochi, V. et al. (eds), *Challenged Borderlands – Transcending Political and Cultural Boundaries*. Aldershot: Ashgate, pp. 123–51.

Hobbing, P., 2005. *Integrated Border Management at the EU Level*. CEPS Working Document No. 227. Brussels: Centre for European Policy Studies.

Houtum, H. and Struever, A., 2002. Borders, strangers, doors and bridges. *Space & Polity*, 6(2), pp. 141–6.

Kepka, J.M.M. and Murphy, A.B., 2002. Euroregions in comparative perspective. In Kaplan, D.H. and Haekli, J. (eds), *Boundaries and Place – European Borderlands in Geographical Context*. Lanham: Rowman & Littlefield Publishers, pp. 50–69.

Marchetti, A., 2006. *The European Neighbourhood Policy – Foreign Policy at the EUs Periphery*. Discussion Paper C158. Bonn: Zentrum fuer Europaeische Integrationsforschung.

Marks, G. and Hooghe, L., 2001. *Multi-Level Governance and European Integration*. Boulder: Rowman & Littlefield.

Paasi, A., 2002. Bounded spaces in the mobile world – deconstructing "regional identity". *TESG* 93, pp. 137–48.

Perkmann, M., 1999. Building governance institutions across European borders. *Regional Studies* 33(7), pp. 657–67.

Richardson, T. and Jensen, O.B., 2000. Discourses of mobility and polycentric development: a contested view of European spatial planning. *European Planning Studies*, 8, pp. 503–20.

Scott, J.W., 1999. European and North American contexts for cross-border regionalism. *Regional Studies*, 33(7), pp. 605–17.

Scott, J.W., 2002. A networked space of meaning? Spatial politics as geostrategies of European integration. *Space and Polity*, 6(2), pp. 147–67.

Weaver, O., 1997. Imperial metaphors – emerging European analogies to pre-national state imperial system. In Tunader, O. et al. (eds), *Geopolitics in Post-Wall Europe: Security, Territory and Identity*. London: Sage, pp. 59–93.

Zielonka, J., 2006. *Europe as Empire – The Nature of Enlarged European Union*. Oxford: Oxford University Press.

Chapter 6

Failed Rescaling of Territorial Governance in Hungary: What Was the Gist?

Ilona Pálné Kovács

Introduction

The European administrative space has become a normative programme relying on the relationship between the different tiers of governance and the elaboration of common procedural and professional standards (Cardona, 1998; Olsen, 2003; Goetz, 2006). This means that there is an aim for some convergence in the national public administrations in Europe. The Europeanization of the public administration territory occurred, among others, through territorial reforms which generally led to strengthening lower level governance (Lidström, 2007). Seemingly this happened in Hungary too, but the result is ambivalent.

This chapter does not aim at describing the almost two-decade long history of territorial reforms in Hungary, it is rather going to analyse the motivations and forces behind the various reform measures. These facts are relevant in understanding what will happen in the future, and also in answering the dilemma whether it is possible to create a real basis for decentralised governance in a country where the centralised model of governance is determined by the legacy of the past and even by the surviving political culture. The Hungarian story provides evidence to the opinion that regionalisation is not just rescaling, but much more an opportunity for shifting power among levels and actors (Swyngedouw, 2000), and not necessarily top down.

The state of the art of the regions is colourful throughout Europe (Pálné, 2005; Baldersheim and Rose, 2010). There are only few really regionalised European countries with regions having constitutional status, autonomy and a real balancing role within the power structure. In most of the regionalised countries regional decentralisation was forced by ethnic movements or other locally rooted political groups in order to counterbalance the central power (Kohler-Koch, 1998). The so-called top-down regionalism, however, is initiated by central governments aiming at modern, cost-efficient administration or regional development under the pressure of the EU Structural Funds regime. In spite of a series of regional reforms, mostly in the 1990s, European countries have different meso-level models and as a consequence of that there is no uniform European scale, status and content at the meso-level governance. Although European local governments tried to push national governments towards decentralisation through, for example, the

European Charter of Self-governments (1985), the establishment of the Committee of Regions or the White Paper on Multilevel Governance (CoR, 2009), there is no uniform landscape of territorial governance and we cannot say that regions 'occupy an important role in the architecture of the EU' (Loughlin, 2007: 400).

The failure or postponing acception of the European Charter of Regional Governments shows that most member states of the Council of Europe do not wish to agree upon any standard. There is no strong doubt about the fact that the formerly fashionable regionalism is declining (Elias, 2008), although many experts are convinced of the advantages of the economies of scale and of more decentralised governance structures. Baldersheim and Rose (2010) used the terminology of 'territorial choice' which always implies the Phoenix dilemma, since it is hopeless to find a final solution for the optimal scale. The task is to understand the internal and external mechanisms and driving forces of territorial reforms in order to fit the appropriate design for the adaptation and change of government models in each country. Hungary has recently started in a completely new direction of territorial governance, referring to the failed reforms implemented or rather postponed in the last two decades. The lessons of the failed reforms could help in avoiding them in the future.

Hungary on the Road of Regionalisation

Systemic Change, Pattern Copying, Path-dependency

The territorial division of public power has always been a hot political and professional issue from the beginning of Hungarian statehood. The counties as sub-national governance units were established together with the central state 1,000 years ago, having the mission to represent the state in the territory occupied and controlled by the king. In the thirteenth century the counties became the frames of defence for the nobility against the king. From that time on the counties have had a dual character, being both self-governments and deconcentrated state organs. This dual character has always caused contradictions between local and national interests.

When the organization and function of counties had been historically stabilised, the scale and borders became the focal point of reform debates between the forces of modernisation and traditions. Interestingly, the supporters of the modernisation and rescaling of counties were mostly dynasties of foreign origin (the Habsburgs for example), therefore the Hungarian nobility defended the county as a symbol of Hungarian independence. The external/foreign pressure for modernising/ rescaling the counties was the main reason why Hungarians were against every territorial reform, assuming that behind the official reform, the real ambition was centralisation and the replacement of the county elite. This was also the case during the Soviet rule around the 1956 Revolution when the communist leaders did not risk changing the county system although there was an idea to follow the Soviet economic districts named 'rayons'. Thus the protection of national sovereignty coupled with the political and emotional support given to the old county system led to a paradox in the sense that the old country system became an obstacle in the way of territorial rationalisation, refusing any change in county division. On the surface debates on the county issue were focusing on the scale (borders, seats), referring to 'big is "strange"', 'small is "our own"', so the territory of the counties remained almost untouched, except after the Treaty of Trianon closing the First World War when the country lost two-thirds of its territory.

During the last systemic change in 1990 the county issue first arose not as a scale problem, but rather as a choice of political value, since the legislator wanted to give preference to values like closeness to citizens and autonomy over economic rationality and the economies of scale. Consequently municipalities were preferred to the county level in the distribution of competences and resources. The issue of scale emerged again in the middle of the 1990s when preparation for EU accession started. The idea of big region instead of small county was not a result of rational recognition of inner necessities; it was rather an external, imported model in order to get access to EU Structural Funds. At that time the slogans of 'Europe of Regions' or 'New Regionalism' (Keating, 2004) were dominating public policy literature and EU regulations, so the Hungarian elite could use it in its argumentation that regionalism would be the only successful way for or road to Europe.

At that time nobody raised the questions: what kind of regions do we really need? How reforms are to be implemented? What will the consequences of the dramatic rescaling of public administration be? What kinds of institutions are appropriate for public administrative tasks, for public services and for development policy in Hungary? Drawing the map concealed the real questions and doubts whether it is really so easy to replace the 19 counties with seven regions and where will the power go among the newly created levels? The only aspect in creating the NUTS2 regions was that these would be eligible for Structural Funds.

Misunderstanding the European Governance Principles

The history of Hungarian regional reforms has not missed the modern European principles of public governance, but unfortunately these principles have not been followed systematically. Analysing how the external patterns were implemented in Hungary is useful in understanding why the context and the political culture matter.

In what regards subsidiarity, it regulates primarily the division of power between the European Union and the member states, so it is not applied automatically to national public administration in the sense of sub-national decentralisation. Thus decentralisation is not a prescribed condition of good governance, although both governance literature and political narrative approach territorial decentralisation normatively in many respects, meaning that it is thought desirable from the aspects of performance, efficiency and democratic legitimacy of the state (Saito, 2011). The criterion of good governance set by international organizations, especially by the World Bank, for the assisted, developing and transitional countries implies that decentralisation in general is seen as a positive and efficient organizational principle (Barlow and Wastl-Walter, 2004).

Regionalism, decentralisation and multilevel governance (MLG) created a very complex governance system in Europe by shifting power and resources generally top down, while, contrary to this, in Hungary regionalisation resulted in more centralised governance. Paradoxically it was the misunderstanding of subsidiarity that led to centralisation. Subsidiarity as a popular slogan was understood, for example, as the preference of municipalities (closest to the citizens), neglecting the meso-level. The bypassed, later continually reformed, meso-level became the reason why municipalities were losing their strong position step by step. Namely, the meso-level self-governments were not able to fill the huge gap between the top and the bottom (being very fragmented in Hungary with 3,200 mostly small municipalities) in order to represent local interests towards the centre. To understand the importance of this we have to keep in mind that the position of meso-level governance almost always determines the extent of decentralisation in the whole governance system: if the meso-level is weak or is owned by the central government, the local level is not able to counterbalance this superiority.

Partnership, horizontal networks and governance are also fashionable, neo-liberal buzzwords, having crucial impacts in the transitional countries. Many mean that the concept of governance is so broad now that it is the source of a number of inconsistencies instead of really contributing to the interpretation of the transformation of government systems (Hughes, 2010). However, there is consensus on the issue that the essence of the governance model is that it goes beyond the borders of hierarchical public administration, involving also the civil and the private sectors as partners. Besides the hierarchy characterising the state, the horizontal and networking elements can also be found here integrating the market, bureaucracy, networking and community-led government models into meta-governance (Jessop, 2011). The previous rigid walls separating branches and levels of power have disappeared and strong, exclusive, non-permeable networks have emerged. Governance has local/regional roots and arenas as well (Bovaird et al., 2002; Jessop, 2011). Yet regional governance has had some fairly contradictory consequences due to significant changes in the functioning of regions.

Democratic deficit, low participation at elections and decreasing trust are getting characteristic at this tier of government too. Under the neoliberal slogan of regional governance we can often find only non-transparent networks. The mainly new regions are actually victims of the institution-building innovations, in the course of which exclusive elite circles, practically a new 'regional service class', appear (Lovering, 2011: 589). It is a general observation that the functioning of partnership, transparency and efficiency of networks depend on the constitutional, political and civil society features of the specific country. Research carried out by the Tavistock Institute has proved that the forms of partnership cooperation required by EU regional policy are best functioning where civil society is strong and where the corporate forms of cooperation with the economic actors fit the community-level decision-making smoothly and in a well-regulated way (Kelleher et al., 1999). This recognition was supported by an inquiry carried out at the request of the European Parliament in 2008 (EP, 2008). Its results corresponded to the social capital theory by Putnam who analysed the management and utilisation of European development resources in Italy at the beginning of the 1990s (Putnam et al., 1993).

This governance level can be generally characterised by strong party dominance and its politicians consider it as a means to enter national politics, although the real impact of regional party organizations on national politics remains rather limited (Fabre, 2008; Stefuriouc, 2009). There are, however, a number of attempts to involve civil society on the basis of recognising the role of social capital and trust, but the success of these attempts is at least questionable (Putnam, 2000). Many share the idea that instead of non-transparent networks the institutions of traditional representative democracy should be rebuilt (Loughlin, 2001: 390–400; Palonen et al., 2008) coupled with deliberative cooperation with the different groups of society (Elster, 1998).

The half federative governance model built on participation, evolved in the European Union, has proved to be an impossible mission, especially in those countries where the state structure is unitary and the corporate and direct forms of interest reconciliation do not function (Grote and Gbikpi, 2002). This is characteristic of the Hungarian government structure as well. In Hungary the regional reform was implemented through the creation of mainly new types of institutions and methods of functioning, because the introduction of elected self-governmental regions, requiring the modification of the constitution, was not supported by the parliamentary opposition. The Act on Regional Development adopted in 1996 established the so-called development councils based on the European partnership model; these were practically semi-public institutions for strategic planning and resource allocation. Such partnership bodies appeared in other fields of public policy as well (such as employment policy, tourism, youth policy and NGO financing system). It became the feature of Hungarian regional governance that it did not fulfil the role of representative self-governmental democracy, and therefore it was not the advantages of partnership but the disadvantages of democratic deficit that became dominant. This fact was revealed by empirical research that analysed the networks established in a Hungarian NUTS2 region, where we found exclusive elitist networks such as grant-coalitions and the complete absence of any publicity (Pálné, 2009).

Structural Funds Regime: The Main Driver of Changes

It is almost a commonplace that Europeanisation was generated by the management of the Structural Funds (Hughes et al., 2004). The European principles of subsidiarity and partnership, applied primarily in Cohesion Policy, involved the regions in the decision-making processes of the European Union and as a result regions have become very active in MLG (Bache, 1998). The so-called experimental governance can also be detected in the rules of allocation of the Structural Funds

(Mendez, 2011). The elements of the open method of coordination (OMC) usually appear where the exclusive competence of the European Commission is missing and therefore it has to negotiate with the member states (Héritier, 2001). This was not the case with the Central and Eastern European countries which proved to be good pupils in order to access the funds. The reason for this is that these countries receive the bulk of the resources allocated for development and therefore they have no alternative but to comply with rules even if Cohesion Policy is the shared responsibility of the Commission and the member states.

The requirements of Cohesion Policy appeared in an extremely extensive system of rules, most of which did contribute to innovating and improving public administration in the member states (flexibility, efficiency, partnership, integration, strategic planning and so on). However, this was not always the case and did not relate to every aspect. One of the most contradictory requirements is the necessity of designating the NUTS2 regions, especially in the so-called cohesion countries (Ireland, Greece, Portugal and Spain before the enlargement, and the Central and Eastern European countries after 2004). These countries are the primary beneficiaries of the Structural and Cohesion Funds. Taking a closer look at the regional reforms implemented in the EU member states we can see that most of the countries have preserved their traditional public administrative units and the new regions were established over and not instead of them (like Greece, France), or the regional development institutions were built outside their normal public administration (Ireland, Portugal). Another important feature is that these reforms were gradually introduced and implemented after decades-long preparation (France, Italy), even in those countries where regionalisation had some historical antecedents or traditional and cultural roots (Larsson et al., 1999). Analysing the consequences of regional structural changes makes it clear that reforms supported from below are more successful and less conflicting, and the new institutions thus created were easier to build and are socially better and more organically embedded (Knodt, 2002; Elcock, 2003).

The candidate Eastern and Central European countries preparing for accession were convinced that regions matter. The European Commission has had a crucial influence on starting territorial reforms in these countries, leaving the national governments enough scope for action in finding the most appropriate model to adapt to European regulations. Paradoxically, the new member states have not made use of this freedom and the new NUTS2 units have become the territorial basis of public administrative reforms in some CEE countries, albeit this was not compulsory according to NUTS regulations.

This was the case in Hungary as well despite that NUTS2 regions had no traditions or identity here and it was only theoretically assumed that they would provide advantages by the economies of scale. The framework of NUTS2 regions was filled up by partnership institutions, development agencies and some public resources at the end of the 1990s, on a parallel with the NUTS3 and 4 units. The government announced the reform programme in 2002, planning to strengthen the status of the NUTS2 regions by direct election of regional self-governments in the next election period in 2006. The accession in 2004, however, caused shock and disappointment. Referring to weak regional capacity, the European Commission insisted on the centralised management of the Structural Funds. Hungary had to realise that the EU did no longer insist on the active role of the regions and did not intend to take the risks of the decentralised structures. As a consequence, the regional institutions almost completely lost their former influence on regional policy. The management authorities responsible for Structural and Cohesion Funds were set up within the central government and regional actors received intermediating functions only. The 2007–13 programming period seemed to be an opportunity for real regionalisation. Although the government strongly emphasised the role of regions in the planning process, in fact it created separate regional operational programmes, and the prospects of the regions became unpromising by the end of the negotiation series with Brussels in 2006. The government again created a fairly centralised management by the National Development Agency having all the competences concerning the management of Structural Funds. The regional development agencies only received an intermediary role, as in 2004–06, and the regional development councils remained no more than consulting partners in planning and project management. Political regionalisation was, of course, simply forgotten, which is a clear evidence of the Hungarian government not having meant the self-governing regions so seriously.

The process described above clarifies that European Cohesion Policy was the main but contradictory and external driving force of regional reforms in Hungary. Furthermore, even the huge amount of European support was not enough to convince the central political elite of the importance of regionalisation, or, more exactly, they insisted on further centralisation and this ambition was supported or at least accepted by the European Commission. Similar processes were characteristic of almost all Central and Eastern European new member states (except Poland) (Bachtler and McMaster, 2008), demonstrating that regionalisation needs a basis broader than the European pattern or the birdlime of Structural Funds, although it is also true that the development aids contributed to massive learning among technocrats and agencies dealing with European funds (Bruszt, 2008). Other observations, however, underline that following EU accession adaptation willingness in the Central and Eastern European countries significantly declined and they rather seek to enforce national characteristics and interests (Bouckaert et al., 2011).

At the same time, if we want to have a complete picture we have to mention that regionalism is no more fashionable in other parts of Europe either. There is a shift occurring in Europe concerning regionalism at least in a political sense (Keating, 2008). Region has ceased to be a miracle; it is time to investigate the processes and the consequences of regionalism in Europe without illusions to be able to envision the future.

Why Have Hungarian Territorial Reforms Failed?

Experiences of decentralisation reforms managed on the basis of a uniform scheme are generally not unambiguous. The expectations and recommendations formulated by the OECD, the European Union and the Council of Europe implied that the public administrative systems of the member states were greatly different, yet they based their policy on the hypothesis that there were some common trends being able to serve as points of reference for the accession countries. However, on evaluating the implementation of the recommendations it was realised that although many Central and Eastern European countries had launched significant reforms, these could not fulfil the expectations. It was thus recognised that the adoption of more developed Western governance solutions and innovations could not be applied mechanically; instead, both the objective and the subjective preconditions of implementation (such as cultural, political and mental) should be taken into account (Tönnisson, 2004). In the course of evaluating the post-accession Europeanisation process, it is admitted ever more often that the models, the best practices coming from old member states can only lead to superficial changes in the new members, since these do not always enable them to carry out a real adoption (Stead and Nadin, 2011).

Therefore, decentralisation also has certain preconditions. In a peculiar way, the national features have been strongly preserved in Western Europe despite the reforms, while in the new member states drastic structural reforms were carried out without launching stable and real modernisation. Although the self-governmental model – its content, tools and its spatial and organizational structures alike – were significantly transformed in the Central and Eastern European transition countries (Wollmann, 2002), it is still an open question what direction they will take in the future.

It follows from the above that the desired European model followed by the reforms of Hungarian territorial public administration is not at all unambiguous, and signs of malfunctions and disillusionment appeared in other countries as well. Consequently, we can assume that the choice of model was not the best. On the other hand, reform capacity was also lacking, the circumstances and consequences of reform implementation were not thoroughly analysed from the aspects of political science and public policy. The process of rescaling in Hungary led to a completely irrational jungle in both institutional and geographical terms as a result of the frequently changing targets, the imperfection of the professional bases and the drifting of the governments between different groups of interests and values. There was no efficient political force and sufficient professional and public policy knowledge to renew territorial governance. Beside the weakening traditional counties the new territorial tiers could only become rivals without having triumphed. Three territorial tiers in a small country are too many and too expensive; moreover, they create extra coordination needs and conflicts. The selection and designation of the optimal medium tier are not issues of belief; neither should they be copied from the European model. They should have been the result of rational consideration and policy analysis of domestic facts and needs.

The missing link in the public administrative reforms in CEE countries was not the fashionable programmes, but the absence of their implementation (Dunn et al., 2006), mainly due to the lack of real political will. The continually repeated reform ideas, the ad hoc efforts and the withdrawals by the next governments show that there was no firm resolution, nor was there recognised interest, to build strong meso-level governance. Paradoxically, anxiety about losing power was strong even in the field of policy where the advantages of regionalisation were the most obvious, namely in the management of European resources. The Structural Funds created opportunity for modernisation and large-scale investments, yet they were unable to contribute to the decentralisation of the country by strengthening the regions. Twenty years after the systemic change we have to admit that without solving the social and economic problems it is not possible to build a stable ground for modern forms of governance (Bayer, 2009). Before someone is given power, one must learn how power should be used. However, this cannot be achieved exclusively by structural reforms or rescaling, especially when structural reforms create only a new sphere of action without adequate competences and resource decentralisation. In such cases no substantial results can be expected.

A further important lesson is that it is not enough to announce reforms, their implementation must also be carefully designed and planned, taking into account possible resistance and the task of persuading those counter-interested. Therefore, identifying opponents is a crucial issue. Our research has proved that even the ruling political groups have not truly supported regionalisation. The mayors of larger towns and the presidents of county assemblies have shown explicit resistance, most of them having been MPs, so they could have strong influence in undermining the reforms (Pálné, 2009). The political resistance of the counter-interested was coupled with the indifference of the ordinary citizens, which was not a Hungarian peculiarity; it is enough to refer to the unsuccessful referendum initiatives about regional reforms in Portugal (Loughlin, 2001) or in England (Curtice and Sandford, 2005). It seems difficult to raise the interest of citizens in regional reforms, except when a region has an ethnic, lingual or historical character and cohesion. However, there are contrary observations as well. Whereas it is a fact that participation is lower at regional elections than at the national ones, this difference is smaller when the regions receive significant resources and power (Blais et al., 2011). Despite the former assumptions, recent research has found that decentralisation has not changed the uniformly national character of political parties. This means that the parties investigated were not compelled to regionalise their politics and organizations, even if there was significant decentralisation carried out in their country (Lago-Penas et al., 2011). Of course, the explicitly regional parties that have won support exactly under the aegis of regionalism are exceptions to this phenomenon (for example the Spanish and Italian regional parties). Regarding the consequences of regionalisation, researchers have also revealed that decentralisation helps in appreciating social capital, human relationships and trust. According to the data of the Word Value Survey, the opportunity of being involved in governance proved to be more important for citizens in decentralised countries than for those in centralised ones (Mello, 2011). Unfortunately Hungarian citizens are not enthusiastic about self-governance and regionalism, and the political actors (especially the parties and mayors) are not convinced of the advantages of regional decentralisation; consequently there were hardly any opponents of strong centralisation.

The Future: Centralisation

As a result of the monetary-economic crisis in recent years and the accompanying social tensions, the outlines of a new governance period are shaping, not only as an answer to the new challenges but also as a criticism of the previous era. The so-called neo-Weberian governance model emerging in some European countries has no illusions about the neo-liberal governance model and it reclaims the order and transparency of the old bureaucratic public administration. Government changes indicate the strengthening of bureaucracy and the central governments, even if there are some theoretical attempts to synthesise the two models (Dreschler, 2009: 13; Osborne, 2010), fearing that the advantages of governance will be lost in the new wave of reforms.

With the right-wing government gaining power in 2010 a new period began in Hungary, both in general politics and in spatial public administration. The previous state philosophy is overtly refused and we can currently witness centralising and nationalising efforts, referring to the strong state which obviously has to cope with the emerging economic crisis too.

The new government passed a new Constitution, officially called 'The Basic Law', as a symbol of beginning a new era, claiming that the former Constitution created during the change of regime 20 years ago was aimed to be temporary only. This implication has a very important message. With the new governance philosophy the new government aims to close the first transitional period, supporting the opinion that the model and the values chosen 20 years ago are not sustainable anymore. The new Basic Law follows the idea of strong, centralised government. It is no wonder therefore that the new law on local governments adopted in 2011 also moved towards a weaker and centrally more controlled model of local government system, giving a definite response to the territorial reform misery of the last decades.

In the course of this process the position and status of self-governments underwent serious modifications with cancelling regionalisation, destroying the regional development institutions and public administrative bodies in the NUTS2 regions and simultaneously consolidating the old counties as meso-level governance. The counties as geographical frames have survived, but not as self-governments. Following the pattern of the French prefect system, government commissioners were appointed in the counties. These commissioners were granted much more power than the county self-governments. The strong county-level state administration is responsible for public services which used to belong to the county self-governments. The elected county self-governments will only be responsible for territorial planning and development policy, but nobody knows what kind of public policy instruments and resources will support this mission.

At the same time, significant reforms are planned to consolidate municipal governments. Although formally the government does not wish to limit the autonomy of self-governments even in the smallest settlements, legal opportunity has been introduced for forced associations. It would be rational, but the marginalisation of the entire system of local governments is a dominant trend which curbs the scope of action not only of the smallest units but also of the cities and counties. According to the most recent legislation, extensive centralising/nationalising processes will start in many local public services (education, health care and so on), since schools, hospitals, homes for the elderly, museums and so on will be run by de-concentrated state organizations. The government has also created new geographical units (*járás* in Hungarian) within the counties, taking over administrative tasks from the municipalities, but it seems likely that they will be assigned to carry out other municipal tasks as well in the future. The result of this process is not clear yet, but the state and its territorial agencies will surely be much stronger in terms of competences, resources and power than the local self-government sector has ever been. Thus we can say that the objective of building a democratic and decentralised governance system has been (temporarily?) cancelled, justifying the iron law of path-dependency in the region.

Conclusions

Over the last decades European public administration has undergone significant transformations and will probably continue to do so in the future. These changes have indicated two main trends: the first is structural, organizational transformation, the second is functional relating to operation. The role of these changes and their interrelationships can hardly be generalised. Despite this, it can be stated that the modernisation of national public administrations and local governments has been typically carried out through structural reforms in Europe during the last decades (Wright, 1997). The new challenges could also be met by functional adaptation, since the impact and consequences of the structural reforms implemented have not been convincing (at least not everywhere).

In the light of the turbulent regional-territorial reforms it is worth raising the question whether the democratic self-value of decentralisation can assert itself automatically everywhere or only within a special context; that is, whether ripe democracies and new democracies are able to decentralise in the same way? The latest Hungarian developments in changing the governance model raise the question whether, after the systemic change, the serious discrepancies in government models can be explained by immaturity or deeper cultural differences?

A further question is whether democratic decentralisation has advantages per se in managing public services and treating territorial inequalities, or, according to the principle of limited rationality, it is only dependent on the particular conditions (Kyriacou and Roca-Sagalés, 2011)? It is especially important to raise the question whether rescaling would automatically entail the benefits of economies of scale and whether the rearrangement of the power structures (centralisation vs decentralisation) is the reason for or the consequence of territorial reforms? Similarly, it is hard to find evidence for the larger scale administrative units, the regions being definitely more efficient or the regionalised, federative countries being more successful economically due to decentralised governance (Müller, 2009).

It is empirically proven that empowerment definitely means the extension of the scope of action, but in itself it does not mean that this empowerment will be exercised in a democratic and efficient way. It is not enough to examine just the content of empowerment, the abilities and ambitions of the local governments should also be known (Johansson, 2000). It is often difficult to judge the real scale and content of decentralisation. It is not accidental that the regulation of responsibility is considered currently as the key challenge in decentralisation (Lago-Penas et al., 2011), so transferring tasks and competences has to be a process based on professional considerations. Furthermore, it is very difficult to decide what kind and scale of decentralisation can be realised at sub-national levels in a given country. If these aspects are neglected, the potential benefits will hardly emerge.

The increasing number of questions and uncertainties imply that there are no axioms or minimum standards in regionalisation and territorial governance. The optimal spatial division of power and the way to manage reforms leading to this optimum are in themselves relevant research topics to be answered in each country. We tend to accept the opinion of Keating (2009) that there is no pure functional or political logic of regionalisation and rescaling.

There seems to be strong relationship between the content and success of governmental policy and the general organizational system of territorial public administration. Not only the quality and adaptive ability of public administration affect the efficiency of public policy, but, conversely, the tasks to be performed also influence public administration being thus shaped in the course of public policy challenges. The choice of political values, attitudes and model of governance also play a significant role in setting the reform targets, and it is also important how the different fields of governance science develop. The professional basis has not an exclusive but an essential effect on the success of public administrative reforms which are normally rare events. Obviously, where performance evaluation is integrated into the public administrative system, that is, where proper information, professionals, appropriate methodology, organizational mechanisms and procedures are available, the preparation of reforms is significantly easier than in a system lacking all these. Furthermore, Western democracies have had a much more stable (and integrated) public sector than the newcomers (Potucek, 2004). In the spirit of incrementalism, that is, slow but deep changes, the model of step-by-step adaptation and modernisation has often been applied.

The adaptation of the governance system in Hungary, similarly to the other CEE countries (Bouckaert et al., 2011), has been carried out in a rather contradictory way. Hungary has established its territorial public administration as influenced by the regional support system of the European Union. The territorial harmonisation of public administration and development policy institutions has not been successful and the replacement of traditional public administrative units by new, larger regions has proved to be an impossible task. Despite structural and organizational changes, the functioning and behaviour of civil servants and politicians have remained almost unchanged and consequently structural reforms have been inefficient. This has been the case in other CEE countries as well where the implemented radical reforms have reshaped only the structure, but not the content, the values and the attitudes of the civil servants (Lazareviciute and Verheijen, 2000). The legacy, the culture and the mechanisms of the past have survived.

One of the most important conclusions is that rescaling/reshaping the territorial governance system has not led to real decentralisation, as recent literature also describes (Scott, 2009). The quality of local democracy and public services depends not only on the general model chosen, but also on national and local socio-economic conditions, public legal fine-tuning, the culture of central and local politicians and on the specific features of local society.

Despite the crucial role of national, regional contexts, the global trends of local/territorial governance do not stop at country borders. Although centralising tendencies gain power cyclically and the position of local authorities and regions in the system of multilevel governance has been changing, local and territorial governments occupy a significant role among public institutions. The extent of decentralisation has remained one of the most important indicators of democracy. The spatial order of governance is an important aspect of power sharing, but the concrete geographical structure and rescaling of territorial governance differ by country and over time (Baldersheim and Rose, 2010).

Returning to the question raised in the title, there is no single reason why territorial reforms have failed in Hungary. Research has to be carried out to contribute to our understanding the reform processes and the factors behind them.

References

Bache, J., 1998. *The Politics of European Union Regional Policy*. Sheffield: Sheffield Academic Press.

Bachtler, J. and McMaster, I., 2008. 'EU cohesion policy and the role of the regions: investigating the influence of Structural Funds in the new member states'. *Government and Policy*, 26 (2), pp. 398–428.

Baldersheim, H. and Rose, L.E., (eds) 2010. *Territorial Choice. The Politics of Boundaries and Borders*. Haundmills, New York: Palgrave, Macmillan.

Barlow, M. and Wastl-Walter, D. (eds), 2004. *New Challenges in Local and Regional Administration*. Aldershot: Ashgate,

Bayer, J., 2009. 'A rendszerváltásról két évtized múltán' ('On the systemic change after two decades'). In. Bayer, J. Boda, Zs. (eds), *A rendszerváltás húsz éve. Változások és válaszok* (*Twenty Years of Transition. Changes and Responses*) Budapest: L'Harmattan, pp. 9–27.

Blais, A., Anduiza, E. and Gallego, A., 2011. 'Decentralization and voter turnout'. *Environment and Planning C: Government and Policy*, 29 (2), pp. 297–321.

Bouckaert, G., Nakrosis, V. and Nemec, J., 2011. 'Public Administration and Management Reforms in CEE: Main Trajectories and results'. *The NISPAcee Journal of Public Administration and Policy*, 4(1), pp. 9–32.

Bovaird, T., Löffler, E. and Parrado-Diez, S., 2002. *Developing Local Governance Networks in Europe*. Baden-Baden: Nomos.

Bruszt, L., 2008. 'Multi-level Governance- the Eastern Versions: Emerging patterns of Regional developmental Governance in the New Member States'. *Regional and Federal Studies*, 1. pp, 629–37.

Cardona, F., 1998. *European Principles for Public Administration*. SIGMA papers, 27. CCNM/SIGMA/PUMA(99)44/REV 1. Paris: OECD.

Committee of Regions, 2009. *White Book on Multilevel Governance*. CdR 89/2009 final Brussels

Curtice, J. and Sandford, M., 2005. 'Does England want devolution too?' In Park, A. et al. (eds), *British Social Attitudes*. London: Sage Publications pp. 201–20.

Dreschler, W., 2009. 'Towards a Neo-Weberian European Union? Lisbon Agenda and Public Administration'. *Halduskultuur*, 10, pp. 6–22.

Dunn, W., Staronova, K. and Pushkarev, S. (eds), 2006. Implementation. The Missing Link in Public Administration Reform in Central and Eastern Europe. Bratislava: NISPAcee.

Elcock, H., 2003. 'Creating new regional regimes?' In Deffner, A., Konstadakopulos, D. and Psycharis, Y. (eds), *Culture and regional Economic Development in Europe: Cultural, Political and Social Perspectives*. Volos: University of Thessaly Press, pp. 87–107.

Elias, A., 2008. 'Introduction. Whatever happened to the Europe of Regions? Revisiting the Regional Dimension of European Politics'. *Regional and Federal Studies*, 5, pp. 483–93.

Elster, J., 1998. *Deliberative Democracy*. Cambridge: Cambridge University Press.

European Parliament, 2008. *Governance and partnership in regional policy*. IP/B/ REGI/FWC/2006-Lot05-C02-SC02. PE 397.245.

Fabre, E., 2008. 'Party organization in a Multilevel System: Party organizational Change in Spain and the UK'. *Regional and Federal Studies*, 4, pp. 309–31.

Goetz, K.H., 2006. *Temporality and the European Administrative Space*. Paper presented at the CONNEX Conference Towards an European Administrative Space. London, 16–18 November.

Grote, J.R. and Gbikpi, B. (eds), 2002. *Participatory Governance. Political and Societal Implications*. Opladen: Leske+Budrich.

Héritier, A., 2001. 'New modes of governance in Europe: Policy-making without legislating'. In Héritier, A. (ed.), *Common Goods: Reinventing European and International Governance*. Lanham: Rowman and Littlefield, pp. 46–59.

Hughes, O., 2010. 'Does governance exist?' In Osborne, S. (ed.), *The new public governance?* London and New York: Routledge, pp. 87–105.

Hughes, J., Sasse, G. and Gordon, C., 2004. *Europeanization and regionalization in the EU's Enlargement to Central and Eastern Europe.* London: Palgrave Macmillan.

Jessop, B., 2011. 'The state: Government and governance'. In Pike, A., Pose A.R. and Tomaney, J. (eds), *Handbook of Local and Regional Development.* London and New York: Routledge, pp. 239–49.

Johansson, J., 2000. 'Regionalisation in Sweden'. In Gidlund, J. and Jerneck, M. (eds), *Local and Regional Governance in Europe: Evidence from Nordic Regions.* London: Edward Elgar Publishing, pp. 125–60.

Keating, M. (ed.), 2004. *Regions and Regionalism in Europe.* Cheltenham: Elgar Reference Collection.

Keating, M., 2008. 'A Quarter Century of the Europe of the Regions'. *Regional and Federal Studies*, 18(5), pp. 629–37.

Keating, M., 2009. 'Rescaling Europe'. *Perspectives on European Politics and Society*, 10, pp. 34–50.

Kelleher, J., Batterbury, S. and Stern, E. 1999. *The Thematic Evaluation of the Partnership Principle.* London: Tavistock Institute.

Knodt, M., 2002. 'Regions in Multilevel Governance Arrangements: Leadership versus Partnership'. In Grote and Gbikpi (eds), *Participatory Governance. Political and Societal Implications.* Opladen: Leske+Budrich, pp. 177–94.

Kohler-Koch, B., 1998. *Interaktive Politik in Europa. Regionen im Netzwerk der Integration.* Opladen: Leske-Budrich.

Kyriacou, A.P. and Roca-Sagalés, O., 2011. 'Fiscal and political decentralization and government quality'. *Environment and Planning C: Government and Policy*, 29(2), pp. 204–24.

Lago-Penas, I., Lago-Penas, S. and Martinez-Vazquez, J., 2011. 'The political and economic consequences of decentralisation. Guest editorial'. *Environment and Planning C: Government and Policy*, 29(2), pp. 197–204.

Lago-Penas, I. and Lago-Penas, S., 2011. 'Decentralization and the nationalization of party systems'. *Environment and Planning C: Government and Policy*, 29(2), pp. 244–64.

Larsson, T., Nomden, K. and Petiteville, F. (eds), 1999. *The Intermediate Level of Government in European States. Complexity versus democracy?* Maastricht: EIPA.

Lazareviciute, I. and Verheijen, T., 2000. 'Efficient and Effective Government'. In Péteri, G. and Simek, O. (eds), *European Union Enlargement and the Open Society Agenda.* Local Government and Public Administration. Budapest: OSI/LGI, pp. 149–63.

Lidström, A., 2007. 'Territorial Governance in Transition'. *Regional and Federal Studies*, 17(4), pp. 499–508.

Loughlin, J. (ed.), 2001. *Subnational Democracy in the European Union. Challenges and Opportunities.* Oxford: Oxford University Press.

Loughlin, J., 2007. 'Reconfiguring the State: Trends in territorial Governance in European States'. *Regional and Federal Studies*. Special issue: Contemporary Trends in Territorial Governance, 17(4), pp. 385–405.

Lovering, J., 2011. 'The new regional governance and the hegemony of neoliberalism'. In Pike et al. (eds), *Handbook of Local and Regional Development*. London and New York: Routledge, pp. 581–95.

Mello, L., 2011. 'Does fiscal decentralisation strengthen social capital? Cross-country evidence and the experiences of Brazil and Indonesia'. *Environment and Planning C: Government and Policy*, 29(2), pp. 281–97.

Mendez, C., 2011. 'The Lisbonization of EU Cohesion Policy: A Successful Case of Experimentalist Governance?' *European Planning Studies*, 3, pp. 519–39.

Müller, U., 2009. *The Power to Shape a Region. Decentralisation of Political Decision*. Basel: Paper for International Benchmarking Forum.

Olsen, J.P., 2003. *Towards a European Administrative Space?* ARENA Working Papers Wp 02/26. http://www.arena.uio.no/publications.

Osborne, S. (ed.), 2010. *The New Public Governance?* London, New York: Routledge.

Pálné Kovács, I. (ed.), 2005. *Regionális reformok Európában* (Regional reforms in Europe) Budapest: IDEA.

Pálné Kovács, I. (ed.), 2009. *A politika új színtere a régió* (*New scene of politics: the region*). Budapest: Századvég.

Palonen, K., Pulkkinen, T. and Rosales, J.M. (eds), 2008. *The Politics of Democratization in Europe*. Farnham: Ashgate.

Potucek, M. (ed.), 2004. *The Capacity to Govern in Central and Eastern Europe*. Bratislava: NISPAcee.

Putnam, R.D., 2000. *Bowling Alone: The Collapse and revival of American Community*. New York: Simon and Schuster.

Putnam, R.D., Leonardi, R. and Nanetti, R., 1993. *Making Democracy Work. Civic Traditions in Modern Italy*. Princeton: Princeton University Press.

Saito, F., 2011. Decentralization. In Bevir, M. (ed.), *The SAGE Handbook of Governance*. London: SAGE Publications, pp. 484–501.

Scott, J.W. (ed.), 2009. *De-coding New Regionalism*. Farnham: Ashgate.

Stead, D. And Nadin, V., 2011. 'Shifts in territorial governance and the Europeanisation of spatial planning in Central and Eastern Europe'. In Adams. N. Citella and Nunes, R. (eds), *Territorial Development, Cohesion and Spatial Planning*. London and New York: Routledge, pp. 154–78.

Stefuriouc, I., 2009. 'Introduction: Government Coalitions in Multi-level Settings-Institutional Determinants and Party Strategy'. *Regional and Federal Studies*, 1, pp. 1–13.

Swyngedouw, E., 2000. 'Authoritarian governance, power, and the politics of rescaling'. *Environment and Planning D. Society and Space*, 18, pp. 63–76.

Tönnisson, K. 2004. 'The applicability of networking principles among Estonian local governments'. In Jenei, Gy., Mclaughlin, K., Mike, K. and Osborne,

S.P. (eds), *Challenges of Public Management Reforms*. IRSPM-BUESPA, Budapest: pp. 193–217.

Wollmann, H., 2002. ‚Die traditionelle deutsche Selbstverwaltung – ein Auslaufmodell?‘ *Deutsche Zeitschrift für Kommunalwissenschaften*, 1, pp. 24–52.

Wright, V., 1997. 'The Paradoxes of Administrative Reform'. In Kickert, W. (ed.), *Public Management and Administrative Reform in Western Europe*. Cheltenham: Edgar Elgar, pp. 7–15.

Chapter 7

Local and Regional Government Reform in Croatia: Subsidiarity and Innovation in an Era of Austerity

Boris Bakota

Introduction

Since the regaining of Croatian independence in 1991 and of a new territorial system, established in 1992 and in operation since 1993, there has been constant public demand for further adjustments and changes. Even though there were numerous small changes in the system of territorial government and in geographical limits of municipalities, towns and counties, there is still dissatisfaction with the current situation.

According to 2011 census[1] there are 4,284,889 inhabitants in the Republic of Croatia in its 56,594 km². The country is divided in 20 counties, 126 towns, 429 municipalities and the Capital City of Zagreb with county status: counties are units of regional self-government while towns and municipalities (555 in total) are units of local self-government. Before 1993 Croatia was divided into 100 municipalities plus the City of Zagreb.

The chapter discusses the reasons behind this dissatisfaction and explores possible solutions for future territorial restructuring of the country. Among other issues, the chapter addresses the matter of the number of local government units, which is considered to be excessive for the size of the country. As the evidence provided will show, this is a rather complex issue, as proven by other foreign examples, but also as a result of the differences within the country: population density is very different from one part of the country to the other, due to many factors (geography, history, economy and so on).

When deciding about borders of specific units certain factors have to be considered: a) homogeneity, b) gravitation, c) complementarities and d) economic and fiscal capacity. It is very difficult to consider all those factors when establishing units. Sometimes it is more important to focus on homogeneity, because that way it is possible to establish a unit predominately inhabited by members of a certain

---

1 Data from 2011 census can be found at www.dzs.hr, but they are still unofficial. Therefore I have analysed most of the information used in this chapter myself and certain data are based on the 2001 census since it wasn't possible to find the information needed.

national minority, thus making it easier for them to preserve their language, tradition, culture and so on. Gravitation is probably the easiest factor to consider, because people's tendency to gravitate around a particular centre is usually obvious. If the law-maker primarily wishes to consider complementarities there are no objections to this decision. This way it is easy to preserve needs resulting from specific living conditions or specific business affiliation due to specific conditions and so on.

However, although it may be relatively easy to respect the first three factors, economic and fiscal capacity could destroy all the previous achievements. Due to many factors (socialist background, war, adaptation to new economic conditions and so on) there are many regions seriously lagging behind in economic power. If we find homogeneity, gravitation and complementarities to be of greater importance, there is often need for central government to help those units in everyday tasks and duties. Some Croatian municipalities would, without central subsidies, only be able to pay salaries to the staff they employ. The law has made provisions for an equalization mechanism to help financially weak municipalities in the implementation of key projects.

As a result of the economic crisis in the last few years there has been growing demand for central government support considering rights and obligations.

Units of Local and Regional Self-government

Counties

Even if accepting that 20 counties is a good solution, we still have to emphasize the differences in their population and area. The most populated county is the Capital City of Zagreb with 790,017 inhabitants (18.44 per cent of the country) while at the same time it is the smallest area in square kilometres, only 641, which represents only 1.13 per cent of the country. On the other hand, the least inhabited county is Lika-Senj with only 50,927 inhabitants but covering 9.46 per cent of the country (5,353 km²). In terms of population, the whole county is smaller than seven Croatian towns. Lika-Senj County is actually a big area comprising forests, mountains, hills, rivers and the most beautiful Croatian National park – Plitvice. The settlements are very small and far away from one another so it was necessary to enable citizens to go to a relatively nearby centre (Gospić) instead of going to some bigger centre which is very far away. Apart from small Lika-Senj County, there are two neighbouring counties in the East part of Croatia with less than 100,000 inhabitants (Požega-Slavonija and Virovitica-Podravina). If the two of them were to join together, the new county would still be smaller than 10 other counties. Since 1992 there have been no changes in the county structure, even though there were many different propositions during the discussion regarding county structure back in 1992. Some even argued that the seats of archdioceses and dioceses should also serve as county centres. This idea was discarded very quickly because the differences between dioceses were even more significant. The final decision was the result of many factors; geographical, historical, economic, but also political ones. The smallest county in area is Međimurje (1.29 per cent) and the decision to constitute that area as a special county was made just one day before passing the law.[2] An even greater problem arose when settling the shape of the southernmost part of the Republic of Croatia. The Croatian coastline is not a single uninterrupted line. Around 20 kilometres of the coastline belongs to Bosnia-Herzegovina.[3] In 1718 the Republic of Dubrovnik, not wanting to have the direct border with Venetians, gave a part of the coast to the Ottoman Empire. Later it was considered to be an integral part of Bosnia-Herzegovina and consequently in 1992 when Bosnia-Herzegovina was recognized as an independent country a big problem arose about how to organize an effective administration with all its organs. The county is a unit of regional self-government whose territory represents a natural, historical, transit, economic, social and self-governmental whole, and it is organized for the purpose of performing tasks of regional interest.

Table 7.1   County population and area

Counties	Population	%	Area (km²)	%
CITY OF ZAGREB	790,017	18.44	641	1.13
SPLIT-DALMATIA	454,798	10.61	4,540	8.02
ZAGREBAČKA	317,606	7.41	3,060	5.41
OSIJEK-BARANJA	305,032	7.12	4,155	7.34
PRIMORJE-GORSKI KOTAR	296,195	6.91	3,588	6.33
ISTRIA	208,055	4.86	2,813	4.97
VUKOVAR-SYRMIA	179,521	4.19	2,454	4.34
VARAŽDIN	175,951	4.11	1,262	2.23
SISAK-MOSLAVINA	172,439	4.02	4,468	7.90

---

2   The justification for establishing Međimurje as a special county exists. It is a geographically established area which has also had a very special history.

3   In the light of Croatia's accession to the European Union on 1st July 2013 a big problem occurred, mostly for the people from Dubrovnik-Neretva County who have to pass a foreign country to be able to enter the rest of their own country. Presently people only have to show their identity cards and are allowed to pass, but in reality there are two border check-points. When Croatia enters the European Union the regime on the border is probably going to be more rigid, and the government is trying to solve this crucial problem. Ideas vary, from erecting a bridge that will go to a Croatian peninsula thus avoiding the necessity of passing through Bosnia-Herzegovina, or building large ferries that will bring passengers and their cars to the other part of Croatia or even constructing a heavily guarded corridor that will only enable traffic to pass without any stopping. But local Bosnia-Herzegovina's municipality of Neum heavily objects to the latter solution.

Table 7.1   *Concluded*

Counties	Population	%	Area (km²)	%
ZADAR	170,017	3.97	3,646	6.44
BROD-POSAVINA	158,575	3.70	2,030	3.59
KRAPINA-ZAGORJE	132,892	3.10	1,229	2.17
KARLOVAC	128,899	3.00	3,626	6.41
DUBROVNIK-NERETVA	122,568	2.86	1,781	3.15
BJELOVAR-BILOGORA	119,764	2.80	2,640	4.66
KOPRIVNICA-KRIŽEVCI	115,584	2.70	1,748	3.09
MEĐIMURJE	113,804	2.66	729	1.29
ŠIBENIK-KNIN	109,375	2.55	2,984	5.27
VIROVITICA-PODRAVINA	84,836	1.98	2,024	3.58
POŽEGA-SLAVONIA	78,034	1.82	1,823	3.22
LIKA-SENJ	50,927	1.19	5,353	9.46
T O T A L	4,284,889	100	56,594	100

Source: Croatian Bureau of Statistics. www.dzs.hr.

Figure 7.1   Croatian counties
Source: hr.wikipedia.org.

Municipalities and Towns

A municipality is a unit of local self-government which is founded, as a rule, for the territory of several inhabited places representing a natural, economic and social whole and which is connected by common interests of the inhabitants. A town is a unit of local self-government where the seat of the county is located, as well as any other place with more than 10,000 inhabitants which represents an urban, historical, natural, economic and social whole. The town as a local self-government unit can include the surrounding settlements that, together with the urban settlement, make up an economic and social whole and are connected with it through the movements of daily migration and the inhabitants' everyday needs which are of local importance.

Exceptionally, where there are special reasons (historical, economic or geographic), a place that does not meet the conditions set forth may be established as a town. Since 1992 all Croatian municipalities and towns have had the same rights and obligations, except that towns were allowed to collect surtax based on a citizen's commodity of living in a town. Later, even the municipalities were given the right to collect surtax, but according to population size. Towns with 35,000 inhabitants and more and all the towns that are county seats received some county prerogatives in 2005. We can accept the fact that towns larger than 35,000 inhabitants can be considered big enough to receive that sort of competence, but a decision that all county seats are also to be considered as big cities may not always be the case.[4] There are actually only 16 towns with 35,000 inhabitants and more.

Table 7.2   Town population and number of towns

Population	Number of towns
less than 10,000	60 (47.62 %)
10,001–35,000	50 (39.68 %)
35,001–100,000	13 (10.32%)
100,001 and more	3 (2.38%)

Source: Own elaboration.

Even though towns can be exceptionally smaller than 10,000 inhabitants, in reality there are currently 39.68 per cent of towns that don't meet the 10,000 inhabitants' prerogative. This stipulation was originally inserted in the law that aimed to differentiate between coastal towns and those in the continental part. Coastal towns even with 2,000 or 3,000 inhabitants do have an urban feeling (town

---

4   It is not very important to citizens themselves whether they go to town or county organs to resolve some of their problems.

parks, public space and so on) while at the same time settlements in the continental part which are even bigger than that are actually villages. Also, there are some towns that should have this status due to their historical importance. According to international regulations there are 79 islands, 520 islets and 624 rocks, in total 1,223.[5] There are 50, or maybe a few more,[6] inhabited islands, islets and rocks which need to be an integral part of some municipalities or towns, but also those inhabited areas need to be part of certain municipality.

This factor enhances the differences between towns and municipalities situated at the seaside from those in the continental part of Croatia. The smallest Croatian town Komiža in Split-Dalmacija County has only 1,526 inhabitants, while the biggest town, Split, also in the same county, has 178,102 inhabitants. Komiža is on a relatively big, but very remote island of Vis and this is the reason for its town status. On the other hand, the most sparsely populated municipality is Civljane (Šibenik-Knin County) with only 239 inhabitants. Civljane municipality is territorially one of the biggest municipalities, but it is almost uninhabited. The biggest municipality is Viškovo (Primorje-Gorski Kotar County) with 14,445 inhabitants. Its number of citizens, according to the law, suggests that it should have town status, since it has more than 10,000 inhabitants. In total there are seven municipalities with more than 10,000 inhabitants, but those municipalities consist of many small settlements which lack urban atmosphere.

Table 7.3   Municipality population and number of municipalities

Population	Number of municipalities
less than 1,000	37 (8.63 %)
1,001–10,000	385 (89.74 %)
10,001 and more	7 (1.63 %)

Source: Own elaboration.

In comparison with town population, we can say that municipalities mostly lie somewhere between 1,001 and 10,000 inhabitants (89.74 per cent). But, we can question whether 1.001 inhabitants are sufficient to make a municipality self-sustainable and logical. Although Croatian law has no regulation concerning the minimum number of inhabitants for a municipality, currently there are discussions whether it should be 1,000 or 2,000 or even more.

Bearing in mind the geographical factors and conditions we must differentiate among many types of Croatian municipalities (island, continental, coastal, mountain and so on). Their different status is not recognized by law, but we cannot decide on

---

5   http:www.hrvatskiotoci.com/hrvatskiotoci.pdf (Accessed 16 July 2012).

6   There are some fishermen not living on the island all of the time.

a minimum number of inhabitants without taking into account their geographical differences, if nothing else. Also, there are many dispersed areas with almost no inhabitants, especially in mountain regions, and they also have to be included in some local self-government units. Due to the low number of inhabitants there is no economically profitable public transport going very often and special care has to be taken so that citizens can have convenient access to their municipality centre.

The law has provided the possibility of setting up a local committee. The local committee is set up by the statute of local self-government for a settlement. They are granted the status of legal entities, but interestingly the law left each municipality or town to determine their jurisdiction by its own statute. In practice, there are big differences among those local committees, depending on which town or municipality they belong to. It is also possible to set up town districts or town blocks in towns as special forms of local self-government. They are set up for the area representing the urban, economic and social whole connected by common interests of citizens. Even though the idea was to bring administrative organs closer to its citizens, the local units haven't used this possibility very much.

Local politicians see their role not as being people's servants, but as a power. That way it is normal not to wish to share power with smaller units. But, even if the municipal authorities see local committees as acting for public good, there is still a budget problem. The amount that local committees will have in their budget is a voluntary decision of the local representative body, even if transfers are set up by some common rules. It is still up to this representative body to set up those rules. Practice has shown that local committees do not like to create tensions with bodies of their local unit, but rather that they usually agree to their proposals. Although the idea was that local committees bring suggestions, ideas, solutions, programmes and so on to the local government body, in practice it is reversed. A local unit decides what to do and how to do it and this is subsequently approved or agreed upon by local committees.

The same situation is with town districts or town blocks, because they are under the same regulations as local committees. The legislative idea was that certain parts of municipalities or towns, due to their special needs or wishes, have the possibility to express such needs and wishes.[7] Inhabitants in certain settlements have the opportunity to express their special needs in those local committees. Some municipalities or towns have their settlements with very differently developed status or in a special geographical area and so on.

Therefore, local committees should be the best way for their inhabitants to be able to make their problems known. Unfortunately, the practice has not been very good. Even though it is expected that municipalities consist of more than just one

---

7 The number of inhabitants, either minimum or maximum, is not prescribed by the law. It is left to an arbitrary decision of local units. Therefore there are big differences between municipalities and towns. For instance, the town of Rijeka has 33 local committees with an average of 4,358 inhabitants, while on the other hand the municipality of Preseka has 12 local committees with an average of 137 inhabitants. This is a very small municipality, but according to law it is necessary for municipalities to have local committees.

settlement, most Croatian towns also consist of more than just one settlement.[8] For instance, the Capital City of Zagreb comprises 70 settlements; Split has 8, Osijek 11, while some smaller towns have even more (Križevci 61, Vrbovec 42 and so on) (Koprić, 2010: 669). On the other hand there are 42 municipalities consisting of only one settlement – the municipality centre (Pavić, 2010: 118). There are still large discrepancies between settlements and as a result local committees should play a bigger role in local unit administration and government.

Table 7.4   Settlements population and number of settlements

Inhabitants	Settlements	Percentage
0	105	1.55
1–100	2489	36.82
101–200	1337	19.78
201–500	1561	23.09
501–1000	719	10.64
1001 and more	549	8.12
TOTAL	6760	100

Source: Own elaboration.

As we can see from Table 7.4, most settlements in Croatia (91.88 per cent) have less than 1,000 inhabitants, while there are only 8.12 per cent of settlements with more than that. This level of population density creates problems, especially in some towns in which certain small settlements are included. They naturally gravitate around the big centre, but their situation, development, interests, wishes and problems are very different, which tends to become another problem that local administration has to solve. Inhabitants of those small settlements incorporated in towns always feel neglected and for that reason tend to protest, asking for better solutions for their problems. It is a difficult situation for these towns, since these problems demand substantial financial resources, besides the fact that the inhabitants of these towns do not seem to agree with having their taxes spent on infrastructures in areas they usually don't have any need to go to.

When we look back to 1992 we realize that there were 488 units (municipalities and towns), in comparison with 555 units in 2006, the year when the last border changes between administrative units were made. This is an increase of 67 units or 13.79 per cent. In 1992 there were 418 municipalities and now there are 429. The main difference lies in the number of towns. There are now 126 towns, in comparison with only 70 in 1992. There are now 56 more towns, an increase of

---

8   There are very few exceptions (for example Rijeka, Županja and Biograd).

80 per cent. For a relatively small country this is definitely an excess. Although there were no major differences between municipality and town regulations, the inhabitants, especially local politicians and officials, wanted their place of living to be considered a town. The main difference seemed to be the fact that a town had the possibility to impose surtax on people living in towns and not on those only coming to work in a town, a possibility later also acquired by municipalities, although in a smaller percentage.[9]

Table 7.5   Number of municipalities and towns

Year	Municipalities	Towns	Total
1992	418	70	488
1994	419	70	489
1995	424	75	499
1997	417	122	539
1998	420	123	543
1999	422	123	545
2000	423	123	546
2001	424	123	547
2002	425	123	548
2006	429	126	555

Source: Own elaboration.

There are different groups of units with special status: i) units on territories of special state concern; ii) units in mountain regions; iii) units in islands; and iv) the cities of Zagreb and Vukovar. The first group comprises units that were completely occupied during the Civil War, parts of units that were occupied and units with a lower level of development according to economic, structural and demographic criteria. There are 175 units completely and 10 units partially in that category. The second group is comprised of 45 units, while the third group is made up of 50 units. The fourth group includes only the City of Zagreb, regulated by a special law, and the City of Vukovar where there is an agency of central government for development and reconstruction.[10] Therefore, there are 272 units totally and 10 units partially under certain special provisions which makes 64 per cent of the total national territory.

---

9   Many municipalities (and towns even earlier), used that possibility, but the fifth biggest city in Croatia – Zadar has just passed a regulation imposing surtax in 2011, due to a difficult financial and economic situation.

10   Vukovar was the most severely destroyed city in whole Europe after the Second World War.

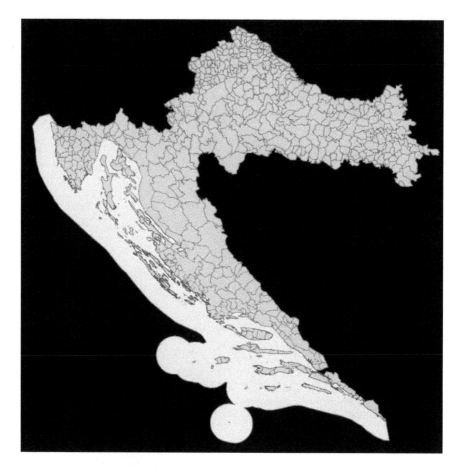

Figure 7.2   Croatian municipalities and towns
Source: hr.wikipedia.org.

Possible Territorial and Administrative Restructuration

The biggest problem in ongoing demands for local and regional self-government reform in Croatia is that there is no strategy or public consensus as to how this reform should be done and what the final results should be. Politicians, depending on which party they belong to, have their ideas, scientists have different perspectives and local and regional politicians, among other stakeholders, also have different visions. However, there is no public debate or a place in which all interested parties could discuss their visions and ideas on this reform.

One of the most intriguing questions is about the future status of counties. Are they going to be replaced by regions or is there a new position for them? Or will they be merely units of state administration? Croatia is not a big enough country to have three levels of self-government and therefore there is almost an agreement that counties need a new role as part of state administration or they need to be abolished.[11]

In the light of Croatia's accession to the European Union in 2013, an agreement has been achieved that regions need to be established. Bearing in mind that Croatia only has a little over 4,000,000 inhabitants and that regions should be between 800,000 and 2,000,000 inhabitants, everybody agrees that five regions are to be established which will correspond to Croatian geographical regions plus the Capital City of Zagreb. Zagreb, with some neighbouring towns and municipalities, will have more than 800,000 inhabitants. In the east there will be Slavonija Region, Central Region and Dalmatia Region, but as to the fourth region, discussions are still ongoing at the time of writing.

Because the borders of counties were not always designed logically, some changes will certainly be necessary. Istria and Kvarner as a maritime region will be joined with Lika, a mountain region. Most complaints are heard regarding this issue. But, it is the only viable solution according to the number of inhabitants. Istria, with its greatest part in Croatia and a smaller one in Slovenia, is the second most developed county in the country. It wasn't damaged by war and since the first local and regional elections in 1993 their ruling government has been formed by a regional party that demands more regional self-government.

Therefore, the voices in favour of the creation of a special region for this case are very loud, but their wishes will probably not be met because the County of Istria only has 208,440 inhabitants. The already mentioned County of Međimurje, the smallest county with only 113,804 inhabitants, also wishes to become a region. Due to historical reasons (most of this territory used to be part of the Hungarian Kingdom) and to the strength of its economy, there is a feeling that they are entitled to have their own regional unit.

Politicians, scientists and journalists have come to the agreement that regions should have at least 800,000 inhabitants, but the problem is where the borders should be drawn. The only consensual proposal is about the City of Zagreb, which will be a special region. However, in order to reach 800,000 inhabitants or more it will be necessary to include some additional areas: in this case, some big towns and neighbouring villages should be incorporated into the Zagreb Region. In each of the other four regions there are also several cases or places that can be part of more than one region and for that reason the decision on the final administrative division is still far from being closed. Since 1993 there have been few changes in the borders between counties.

As mentioned before, accessibility and transport infrastructure are other factors to take into consideration in the definition of county borders. Due to the accessibility criteria major changes have been introduced in the recent past. For

---

11 Although in 1992 present counties did not have many connections with historical counties (until the end of the nineteenth century) people got used to them and there are a lot of organs and other structures constituted according to county borders.

instance, a significant part of the County of Požega-Slavonija opted in 1997 to shift to Osijek-Baranja County. The reason was the fact that it was necessary to cross a mountain to get access to the county capital, which during the winter season was a rather difficult and dangerous task. Osijek, as the seat of Osijek-Baranja County is a bigger town, a university centre and it is also the place to which they gravitated in the past. Another example occurred in the period from 1993–97 with the then counties of Zadar-Knin and Šibenik. Knin and the neighbouring places left Zadar-Knin and moved to the county of Šibenik and now there are two different counties: the Zadar County and the Šibenik-Knin County.[12]

Another interesting example is the island of Pag, which is divided between two counties: Zadar and Lika-Senj. Lika is the name of a geographical region and Senj is a town on the coast. Lika is the most undeveloped and least inhabited region in Croatia and there was a decision that such a region, being an independent county, would not have sufficient economic and financial strength to function normally. Therefore, some coastal areas were merged with Lika. Revenues from tourism represent a big part of their budget. There were many protests against this decision, because people living at the coast wishing to go to their county seat would have a difficult journey across the biggest mountain regions in Croatia.[13] A referendum was organized and a few villages opted to merge with Zadar County, but the biggest part decided to stay in Lika-Senj County.[14]

Since 2007 Croatia has been divided into three statistical regions, but there are ongoing negotiations with the European Union for the establishment of only two regions, starting in early 2013. Right now two are underdeveloped regions, but the one that comprises the Capital City of Zagreb comprises over 75 per cent of European Union GDP. With only two regions, both of them will be eligible for more money from European Union structural funds.[15] This solution resulted in a lot of protests from underdeveloped counties in the region that now includes Zagreb, fearing that its presence will raise the GDP thus making it harder for them to get their projects financed by the European Union structural funds. Nonetheless, it is important to note that Zagreb also has the possibility to claim to be underdeveloped and to get, due to that status, financial aid from the European Union structural funds. The city administration in Zagreb has much more organizational and

12   It is the only example where the county name changed due to border changes.

13   In 1999 a tunnel was built going through the mountain; a few years later a modern high-way was built and now this is not an important factor as it used to be before.

14   Registration plates in Croatia start with two letters representing towns in which owners of the vehicles live. In some counties there are a lot of towns having their own registration plates (covering neighbouring municipalities also), but some smaller ones only have one town with registration plates for the whole county. All vehicles from Lika-Senj County have the letters 'GS' (representing Gospić). Therefore even the people from the coast have the registration plates of the town in a relatively remote area.

15   Although it might look unjust, the truth is that only the Capital City of Zagreb is above the average GDP and the other counties in that statistical region are below average, but in total they are above. Therefore they are not eligible for certain financial grants.

technical capacity and for that reason they have more possibilities to get their projects approved than some poorer municipalities with only 2–3 employees.

The unusual shape of the Republic of Croatia, in spite of many challenges facing the organization, structure and functioning of certain local and central bodies, has some advantages. For instance, there is the possibility to benefit from the resources available in the EU cross-border cooperation programmes. Out of 20 existing counties there are 18 which are border counties with Bosnia-Herzegovina, Hungary, Italy, Montenegro, Slovenia or Serbia. The 19th county is also eligible for cross-border cooperation programmes as it is less than 50km away from the Bosnia-Herzegovina border. Although there are numerous activities already underway, there are still many unused opportunities in this field.

Every new government in Croatia tended to perceive itself in the past as the only solution to the problems of the country and they usually tended to cut completely with the past. In 1992, when Croatia adopted a new law that defined the new territorial structure, old and big municipalities were broken apart and incorporated into towns and smaller municipalities. Older municipal buildings in towns that are county seats were taken by the new county offices. Even now, some older people tend to say that they go to the municipality instead of saying that they go to the county. However, by younger generations those buildings are always referred to as the county.

When some county prerogatives were passed to big towns, nothing changed in practice: offices only changed names and employees their employer. The place to get certain documents is still the same. So, younger people will say that they are going to the county while the older ones will say that they are going to the municipality. Nobody will say that he/she is going to the town office. This amendment actually hasn't made any change to the inhabitants' everyday life. It is not the substance that has changed, just the structure. The procedure is still as complicated and time-consuming as it was before. Also, geography is one of the factors usually taken into consideration less when restructuring a country's territorial structure.

These factors are very important, but let us not forget Croatia's peculiar shape and the numerous inhabited small islands. All these settlements, no matter how small or economically unimportant they are, still have inhabitants (even one or two) who are tax payers wanting their needs to be met by administrative actions. After disintegration of the former Yugoslavia in 1991 some problems arose in small villages without road contact with the rest of Croatia or being on the other side of the river. This was mainly on the border with Slovenia, but also in some places bordering with Bosnia-Herzegovina. When former borders between republics became international and border check-points were erected, this issue was not deemed an important aspect to be considered in the negotiations. Those villages belonged to a Croatian municipality but nobody gave importance to the fact that some of them had to cross another republic while going to a certain destination in Croatia. There are still some parts of Croatia which are considered Croatian in land property books and which are owned by Croatian citizens but which are still disputed by Serbian authorities which have direct land contact with them.

Even though the principle of subsidiarity has been very much appraised by politicians and scientists, the fact remains that it has not been used in practice and that is more important. The principle of subsidiarity is a dynamic principle which requires everyday judgement and therefore is connected with efficiency, solidarity, uniform action and uniform appliance. Local governments perform certain duties and it is normal to implement uniform action in all parts of the national territory. Central administrative organs therefore have a regulatory role in ensuring uniform action all over the country. The subsidiarity principle is not opposed to economic results although it is the human factor and one's welfare that is more valued. Bearing in mind that the subsidiarity principle demands local action of those who are more familiar with local conditions, uniform appliance all over the country needs to be examined.

From a moral point of view equality is of one of the highest values, and it is therefore necessary to decide in which sectors uniform appliance all over the country has to be considered, assigning these functions and roles to higher levels of public administration. Apart from those where individual judgement, according to local conditions, is more important, it is admitted that proper support by higher levels of public administration, on one side, and joint coordination of local units on the other will ensure solidarity across the country and prevent the rising of further differences among developed and less developed local units. The principles of solidarity and subsidiarity are in contrast, because the former requires greater solidarity between the rich and the poor, while the latter requires actions to be performed at levels as close to citizen as possible. The consequence is that performance has to be different from one local unit to another. In order to ensure solidarity it is necessary to clearly differentiate prerogatives of each level and enable the development of local units.

The subsidiarity principle invokes freedom, difference and responsibility. These principles demand a new system of societal organization in which the accent is not on top-down solutions, but on bottom-up approaches instead. Subsidiarity takes into consideration differences stemming from many factors, especially geography and economy.

Conclusion

Every change has certain advantages and disadvantages and brings uncertainty and a feeling of unease in some circumstances. There should be a joint public debate in Croatia on the future of the decentralization process, engaging politicians from local and central government, scientists, experts and NGOs, among other stakeholders. These debates should bring a widely accepted and well-thought-through local government reform.

The subsidiarity principle should be seen and practiced as the guiding norm for this administrative reform in Croatia, taking into consideration the lessons learned in the current economic and financial crisis. The subsidiarity principle is actually already incorporated in the Croatian legislation and it is an obligation stemming from the Council of Europe Charter for Local Self-Government. However, in everyday practice it is not well applied or simply not applied at all. This principle should help to define the differences between units of the same level and to grade them at a certain task-obligation-duty level. Although it is better to have similar units in the same administrative tier (e.g., according to number of inhabitants, area, duties, tasks, obligations and so on) it seems inevitable to introduce changes in the current sub-national tiers of self-government in Croatia.

The evidence available on the Croatian local and regional governance recommends a solution that makes compulsory the cooperation between sub-national administrative units. The demographic size and the functions of these units shall be defined by law, including the list of compulsory functions that each administrative tier has to implement. For instance, the law should define how many inhabitants are needed for certain tasks to be undertaken, among other aspects.

The current economic and financial crisis that has struck numerous European countries since 2008, as is examined in other chapters in this book, in particular in countries under structural adjustment programmes, and which is forcing reforms in the respective systems of local and regional governance, should be considered by policymakers in the ongoing debate for a reform of sub-national government in Croatia. The post-crisis local governance model in Europe seems to require new approaches and innovations, namely in local government finance systems and in the division of competences between central government and sub-national tiers of public administration. As a relatively new republic, Croatia has much to benefit from the experience of other European Union countries in the field of local governance reform and local governance innovation in this era of fiscal austerity and scarcity of public finance resources.

References

Babac, B., 1994. Obnova hrvatskoga gradjanskoga društva – politička kontrola i državna uprava (Reconstruction of Croatian civil society – political control and state administration). Osijek: Pravni fakultet

Bakota, B., 2011. 'Pravo građana na sudjelovanje u poslovima lokalnih vlasti' ('Citizens' right to participate in the affairs of local authorities'). In *Zbornik Međunarodne konferencije 'Razvoj javne uprave'*. Vukovar: Veleučilište Lavoslav Ružička.

Bakota, B. and Ljubanović, B., 2011. *Citizen Participation as a Form of Active Control of Public Administration*. Pécs: Pécsi Tudományegyetem Állam- és Jogtudományi Karának Doktori Iskolája.

Bakota, B., 2007. *Problemi primjene načela supsidijarnosti* (*Problems in the Appliance of the Principle of Subsidiarity*). Osijek: Pravni fakultet.

Garralda, J.F., 2000. 'Europa y el retorno del principio de subsidiariedad' ('Europe and the return of the principle of subsidiarity'). In Banús, E. (ed.), *Subsidiariedad: historia y applicación*. Pamplona: Centro de Estudios Europeos, Universidad de Navarra.

Koprić, I. 2010. 'Stanje lokalne samouprave u Hrvatskoj' ('Current state of local self-government in Croatia'). *Hrvatska javna uprava*, 10(3), pp. 665–81.

Millon-Delsol, C., 1992. *L'État subsidiaire* (*Subsidiarity state*). Paris: Presses universitaires de France.

Pavić, Ž., 2010. 'Veličina lokalnih jedinica – europske tendencije i hrvatske nedoumice' ('Size of local units – European tendencies and Croatian doubts'). *Hrvatska javna uprava*, 10(1), pp. 81–131.

Pusić, E., 2002. *Nauka o upravi* (*Science of Administration*). Zagreb: Školska knjiga.

Chapter 8

Local Governance in Belarus: The Impact of the Economic and Financial Crisis on the Administrative Division Reform

Bahdan Sarazhynski

Introduction

Local governance institutions are an essential part of every modern state regardless of the political regime or territorial size of the country and their functioning varies significantly due to political, economic and cultural factors. The chapter examines the notion of local governance in Belarus, the legislation on local governance and its application and the actual functioning of local governance in the country. The main research question that the chapter aims to address is whether the current system of local governance in Belarus corresponds to the needs of the society in Belarus and to what extent does the current economic and financial crisis limit the direction and the rate of the administrative division reform in Belarus.

The first part of the chapter deals with the notion of local government in Belarus; the second part examines the system of local government; and the third discusses the possible reform of the administrative division of Belarus and the impact of the economic and financial crisis.

The Notion of Local Governance in Belarus

It's necessary to clarify the notions of local government and self-government, as some difference exists in understanding this concept in, for example, the US, France and post-Soviet countries.

The Belarusian legal system has much in common with the Soviet Union system. The Belarusian system of local governance has its roots in the USSR system. It's worth mentioning that in the Constitution of the USSR of 1936 it was stated that the power on local level belongs to soviets of deputies (representative bodies) and so-called *ispolkoms* of these soviets (executive bodies). The notion of local self-governance was not mentioned, though in 1974 in the Soviet Encyclopedia (Yandex Dictionary, 1978) a new term was used – local self-governance – that meant the participation of citizens in public administration affairs directly or through elected representatives. The notion of self-governance was firstly introduced into the legal system in 1990 in the law on principles of local self-governance and local economy. It didn't change the situation in part due to the fact that the USSR soon split in 1991.

In what concerns the relations of soviets of deputies and *ispolkoms*, according to the 1936 Constitution of the USSR, these soviets of deputies were elected by citizens, by workers to be precise. The disguised task of the communist system was not to give much autonomy to the elected representatives and, for that reason, the *ispolkoms*, or executive bodies, had much more real power. These bodies used to take decisions that were prepared by themselves and not discussed in the soviets of deputies. This institutional model was neither democracy nor self-governance.

On the contrary, in the Belarusian system there is a special law on local governance and self-governance (Law No. 108–3) which defines local governance as a 'form of organization and activity of the local executive and administrative bodies for solving the questions of local importance, according to the national interests and the interests of the people', and local self-governance as the 'form of organization and activity of the population, living on the corresponding territory, for the independent resolution of social, economic and political problems through elected organs, according to the national interests and the interests of the people, the specific characteristics of each administrative-territorial unit, on the basis of material resources and funds available'.

In other words it can be said that local self-governance is when a population makes decisions directly or through elected representatives (in soviets of deputies (English equivalent – local council)) and local governance is an activity of executive\administrative organs (*ispolkoms* (English equivalent – executive committees) and local administrations).

The current system of administrative divisions in Belarus is composed of three levels: six *oblast* (region) and the capital (Minsk) are on top of the system; the next level consists of 118 districts and 12 cities of *oblast* subordination; and the lowest level comprises 98 cities of district subordination, 95 settlements, 1,365 soviets of the villages and 25 city districts (Ministry of Sport and Tourism of the Republic of Belarus, 2013). Local governance bodies exist on each level, but in city districts *ispolkoms* are called local administrations. It's interesting that before 2000 *ispolkoms* were considered local self-governance bodies. The reason for this change will be discussed in one of the next sections.

The Legal Regulation of Local Governance

The law on local governance and self-governance (Law No. 108–3) came into force on 4 January 2010, with the last changes made on 28 August 2012. The law contains a long list of principles (Article 3), according to which local governance and self-governance is put into effect: legality; social justice; protection of rights and lawful interests of citizens; combination of national and local interests;

participation of institutions of local governance; and self-governance in matters affecting rights and lawful interests of citizens; unity and integrity of system of local governance and self-governance; cooperation of institutions of local governance and self-governance; distribution of authority of institutions of local governance and self-governance; electiveness of institutions of local self-governance, their accountability to citizens; publicity and public opinion; keeping citizens informed about decisions taken on the most important question of local importance; responsibility of institutions of local governance and self-governance for lawfulness and reasonableness of decisions taken; obligation of implementation of decisions of soviets, administrative and executive organs on the corresponding territory; independence of institutions of local self-governance within the limits of their competence of solving local questions; denial of limitation of competences of institutions of local governance and self-governance with exception of the cases defined in this law or in other legal acts.

Although these principles seem obvious for everyone, they are useful in the sense that citizens can refer to these written norms in complaints to local authorities and in court disputes.

Local Governance vs Self-governance

It should be taken into consideration the fact that before the law on local governance and self-governance of 2000 came into force, both soviets of deputies and *ispolkoms* were bodies of local self-governance. According to UN Public Administration Country Profile (2004: 7), the 2000 changes in the law were 'primarily concerned with the relations between local representative and executive bodies'. Executive committees lost their former status as bodies of self-government, instead becoming a component in the system of the executive power and defined as the 'local government'. Local government bodies are required by law to act primarily in the interest of the state in the resolution of local issues. As Miroslav Kobasa, Alexander Karamyshev and Valentin Dritz (2001: 55) note: 'thus, the principle of autonomy is no longer extended to executive bodies, which are now commonly referred to as the Presidential vertical'. This term, although not entirely correct from an administrative and legal point of view, reflects the true role of these bodies within the state administrative machine.

The Competences of Local Government Bodies

The overlapping of competences is an important issue in local government in Belarus. Changes in the competences of local government in Belarus have been made almost in every new edition of the law. For instance, Kobasa et al. (2001: 53) refer that 'functions were not clearly distributed among levels of government according to the principle of subsidiarity. Thus, overlapping areas of competence remained from the previous system, in which higher-level bodies controlled the lower-level ones and took responsibility for the results of their work. Local bodies did not achieve real independence, since higher-level bodies retained the overwhelmingly important functions of control and resource distribution'.

Article 41 of the law on local governance and self-governance contains a long list of competences of *ispolkoms* in all three tiers of the administrative structure. The competences of *ispolkoms* are very broad, though often it's not clear what effective means *ispolkoms* have to achieve the goals. For example, what competence do they have to take counteraction on terrorism or to secure nuclear safety? The competences of *ispolkoms* in the different tiers are regulated by Articles 42–5 of the law on local governance and self-governance.

Oblast-level *ispolkoms* have the following competences (only the most important ones are listed): to assist the employment of citizens; exercise control of public health system; work on master plans of Minsk and *oblast* centres and cities of *oblast* subordination; provide credits on favourable terms; do registration and liquidation of legal entities; issue licenses; examine business plans of investment projects; determine prices (tariffs), markups (discounts) on goods (services); provide guidance for the activities of registry offices; solve the questions of dismissal of administrative staff; hold annual regional programs on the cadre; and to cancel decisions of subordinate bodies.

The *ispolkoms* at the district level have, among others, the following competences: to solve employment questions; to provide credits on favourable terms; to organize the functioning of libraries; to provide the beautification of the territory; to provide illumination of streets, street names and numbers; to organize waste collection and disposal; to organize activities of public registry; to organize traffic safety, registration and liquidation of legal entities; and to issue licenses.

The *ispolkoms* at the lower tier have, among others, the following competences: to steer motions on social security issues in the soviets of deputies; to organize the work of local self-governments; to provide the beautification of the territory; to provide illumination of streets, street names and numbers; to organize waste removal; to organize the activities of public registry; to function as notaries; to register citizens in the place of domicile, permanent residence; military registration in places where there are no military commissariats (military service (12–18 months) is obligatory in Belarus for men at the age of 18–27); to take measures to stimulate small enterprises; to lead administrative procedures; to create municipal services (for example, the renting of agricultural equipment).

Local administrations in city districts are a peculiar organ of local governance. The president abolished city district councils and their executive bodies by the Presidential Decree No. 383 on the Reform of Local Government and Self-government Bodies, issued on 19 September 1995. They were replaced by local administrations, which were government bodies of general competence (Miroslav Kobasa, Alexander Karamyshev and Valentin Dritz, 2001: 73). It means that there are no representative bodies and separate budgets on city district level.

The competences of local administrations are the following: represent the interests of districts of cities; make and execute local budgets; are in command of municipal property; secure minimal social standards (social support, social services, wages, pensions); cooperate with other *ispolkoms* and soviets on local questions; inform citizens on various issues; assist local self-governance; solve questions of demographic security, improvement of socio-economic conditions of families; make decisions on construction projects and development of housing resources; provide credit in favourable conditions; create conditions for the provision of communication services, public catering, trade and consumer services; create conditions for the implementation of the right to education, control the quality of education and cultural events; organize sports facilities and events; coordinate health improvement, sanatoriums; promote the development of non-government organizations; coordinate state youth politics (mainly through BRSM);[1] maintain public order (with close cooperation with police); take counteraction to terrorism, extremism; secure fire, nuclear and radiation safety; provide traffic safety; organize the activities of public registry; organize waste removal; organize libraries; provide the beautification of the territory; provide illumination of streets and street names; take measures to preserve the environment; explain the legislation to citizens; conduct cultural events on public holidays; create local media; and supervise labour safety.

It's evident that many competences are overlapped in the spheres of beautification of territories, waste removal, libraries, illumination of streets, street names and numbers, registration and liquidation of legal entities, provision of credit and licensing. It leads to disorder when *ispolkoms* and local administrations cannot determine their own responsibilities.

As we may observe, such verbs as coordinate, provide and organize are used by the legislator. As Cheburanova (n.d.) writes, optional competences are based on law, but are used in view of the absence of concrete legal norms. These optional competences are used to achieve a closed list of goals. Words like 'coordinate', 'provide' and 'organize', identifying only the spheres of activity, but not concrete rights and obligations, allow *ispolkoms* and local administrations to use optional competences.

The Structure of Local Government Bodies

According to Article 38 of the law on local governance and self-governance, *ispolkoms* at the *oblast* and district levels are composed of head, deputy heads, business manager and committee members. *Ispolkoms* at the lowest administrative tier may have no deputy heads. The typical structure of *oblast*-level and district-level *ispolkoms* is set by the president, as well as the quantity of local governance workers.

Oblast ispolkoms are subordinate and accountable to the president and to the government on issues that are the competence of government. Other *ispolkoms*

---

1   The Belarusian Republican Youth Union is a youth organization in Belarus. Its goals are to promote patriotism and to instil moral values into the youth of Belarus, using activities such as camping, sporting events and visiting memorials (Reddif.com, 2013).

and local administrations are subordinate and accountable to the president and higher level *ispolkoms*. Local executive bodies are not accountable to the local representative branch or to local citizens. The executive committee makes decisions within its competence through a simple majority of votes by committee members.

According to the Presidential decree No. 66, 'On questions of local governance and self-governance', published in 2011, the president directly appoints and dismisses the heads of regional executive committees and approves the appointment and dismissal of heads of district executive committees. Executive committees of the first tier are governed by the head of the local soviet of deputies. The head of local administration is appointed by the head of the city executive committee after consultations with the president.

At the *oblast* level all executive committee members are appointed and dismissed by the head in coordination with the president. Such influence of the president on local governance violates the principle of autonomy of local governance.

The Problems of Local Governance: View from the Inside

To understand how the system of local governance works, the feedback from office employees is useful. Unfortunately, members of the administrative staff are not willing to speak openly as they can be sacked. In this circumstance, the research published on the website Regnum is a valuable source of information (Malishevsky, 2012). In this case, the opinions of members of administrative staff during refresher courses in The Academy of Public Administration under the aegis of the President of the Republic of Belarus were published. The real names and surnames of the speakers were not written. The office workers took a serious approach towards these courses and took the initiative; they spoke openly, trying to identify the most significant problems of local governance.

The most important issues mentioned were: 1. Centralization of power that led to passiveness of civil initiative and weak development of local self-governance. This may be explained by the lack of a tradition of local self-governance and also by the political will of the regime in favour of centralization; 2. Lack of real power at the district level; 3. Loss of contact between central and local government that leads to planning of unreal programs and requirements that must be fulfilled by lower level bodies; 4. Soviets of deputies (organs of local self-governance) always vote in favour of the decisions proposed by local administration. The real decision is taken beforehand by the executive body. The deputies can lose their workplace if they disagree with the proposed laws; 5. Local officials in their attempts to fulfill the plan produce false records, being the root of this problem in the so-called planned economy of the USSR period, when only the numbers mattered; 6. Duplication of functions; 7. No cooperation between local governance and law-making bodies. Laws are made by people that do not understand how the norm will be implemented and used in practice; and 8. Another important issue is the problem of double or triple subordination.

The most notorious example is Minskoblgas. It is included in the Ministry of Energy but at the same time is subordinate to the production association Beltopgas and is subordinate to Minsk *oblast ispolkom* (local government body). The main task of Minskoblgas it to provide gas to consumers, both persons and entities. But three organs control and regulate the activity of Minskoblgas which leads to disorder. Minskoblgas has also to build the gas systems, to work in the livestock sector, the crop sector and the peat industry.

The Reform of the Administrative Division of Belarus

The History of Administrative Division in Belarus

Belarus became an independent state only in 1991 and throughout its history the administrative division was usually influenced by the wars that affected the country. The administrative division of the Great Duchy of Lithuania and Rzeczpospolita could not be fully or partially used nowadays as the density of the population was significantly less, the socio-economic conditions varied significantly from contemporary ones and the constant territorial expansion processes, not the interests of population, determined territorial units.

After the split of Rzeczpospolita, Belarus became a part of the Russian Empire. At the very beginning only two *gubernias* (regions) were created. The aim was to concentrate the power in the hands of the heads of those territorial units, in order to make it easier to control potential rebel territories. Later five *gubernias* instead of two were created.

In the twentieth century after the Russian Revolution and the Peace of Riga, half of the territory of Belarus was acquired by Poland. The other part, the soviet sector, was divided into 12 districts. Later, at the beginning of the 1930s, the district division was abolished. In 1938 five *oblasts* were created. After the start of the Second World War in 1939, when the USSR and Nazis divided Poland, the former Belarusian territories were included into the BSSR (and USSR) and on these territories five *oblasts* were created. In total, BSSR was divided into ten *oblasts*. In 1944, three new *oblasts* were created. After the Second World War the number of *oblasts* gradually diminished – minus one in 1945, minus five in 1954 and minus one in 1960 (archives.gov.by, 2013). The reason for the reduction was to make *oblasts* bigger – so they would be more similar to Russian and Ukrainian *oblasts* – which would probably facilitate the functioning of the planned economy. After the 1960s the structure remains stable: six *oblasts* plus Minsk, the capital. It can be observed that at some historical periods Belarus was composed of territorial units 2–4 times smaller than current ones.

The Complexity of the Current System

The current system '*oblast*-district-settlement' is complex: the responsibilities of different organs are often overlapped, as stated previously in the chapter. The second level especially has efficiency problems. It doesn't possess the powerful resources of the *oblast* level and doesn't solve local questions that are the responsibility of the lowest level organs.

The governors of the six *oblasts* have strong powers and may try to use this authority to create clans and to take personal benefits from these economic activities (for example, to profit from the ongoing privatization process). Reducing the amounts of power in these sub-national units will decrease the chances of corruption and oligarchy – as stated by Ales Mihalevich, the former presidential candidate (Naviny.by, 2011).

Soviets of the villages are small in area and in population and don't have enough economic resources to provide services even of a minimum quality (Fateev, 2008: 6). Small territorial units (especially of the lowest level) don't have financial and administrative resources that lead to the development of social, engineering, market, transport and other infrastructure. Around 60 per cent of the budgets of the entities of the lowest level are subsidized, although in some regions this figure can go up to 85 per cent (Fateev, 2008: 6).

If we take a look at the map of the Republic of Belarus, we can observe that 4 of 6 *oblast* capitals (Grodno, Brest, Vitebsk, Gomel) are located near the borders of the corresponding *oblast*. It leads to the formation of the alternative centres of development in other parts of *oblast* and the growing influence of the capital, Minsk, which is located almost at the centre of the Republic of Belarus. For example, it takes twice as long to get from Smorgon to Grodno than to Minsk, though Smorgon belongs to Grodno *oblast*.

The size of the *oblasts* make it difficult to solve social and economic problems efficiently at the meso-level, and to use the economic potential of big and medium cities, such as Lida, Borisov, Mozyr, Baranovichi, Molodechno and Soligorsk, as a tool to enhance the development of the neighbouring territories (Fateev, 2008: 7).

The EU Experience

The experience of other European states should be considered and compared. Unfortunately, there are no EU countries with a similar area and population density. The most similar ones are Portugal, Czech Republic, Romania, Hungary and Bulgaria (Table 8.1).

Table 8.1   European countries: area, population and NUT division

Country	Territory	Population	NUTS2	NUTS3	N	NUTS2B	NUTS3B
Belarus	207 595 km2	9 503 807 (2009)	6*	-	-	-	-
Portugal	92 212 km2	10 561 614 (2011)	7	30	1,35	10	41
Romania	238 391 km2	19 042 936 (2011)	8	42	0,62	5	26
Bulgaria	110 994 km2	7 364 570 (2011)	6	28	1,48	9	41
Czech Republic	78 866 km2	10 562 214 (2011)	8	14	1,48	12	21
Hungary	93 030 km2	9 982 000 (2011)	7	20	1,38	10	28

Source: Geographical statistics, obtained from http://en.wikipedia.org/wiki/Romania, http://en.wikipedia.org/wiki/Bulgaria, http://en.wikipedia.org/wiki/Czech_Republic, http://en.wikipedia.org/wiki/Portugal, http://en.wikipedia.org/wiki/Hungary and http://en.wikipedia.org/wiki/Belarus are used in the present table.

*As Nomenclature of Units for Territorial Statistics is a standard developed and regulated by the EU, it doesn't cover Belarus. The number in this cell is an equivalent from the Belarusian system.

From Table 8.1 we may observe that three of the comparable states (Portugal, Czech Republic and Hungary) have the same population as Belarus, but their territory is 2–3 times smaller; Romania has similar a territory to Belarus, but its population is two times bigger. Bulgaria is smaller and less populated than the Republic of Belarus, but has a similar density of population.

One of the main questions is what factor is more important while determining the sizes and borders of regions and districts – population or territory? Our hypothesis is that population is more important than area as it influences economic relations more significantly. And therefore districts should be of similar population rather than similar territory. Without any doubt, historical, cultural and economic factors should play a significant role in determining the number and size of territorial units rather than only maths formulas.

To assess the situation in other European states it is necessary to make the data comparable. To compare the data more efficiently, the coefficient N that equals $(TB/T+2*PB/P)/3$ is used, where TB is territory of Belarus, T is territory of EU state, PB is population of Belarus and P is population of EU state. Using this coefficient N we may find how many NUTS2 and NUTS3 units Belarus would have, applying each state division (NUTS2B=N*NUTS2, NUTS3B=N*NUTS3).

Belarus would have approximately 10 NUTS2 units in 4 out of 5 cases (except Romania). NUTS3B units vary significantly (from 21 to 41) but this may be explained by national peculiarities of each scrutinized state.

The necessity of NUTS2 level is not evident – it's often used for coordinating EU regional development projects and statistical purposes and doesn't have administrative capacity (Romania VET in Europe – Country Report, 2011).

The main conclusion is that Belarus would probably have 10 NUTS2 units, but another way is to have around 20 NUTS3 units. The second variant (with no NUTS2 equivalent level) has a serious advantage – it's simpler and the advantages of NUTS2 are not clear.

A Proposal for the Reform of the Administrative Division of Belarus

In the paper 'Perspective areas to improve regional policy and local self-governance in the Republic of Belarus', V.S. Fateev, professor at the Belarusian State Economic University, introduced a draft model for the new administrative-territorial division (2008: 7), a proposal with which I tend to agree. The *oblast* and district levels should be merged. Instead of six *oblasts* and 118 districts, around 15–25 new *oblasts* should be created. In 2011, the former presidential candidate in the Republic of Belarus Ales Michalevich suggested that the number of new *oblasts* should be 17 (Naviny.by, 2011). The exact number has to be determined after national deliberation supplemented by expert research. At the same time, on the lowest level, units should be merged. As mentioned earlier, current soviets of the villages are so small that they often don't have economic resources to function properly. Fateev suggests that there should be around 300–600 new units. Their minimal population will be 3,000 people with an average of 7,000–10,000.

This new reform will require the adoption of new or changes in current laws on regional development, local governance and self-governance, as well as changes on the financial basis of local self-governance, associations of organs of local self-governance, administrative-territorial division, civil code, tax code and others.

Conclusion

Belarus has a complex system of local governance and self-governance. Before 2000 all local bodies were called 'local self-governance', but after that a new law renamed the executive bodies (*ispolkoms* and local administrations) as 'local governance'. This was probably done with the aim to centralize the power on the president and on central government, in order to better control public policies in the regions and districts. If we take into account the long-established tradition that dates back from the USSR, when local executive bodies played a more significant role in local politics rather than soviets of deputies (local councils, representative bodies), the conclusion is that the system of local governance is not autonomous.

The law on local governance and self-governance is very detailed. It contains a long list of principles, according to which the local governance and self-governance system is put into effect. However, there are problems in the application of the law. During refresher courses in The Academy of Public Administration, members of administrative staff spoke openly and tried to identify the most significant issues: centralization of power; lack of cooperation between central and local government, local governance and law-making bodies; loss of independence of soviets of deputies; doctored records; double or triple subordination. There is also overlapping of the competences of local governance bodies at the different levels, for instance in the areas of beautification of territories, wastes removal, libraries, illumination of streets, street names and numbers, registration and liquidation of legal entities, provision of credit in more favorable conditions, licensing. This overlapping of competences and duplication should be eliminated.

The president has a significant influence on the local governance system, since it is his/her responsibility to appoint the heads of the regional executive committees and to approve the appointment of heads of district executive committees. He also participates in the appointment and in the dismissal of other executive committee members. All *ispolkoms* are subordinate and accountable to the president. The principle of autonomy of local governance is violated.

A very important issue for the Republic of Belarus is the administrative-territorial division. The current division was influenced by the USSR's intention to make *oblasts* similar in area to those that existed in the other soviet republics. The current system of three levels is complex and has several problems: it doesn't take into account the development of new economic centres; governors have too much power that can lead to corruption; the 2nd district level has little real powers; and the small size of the units of the lowest level hinders economic development.

The experience in the EU countries suggests that Belarus would have around 10 NUTS2 units and/or 20–40 NUTS3 units. According to the proposals of Fateev and the former presidential candidate Michalevich, the *oblast* and the district levels should be merged and around 10–20 new *oblasts* should be created, a proposal with which I concur. At the same time, on the lowest level units should be merged. Though the reform will require funds, the elimination of administrative staff on the district level (now 118 districts) would lead to a reduction in public expenditure.

The probable changes in the system of local governance will require, firstly, a political will (the current intention of Alexander Lukashenko of centralization hinders the independence of local governance) and, secondly, a stable economic and public finance situation.

In other words, the reform of the administrative division of Belarus needs to become a central topic in the national political agenda which is far from being the case at the time of writing. On the contrary, all the evidence collected suggests that it is not the case, mainly due to the current economic and financial crisis. As in the cases examined in the other chapters, the current economic and financial crisis that affects European countries emerges in Belarus also as a key determinant in the reform of local governance, in particular the reform of the sub-national administrative division, in this case slowing down a much needed administrative and territorial reform.

References

Archives.gov.by, 2013. Административно-территориальное деление Беларуси, [online]. Available at: <http://archives.gov.by/index.php?id=989746> [Accessed 1 August 2012].

Cheburanova S.E., n.d. 'Theoretical and practical problems of regulating the legal status of local government and self-government' [online]. Available at: <http://www.lib.grsu.by/library/data/resources/catalog/163876-357088.pdff> [Accessed 1 August 2012].

Decree On some issues of local government and self-government from 22 February 2011 г. No. 66, [online]. Available at: <http://pravo.by/main.aspx?guid=3871 &p0=P31100066&p2=%7BNRPA%7D> [Accessed 1 August 2012].

Fateev V.S., 2008. 'Promising directions of improvement of regional policy and local self-government in the Republic of Belarus' [online]. Available at: <http://ekonomika.by/downloads/fat5.pdf> [Accessed 1 August 2012].

Fateev V.S., 2002. 'About the reform of local governance and self-governance in the context of world trends and processes' [online]. Available at: <http://ekonomika.by/downloads/fat10.pdf> [Accessed 1 August 2012].

Kobasa M., Karamyshev A. and Dritz, A., 2001. 'Local Government in Belarus, Local governments in Eastern Europe, in the Caucasus and Central Asia' [online]. Available at: <http://lgi.osi.hu/publications/2001/84/Ch2-Belorussia. pdf> [Accessed 1 August 2012].

Law on administrative-territorial structure of the Republic of Belarus from 5 May 1998 г. No. 154–3 [online]. Available at: <http://www.pravo.by/main.aspx?gu id=3871&p0=h19800154&p2=%7BNRPA%7D> [Accessed 1 August 2012].

Law on local governance and self-governance in Belarus from 4 January 2010 г. No. 108-3 [online]. Available at: <http://www.pravo.by/main.aspx?guid=3871 &p0=H11000108&p2=%7BNRPA%7D> [Accessed 1 August 2012].

Malishevsky D., 2012. 'The problems of local governance in the eyes of Belarusian officials' [online]. Available at: <http://belarus.regnum.ru/news/1496656. html> [Accessed 1 August 2012].

Ministry of Sport and Tourism of the Republic of Belarus, Administrative Division [online]. Available at: <http://www.mst.by/ru/tourists-belarus/about_belarus/ administrativnoe_delenie/> [Accessed 1 August 2012].

Naviny.by, 2011. Ales Mikhalevich – Administrative reform – the first duty of a democratic government [online]. Available at: <http://naviny.by/rubrics/ opinion/2011/07/12/ic_articles_410_174347/> [Accessed 1 August 2012].

Reddif.com, Belarusian Republican Youth Union [online]. Available at: <http:// pages.rediff.com/belarusian-republican-youth-union/1151483> [Accessed 1 August 2012].

Republic of Belarus Public Administration Country Profile [online]. Available at: <http://unpan1.un.org/intradoc/groups/public/documents/un/unpan023207. pdf> [Accessed 1 August 2012].

Romania VET in Europe – Country Report 2011 [online]. Available at: <http:// libserver.cedefop.europa.eu/vetelib/2011/2011_CR_RO.pdf> [Accessed 1 August 2012].

Tagunov D. and Marhotko E., 2008. 'Urgent questions of local government legal provision enhancement in the Republic of Belarus' [online]. Available at: <http://pu.by/iss/n28/Tagunov_Marhotko_28.pdf> [Accessed 1 August 2012].

USSR Law from 09 April 1990 on principles of local self-governance and local economy [online]. Available at: <http://zaki.ru/pagesnew.php?id=1687> [Accessed 1 August 2012].

Yandex Dictionary, 1978. Самоуправление [online]. Available at: <http://slovari. yandex.ru/~книги/БСЭ/Самоуправление/> [Accessed 1 August 2012].

1936 Constitution of the USSR [online]. Available at: <http://www.departments. bucknell.edu/russian/const/36cons03.html#chap08> [Accessed 1 August 2012].

PART III

Chapter 9

Non-governmental Organizations (NGOs) and Citizen-Authority Engagement: Applying Developing World Solutions to Europe in an Era of Fiscal Austerity

Stephanie Steels

Introduction

The last few decades have seen a large increase in the number of non-governmental organizations (NGOs) operating globally. NGOs can play an important and significant role in the developing world. Limited financial resources and poor (or basic) infrastructure allow NGOs to provide a supportive role in managing, implementing and delivering health- and non-health-related programmes and policies (Kates, Morrison and Lief, 2006). NGOs are also better placed to act as an intermediary body between a local community and the local government. They can provide a neutral platform to encourage dialogue and facilitate community and citizen-authority engagement between the different actors.

The present global economic downturn has placed additional burdens and challenges in the way health policy is formed and implemented. The situation in Europe is complicated by other factors which will not be discussed here. Whilst European governments make cuts to reduce country level deficits, these in turn create a domino effect, impacting on regional and local authorities. With reduced budgets, local as well as national service providers and other organizations must deliver more for less.

In terms of health, there are increased demands on health services due to the changing demographic landscape of an aging population and the lifestyle effects of modern living. Furthermore, reduced financial budgets and further spending cuts mean that more communities are at a higher risk of losing access to health care providers and health centres. At the same time, screening programmes and other health intervention programmes may be scaled back, yet health care providers will still have to meet the same targets but with limited financial and personal resources.

In the UK, the National Health Service (NHS) is undergoing a series of reforms as part of the new Health and Social Care Act 2012. Primary Care Trusts (PCTs) and strategic health authorities will be abolished as part of a major structural reorganization taking place over the next year. Instead, new health and wellbeing boards will be established to improve integration between NHS and local authority services. Clinical commissioning groups will take over commissioning from PCTs and will work with the new NHS Commissioning Board. A new regulator, Monitor, will be established to regulate providers of NHS services in the interests of patients and prevent anti-competitive behaviour. The influence of patient feedback will be strengthened through the setting up of a new national body called Health Watch, which will also operate at the local level.

Public health is also experiencing immense changes. At a national level, Public Health England will be established in April 2013 to work across government departments on health improvement and provide specialist functions for public health. These functions include: delivering services to national and local government, the NHS and the public; leading public health; and supporting the development of the specialist and wider public health workforce. Local authorities will take charge of public health responsibilities at a local level. Funding for public health will also be transferred from the NHS to local authorities in line with these changes. It is expected that local authorities will work closely with NHS organizations in their new public health duties.

There has been much debate about the 2012 Health and Social Care Act both within the health care profession and in the general press. There are concerns about fragmentation of the NHS and a loss of coordination and planning. In particular, medical and health professionals are concerned about the new reforms causing long-term harm to patient outcomes, especially in cases of children with disabilities, those with multiple co-morbidities and the frail and elderly. There are also further issues surrounding the accountability of the NHS. Even with national regulatory bodies such as the Department of Health, the National Institute for Health and Clinical Excellence, the Care Quality Commission, the NHS Commissioning Board and the newly formed regulator Monitor, it is not clear how these national bodies will interact or how they will provide coordinated and consistent governance of the NHS.

Despite this, the seismic changes within both public health and the NHS provide an exciting opportunity in which to explore the potential opportunities that exist within the UK for NGOs to support health providers under the new reforms. In particular, the following two questions will be examined in this chapter:

- What are the current health challenges that health policymakers face in the UK?
- What potential opportunities exist for civil society organizations, such as NGOs, to support health care providers under the new UK health reforms?

The structure of this chapter is as follows. First, we begin with an overview of the current health challenges in the UK, with particular reference to the increase in urbanization and the specific health problems of urban populations. Next, we present a summary of how civil society organizations, with emphasis on NGOs, operate in the developing world. In particular we explore NGO motivations, the multiple roles played by NGOs and some future challenges. Finally, we will outline and discuss some of the key opportunities that exist for NGOs under the new NHS reforms. Examples of pre-existing NGO roles from both the developed and developing world will be used to highlight these opportunities. This is followed by our conclusions.

Current Health Challenges: Urbanization and the Urban Penalty

Current trends in population growth have shown that, on the whole, urban populations are increasing. Since 2008, more than half of the world's population now live in an urban area (World Health Organization and United Nations Children's Fund, 2008). Living in a city can bring about improved access to clean water, better sanitation services and access to health care facilities. However, the positive aspects of urban living are accompanied by what can be described as potential urban health penalties.[1] Increased risk of infectious disease, exposure to air pollution and injury from traffic accidents are just some of the health risks associated with urban living (Galea and Vlahov, 2005c). Whilst the growth in urban populations has largely levelled off in the developed world, the consequences of this still exist (Galea and Vlahov, 2005b). Strains on existing resources such as access to health care, housing and infrastructure are under pressure from multiple factors.

In particular, the urban physical environment which includes the built environment, air and water quality and noise pollution, has been linked to specific health outcomes (Galea and Vlahov, 2005a). For example, specific features of the built environment such as access to green spaces (such as parks) and some features of urban planning may affect the amount of physical activity of an urban population (Boone-Heinonen and Gordon-Larsen, 2010; Handy et al., 2002). Without designated spaces in the external environment, a person may find it difficult to undertake exercise especially if a park cannot be reached easily on foot or by public transport. Furthermore, persons may be discouraged from undertaking exercise if a space is not deemed safe. This in turn can lead to increased risk of obesity and cardiovascular disease in both children and adults due to sedentary behaviour (Reddigan et al., 2011; Sallis et al., 2012). Additionally, lifestyle factors such as long working hours, stress, unhealthy eating habits through consuming too much convenience foods and binge drinking can impact on both our physical and mental health. There is substantial literature on the relationship between these lifestyle factors and health (for example (Malyutina et al., 2002; McEwen, 2008; Mirowsky and Ross, 1998; Rueggeberg, Wrosch and Miller, 2012; Stacy, Bentler and Flay, 1994).

---

1   In its broadest definition, urban health can be described as the study of the health of urban populations. Or more simply, urban health can be defined as 'public health for urban areas' (EURO-URHIS, 2008).

As a consequence of urban living, the treatment for poor physical and emotional health can be costly to both patients under treatment and health care providers. Similarly, the provision of health and social services within the urban setting is complicated and varies between cities and countries. Many cities are characterized by disparities in wealth between neighbourhoods. The aggregating effect of wealthy neighbourhoods can mask the difficulties and barriers faced by low-income residents in finding health care facilities. Issues such as lack of health insurance coverage, unemployment and homelessness can result in those from low socio-economic groups receiving poor quality health care or, in some cases, unable to utilize health services due to lack of affordability. Furthermore, increased life expectancy and aging populations place additional burdens on existing health care resources (Crystal and Siegel, 2008; Garrett and Martini, 2007; Lin et al., 2010; Saarni et al., 2007). Thus, the complex nature of the relationship between the urban environment, urban living and health makes it difficult for health policymakers to address these issues because a one-size-policy does not necessarily fit all.

The complexity of studying health within the urban environment has led to a shift in the way researchers consider population health. Historically, the health of urban populations was considered within the context of prevalence and mortality rates (Canadian Institute for Health Information, 2010). More recently, population health is being considered as more than just the sum of individuals' health in a population. Instead, the health of an individual can be characterized and influenced by other factors, often described as determinants. These determinants can be described and emphasized through interactions between individual lifestyles and how these relate to social norms and networks; living and working conditions; and how these in turn are related to the wider socio-economic and cultural environment in which we live (Dahlgren and Whitehead, 2007). Thus, when we consider the health of urban populations, the impact of the surrounding environment (including physical, cultural and political factors) can create a more complex setting in which to investigate population health. As highlighted by Galea and Vlahov (2005c), cities are not just geographic places. Instead, each city has its own defining features which may or may not have an impact on the health of its population.

Civil Society and the Emergence of NGOs

The last few decades have seen an increase in numbers of non-governmental organizations (NGOs) involved in the development process. This can be attributed to what some believe as the frustration and impatience of governments in the developing world failing to assist or generate growth to assist the poor (Barr, Fafchamps and Owens, 2005). A renewed increase in civil society by donors and the general public, as well as the expansion and significance of larger international NGOs has also been attributed to the rise and popularity of the NGO sector (McCoy and Hilson, 2009).

Traditionally, NGOs have been discussed within the discourse of civil society. This is because NGOs are seen as a product of civil society. Civil society is a broad and difficult concept to define. There has been much debate over its definition and use, especially as the term depends on other theoretical influences. Many of these theoretical influences can be found in the social sciences where it is understood in different ways (Hulma and Turner, 1990; Kidd, 2002; Oxhorn, 1995). This makes it difficult to generalize the concept of civil society, even though this has happened to some extent within the literature.

Defining NGOs

In essence, civil society can be defined as a space between the state, the market and family where people can debate and tackle action. By this definition, the civil society sector comprises the residual domain outside the realms of the state and market. This is sometimes referred to as an 'independent sector', third sector' or 'voluntary sector' (Anheier and Seibel, 1990). Civil society organizations can include charities; international bodies (such as the United Nations and the World Health Organization); human rights campaigns; neighbourhood self-help groups; and non-governmental organizations (NGOs). Thus, civil society involves a wide range of self-governing and self-generating private organizations in which citizens can exercise their initiatives in their own right for what is often described as 'the greater good'.

Despite the rapid expansion of NGOs, there has been no specific definition for defining them. Instead, the term NGO has been used in different ways. NGOs are often defined as organizations that are institutionally separate from the government (Garonne, 2012). There are, however, several difficulties with this definition. First, some NGOs are contractors of foreign government agencies, acting as tax shelters or providing a cover for a political organization (Green and Matthias, 1996). Second, organizations such as charities, whilst being outside the government structure, are not strictly classified as NGOs (Akukwe, 1998). Finally, local NGOs (especially those in the developing world) often have former government officials as members. This makes it difficult to distinguish between government and non-government operations (Akukwe, 1998). For the purposes of this chapter, we define NGOs as non-governmental organizations that provide assistance or services to local communities.

There is substantial literature devoted to NGOs and their role in development. The literature has outlined the many different roles that NGOs can play in society.

In the developing world NGOs have become an undeniably powerful third sector. In particular, NGOs have a long tradition of local-level community engagement, providing services, social capital and advocating for vulnerable groups (Barr, Fafchamps and Owens, 2005). They are widely known as serving an intermediary role between governments and communities, and have begun to establish themselves at different levels within and across the decision-making process, from local to global. They are very well placed with networks across different sectors to advocate sustainable and cost-effective development activities and projects. The involvement of NGOs in humanitarian interventions is also well documented. They are known as providers of humanitarian assistance, particularly during times of natural disasters, human conflict and epidemic disasters (Yoshida et al., 2009).

The types of work that NGOs undertake can be grouped into six broad categories (Carrard et al., 2009; Clark, 1995; Gellert, 1996):

– NGOs that facilitate service delivery (directly and indirectly) or play an intermediary role between communities and service providers. They may try and change official policies and programmes towards public needs by reporting on public opinion and local community experiences.

– Community education, marketing, gender-sensitive approaches and implementing behaviour change programmes, as well as educating the public as to their rights and entitlement under state-run programmes.

– NGOs that build partnerships and promote different networks between different sectors, such as the government and service providers. They may also assist in translating and implementing policies and regulations at the local level.

– Assisting capacity building for different groups. In particular, they may assist governments and donors in developing more effective development strategies through strengthening institutions, staff training and improved management capability.

– Assisting or undertaking research of new technologies that have been adapted at the local level.

– NGOS that engage in policy dialogue through promotion of successful programmes, communicating lessons learnt and monitoring programmes and government initiatives. They may also promote decentralization and local government reforms.

In recent years there has been a shift from supply-side to demand-side activities, characterized by the way NGOs have developed new skills and partnerships. In some cases changes in the way of working have allowed NGOs to manoeuvre into more senior negotiating positions with government officials. They are also better placed to utilize their technical and operational know-how of information technology to communicate advocacy and promote their networking skills (Clark, 1995). As a result, NGOs are becoming increasingly powerful agents within the international development process. This is particularly visible within the areas of health and environmental conservation. However, in the present economic climate it is difficult to ascertain how much more power NGOs will garner in global issues.

In some developing countries, there has been the development of a stronger NGO sector. For example, in India a large number of hospitals outside of the government health sector are run by NGOs. This was because facilities were not properly utilized through the lack of community participation and poor quality of services. As a result, NGOs have carved out a niche in the areas of training and research (Tekhre, Tiwari and Khan, 2004). A further shift towards the demand-side approach is the way in which NGOs assist citizens in finding out about government activities (or lack of activity) and other policies which may affect them. Here, NGOs are often better placed to use advocacy and political influence to hold local officials accountable to activities or policies which create further damage towards the poor. They can construct fora in which both local authorities and communities can consult on government decisions and negotiate policies (Clark, 1995).

NGO Controversies: More Harm than Good?

Despite the good intentions of NGOs, it is also true that harmful conduct through their programmes can at times potentially have a detrimental effect. There is a growing body of literature that have highlighted these weaknesses and harmful effects (Barber and Bowie, 2008; Garonne, 2012). The breaking of local economies and aid dependency are two of the biggest issues. However, the extent of the negative effects of some NGO activities remains unknown.

In her controversial book *Dead Aid*, Dambiso Moyo (2009) uses a hypothetical scenario to provide a critical overview of a reality that occurs with many INGOs (international non-governmental organizations) in Africa. Moyo describes a mosquito net maker who manufactures around 500 nets per week, employing ten people, all of who have large families to support. Despite their best efforts, they struggle to beat the malaria-carrying mosquito. An INGO delivers 100,000 mosquito nets to help the affected region. However, the local market is now flooded with INGO mosquito nets and the local net maker is out of business. In turn, the net maker's employees are made unemployed and they are unable to provide for their families. Within the next five years, the majority of these nets will be torn and damaged and no longer effective in preventing malaria. Here, the act of giving is described as a potentially detrimental act of providing assistance. An another example is the food, medical equipment, toys and school supplies which are often imported by INGOs when resources are often available locally (Gray, 2012). The key issues raised here illustrate the harm caused to local businesses by the flooding of markets with foreign goods and supplies. When foreign aid and the INGOs disappear, there are no local resources available to fill the gap.

Concerns have also been raised with regards to the use, maintenance and operation of initiatives (such as financial co-operatives) once an INGO leaves the area at the end of the project. This has led to numerous projects, organizations and websites being created to score NGOs on the sustainability of their projects. Strengthening Health Outcomes through the Private Sector (SHOPS) is one such project working in partnership with USAID (United States Agency for International Development), Marie Stopes International and other groups and consultancies which score NGOs working in the health sector (SHOPS, 2012). Although they provide reports of how to make projects more sustainable, this comes at a cost, which most NGOs, particularly small community projects, could not afford.

Furthermore, there has been a rise in demand for greater transparency within the NGO sector. This is because in some countries, donors play a role in financing, designing and delivering services (Carrard et al., 2009). This can have a negative impact in the way NGOs carry out their activities as donors will prefer to see successful activities rather than unsuccessful ones. As a result, some NGOs have begun providing donors with false reports to ensure future financing (Garonne, 2012). Thus, there is much to be done to encourage transparency within the NGO sector so that mistakes can be learnt from unsuccessful projects as well as giving donors a true report of how their finances were used. Despite this, NGOs, whether at the local or international level, still play an essential role in addressing issues of global poverty and development.

Potential Opportunities and Roles for NGOs Post-reform

NGO, private and governmental partnerships are a common feature in developing countries. Within the area of health, it is a paradigm that has been widely promoted as a solution to the perceived failings of government responsibilities. It can harness NGO and civil society power to support effective health policy-making and delivery of health programmes and services (McCoy and Hilson, 2009). Examples within the global health landscape include the GAVI Alliance and the Global Fund to Fight AIDS, TB and Malaria. However, the success of these health programmes relies on wider changes in government structures and institutions, and not just NGO involvement.

The recent and ongoing NHS reforms in the UK provide potential opportunities for NGO involvement and support. This is because there has been a shift in the traditional hierarchies of the health care system. These have now been replaced by a more complex and multilevel balance in power where local authorities, GPs, hospitals, regional and national health authorities will play an active role in the decision and policy-making process. Furthermore, the good governance debate has highlighted the need for the citizen's voice in the continuing development of the UK health care system and the quality of health care on offer to patients. The establishment of a new national body called Health Watch will allow patients to feed back their concerns and ideas for improvement at the local level.

The NHS reforms are also meant to encourage greater involvement from the private sector and civil society organizations. However, financial issues make it difficult for civil society organizations to compete with wealthier private health organizations, such as BUPA, who may already offer high quality health care services. However, since the UK government will be seeking to provide quality health services through the new health care infrastructure, there is the potential to explore opportunities for NGOs to support health care providers under the new UK health reforms.

Advisory Role

NGOs might participate within or alongside the new decision-making structures in an advisory capacity. By providing a supportive advisory role, NGOs can be utilized and incorporated into the decision-making process of new policies or health programmes. By operating outside the formal management structures, NGOs have a greater freedom to express their opinions without the burden of responsibility to others within the debate. This leaves them open to criticize existing health policies and programmes as well as suggest potential solutions from their own experience of community-based work. Being independent and relatively free from political entanglements, NGOs can promote greater acceptance from both the government and local communities.

Furthermore, General Practitioners (GPs), hospitals and government health institutions and organizations may also informally consult with NGOs who specialize in a specific health area, such as working with ethnic minority groups or elderly people, thus creating a bottom-up approach to both the decision and problem-solving processes. To some extent, this is already taking place between health care providers, health institutions and charities. For example, UK charities such as Help the Aged and Age Concern already work across several sectors and local authorities to ensure elderly members of the population are able to utilize existing services, as well as providing guidance and information about individual benefit entitlements (such as reduced council tax and fuel allowance) and access to care facilities.

Monitoring and Evaluator Role

NGOs could also provide support in the form of monitoring and evaluating the new NHS reforms. The information generated can then be used to inform the different levels of actors involved in the decision-making process, as well as providing an opportunity for patients to feed back their opinions. This could include suggestions for improvements to existing health services, opportunities to develop and test new health policies and interventions and could highlight failing areas or services. It could also include monitoring government spending on intervention and prevention programmes within communities, as well as general spending within the health care system so that all actors remain accountable for their spending budgets. Using NGOs in a monitoring and evaluator role also improves accountability and transparency within the NHS through the publication of reports to the general public as well as government.

This is a role that has been used widely within global health governance. Social Watch, for example, is an international network informed by citizen's groups in each country which monitor and report on the fulfillment of national, regional and international commitments to eradicating poverty and ensuring equality (Social Watch, 2012). In the UK, the Bretton Woods Project monitors and critiques the IMF and World Bank through a social justice viewpoint (McCoy and Hilson, 2009), whilst Citizens UK provides guidance for people who wish to form a community organization to create change in their neighborhoods, as well as nationally.

Mediation Role

The freedom of independence that NGOs have also lends itself to them providing an intermediary role for facilitating disputes or debates. This role can encourage dialogue between patients, local communities, local health care providers, other health institutions and organizations as well as politicians and national government. This is a role that is widely undertaken by NGOs in the developing world and there is a substantial body of literature that illustrates this.

Tekhre's study of NGOs in Indonesia (Tekhre, 2004) found that NGO collaboration with policymakers, local communities and Indonesian government officials promoted the use of primary health services in the state of Arumchal Pradesh. In Carrard et al.'s (2009) study of NGOs working within the sanitation sector in Vietnam, they found that building partnerships and engaging in policy dialogue helped to promote networking and discussions between the different levels of actors involved in providing clean water and sanitation facilities (Carrard et al., 2009).

Within the health policy environment, it is important that consultation is encouraged. To some extent, this is a strategy that the UK government is already following; however improvements can still be made to the current process. A more constructive dialogue between local communities, health care providers and all government actors needs to take place. NGOs have the potential to create a collaborative relationship between all actors involved in the policy-making process. Inviting NGOs and community-based organizations to public consultations could result in better informed government planning and policies.

Support for Services Role

The final opportunity for NGO involvement suggested in this chapter is that of a supportive role for existing services, both in health care service provision and training needs. This is one of the key roles that NGOs fulfil in the developing world from a health viewpoint. This can occur in many ways, such as in the provision of basic shelter after a natural disaster, to administering vaccinations for childhood diseases on behalf of the World Health Organization, such as the Roll Back Malaria (RBM) partnership.

NGOs are generally low-cost operations with motivated and committed staff. Low staff costs combined with streamlined services allows NGOs to work effectively on low budgets. Thus they are well-placed to add value or work in partnership with existing health care services which may be under pressure to either reduce costs or be on the receiving end of budget cuts. Through innovative programme operation and improving existing services and infrastructure, NGOs can potentially reduce resources and costs whilst trying new approaches for service delivery.

Training itself is not just limited to providing further training to health professionals. Local communities can be involved in training programmes to promote health education programmes. These could be run in schools or in local hospitals or GP practices by volunteers in partnership with more localized organizations. Opportunities also exist for qualified health professionals working within NGOs to offer staff support to health clinics as well as assisting in promoting public health initiatives and education programmes.

An example of this in the international setting is Project HOPE, an NGO whose primary mission is health education. Its training programmes range from tertiary care training to hospital-based skills, to health policy and management training (Project HOPE, 2012). In addition, Project HOPE tackles issues and problems that are not always perceived to be directly linked to health. An example of this is their income-generating programs which provide short-term loans, job training and assistance to mothers seeking employment, thus generating revenues so that changes in health behaviour and reduction of risk for their families can be effectively implemented and sustained.

Conclusions

Despite the uncertainty surrounding the UK NHS reforms, the potential exists to encourage and promote the participation and partnership of NGOs within the health care sector. Civil society and NGOs already exist and operate within the UK. The most abundant of these are charities; however, the ongoing NHS reforms provide an opportunity for NGOs to take an active role within the health sector. Furthermore, the good governance debate has highlighted the need for a citizen's voice in the continuing development of the UK health care system and the quality of health care on offer to patients. The influence of patient feedback will be strengthened through the setting up of a forthcoming new national body called Health Watch, which will also operate at the local level.

The literature has highlighted the different roles played by NGO in the developing world. These range from assessing and monitoring interventions to providing training opportunities to local communities. The literature also suggested that despite the good intentions of NGOs, harmful conduct can arise through their projects. However, lessons in harmful conduct can be used to ensure that future failures, whether in the UK or in the developing world, can be minimized.

Despite this, these roles played by NGOs in the developing world have the possibility to be utilized and implemented in the newly reformed UK health sector. Encouraging NGO partnerships and public accountability of the health care system, as well as promoting community engagement, can foster better relationships and create a more grassroots strategy of public consultation. This in turn would enable the government to create better informed decisions for health policy and health programmes. Of course, the degree to which NGO potential can be both utilized and realized is dependent on many factors. The most principal factor is the nature of the relationship between the NGO sector and the government. If both parties can look to complementary rather than competing contributions, the potential for collaboration becomes possible.

Acknowledgements

The author would like to thank the University of Manchester for providing financial support to attend the IGU-Commission on Geography of Governance conference, at the Institute of Geography and Spatial Planning, University of Lisbon, Portugal.

Chapter 10

Regional Effects of Urban Development Projects: An Innovative Tool to Support Fiscal Sustainable Urban Planning

Anja Brauckmann

Introduction

Residents and companies are key factors in urban development processes. They affect urban development in what concerns settlement development, requirement and use of infrastructure or the labour market. The focus of this chapter lies on the impact which urban development projects have on local government finance, namely municipalities and regions illustrated by case studies located in Germany.

In Germany, the municipal financing system is regulated at the federal level, but the federal states (German: Bundesländer) are able to exert limited influence. The following figures are related to the federal state of North Rhine-Westphalia (NRW) where the case studies are located.[1] They give evidence of the situation in 2008, but they may slightly deviate from year to year. On the one hand residents and companies influence the most important municipal taxes (Figure 10.1):

The trade tax (German: Gewerbesteuer) takes on average 17.1 per cent of the municipal revenues in NRW (IT.NRW, 2008). It is calculated on the basis of the companies' yields and is directly paid to the municipality where the company is located. The municipalities are able to influence the revenues of the trade tax to a certain extent by defining a fee rate. Due to the dependence on the companies' yields, the trade tax is characterized by a wide range both in comparison with the single municipalities and different periods of time.

The income tax (German: Einkommensteuer) (10.7 per cent, ibid.) is paid by the working people on the basis of their income to the state and partly redistributed to the municipality where the taxpayers reside.

The property tax (German: Grundsteuer) as another important revenue (4.5 per cent, ibid) is also paid directly to the municipalities. The standard value of a plot forms the basis for taxation. Municipalities define a fee rate for the property tax as well. The tax on a built-up plot is higher than the tax on an agricultural plot.

---

1 The tax calculation system in the other federal states is identical. The following average values vary between the federal states but the ranking remains the same.

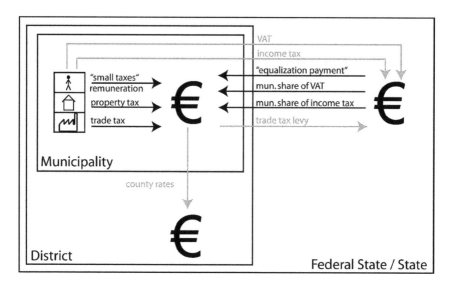

Figure 10.1   Structure of the main sources of municipal revenues and levies in Germany

On the other hand residents and companies are important for the equalization payments (German: Schlüsselzuweisungen) which amount to 27.3 per cent of the municipal revenues on average (ibid.). Their objective is to equal the municipalities funding per resident. The equalization payments are mainly calculated by the number of residents in a municipality: the arithmetical definition of a need (annual determination by the federal state) is compared with the municipalities' taxable capacity. Municipalities do not receive equalization payments when their taxable capacity exceeds the arithmetical need. 83.8 per cent of the 396 municipalities in NRW received these kinds of payments in 2011 (MIK NRW, 2010).

The majority of the German municipalities or districts[2] are affected by population decline. From 2005 to 2010 80.7 per cent of the districts in NRW and 70.3 per cent of the districts in Germany lost residents (database enquiry Regionaldatenbank). At the same time, 95.7 per cent of the municipalities in NRW are indebted with 1,663 EUR per resident on average (database enquiry IT.NRW).

In spite of the decreasing population and high level of debt, municipalities keep on developing new urban development projects such as housing or commercial areas. They are seen as one strategy to affect these key factors and increase or at least maintain the revenues. This strategy can be successful if only the municipal level is regarded. On the regional level, however, these developments lead to a competition for residents or companies when neighbouring municipalities act

_____

2   Districts consist of several municipalities; their purpose is to take over responsibilities if single municipalities are not able to carry them out.

equally. This competition is founded in the fact that the group target of new urban development projects is limited in its quantity (BMVBS and BBR, 2007: 154–63) because people mainly tend to move within the region (Bauer et al., 2005: 269). Companies tend to move within the region too, especially to hold their position on the market and employees (IHK Region Stuttgart, 2009; IAB, 2008).

Various mechanisms interact within the municipal financing system. Therefore, fiscal effects of new urban development projects cannot be estimated by a single formula to answer the question whether a planned urban development project has the desired effects. Hence the research deals with the following question: to what extent do urban development projects affect municipal and regional revenues?

New Cost-efficiency Instruments

The topic of costs of urban sprawl gained more and more importance in public discussion in recent years. The USA took a pioneering role as they already decreed the need to analyse the costs of large urban development projects in some states (Reidenbach et al., 2007: 12). In Europe, Switzerland and Austria are examples of countries that attempted to analyse the costs of supplying technical und social infrastructure in the context of new urban development projects (Ecoplan, 2000; Dittrich-Wesbuer and Osterhage, 2010).

In the last years some instruments or studies to support planning-related decisions concerning the projects' effects on the costs have been developed. The main objective of these instruments is to increase transparency as well as cost-awareness and to offer additional reasons for decisions in planning processes.

Widespread arguments concerning positive effects of urban development projects can therefore be checked. A variety of instruments has also been developed in Germany; some of them were promoted by the REFINA-Program.[3] On a long-term basis these instruments should support economical and sustainable land-use policies by reducing the drain of land resources. The instruments are mainly focusing on the topic of cost-efficiency and housing projects (Preuß and Floeting, 2009; Bock et al., 2009). Most of these instruments calculate costs for the initial implementation of a particular urban project and subsequently the follow-up costs associated with the operation of the infrastructure. Only some of these instruments can also calculate the benefits associated with the project. One example of this is an instrument named LEANkom, inter alia, developed by the Research Institute for Regional and Urban Development gGmbH (ILS), which calculates both costs and benefits (Dittrich-Wesbuer and Osterhage, 2010).

All these instruments function as decision support systems and can be differentiated according to their different target groups (Preuß and Floeting,

---

3 'Research for the Reduction of Land Consumption and for Sustainable Land Management' funded by the Federal Ministry of Education and Research within the German National Strategy for Sustainable Development.

2009). On the one hand there exist highly complex instruments that often require the collaboration of experts and consultants for the interpretation of the results, a task not always accessible to the municipal staff. These instruments require a large amount of detailed information, a long processing time and the results are mainly quantitative. On the other hand there are instruments which are easier to handle and for that reason can be more easily used by politicians, planners or even residents looking for information that can support a decision, for instance, on the location of a new residence. By depicting possible rough trends, they need less information and often use average values to accelerate processing time. Their results are often point systems or traffic light rating systems. These kinds of instruments should be applied in different stages of the planning process because they address different questions and people. A combination of both kinds of instruments is possible in different stages of the planning process.

Some of the first applications of these instruments show that planners and decision-makers are mainly interested in strategic planning processes. A chronological order is often demanded for the development of certain areas in the context of formal and informal land-use plans. In addition to that, issues related with the use of infrastructure have great interest for the actual users of these infrastructures (Dittrich-Wesbuer and Osterhage, 2010). Demographic models are essential elements in these instruments, although the experience so far shows that these instruments provide a rather limited view of the demographic trends. They rarely cover topics related to companies and retail, two crucial issues in municipal and regional development. In addition to that, these models tend to focus only on a single municipality (Preuß and Floeting, 2009). Interactions among neighbouring municipalities and the effects on each other can hardly be depicted, a characteristic that certainly adulterates the results on a regional perspective.

RegioProjektCheck – an Instrument to Evaluate New Projects in Urban Development

Based on these experiences the project team[4] is currently working on a follow-on project, inter alia, based on LEANkom called RegioProjektCheck. The new instrument illustrates the effects for both the neighbouring municipalities and the region and hence expands the existing instruments. Besides the fiscal topics it also covers topics of ecological (energy consumption, transport emissions, ecological values) and social effects (participation, accessibility). In addition to housing, models for companies and retail are included (Figure 10.2). Due to this complexity the model has been developed to be used primarily by experts or consultants who will interpret the results and use them to advise municipalities and regions on the

---

4   The project team consists of HafenCity University Hamburg, Research Institute for Regional and Urban Development, the office of GertzGutscheRümenapp and Institute 'Raum und Energie'.

multidimensional effects in strategic regional planning processes. Single values as well as joint evaluations should be available depending on the topic of the effects. Technically this instrument will be implemented via a toolbox in a Geographic Information System (GIS). The project will be completed in the autumn 2013.[5]

During the development stage of this new instrument the project team cooperates with two administrative districts, the district Rheinisch-Bergischer Kreis close to Cologne in the west and the district Landkreis Harburg close to Hamburg in the north of Germany. These experimental projects are tested to gain experience on the applicability of this sort of instrument in local and regional planning processes and on the data.

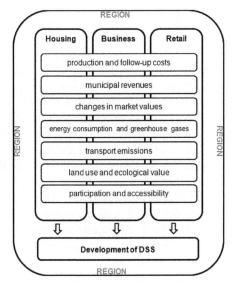

Figure 10.2　Components of the model RegioProjektCheck

By using this kind of instrument the knowledge of the consequences of each particular decision can be assessed and cooperation on regional development issues can be encouraged. One possible result might be the fact that in one municipality there is profit regarding one policy issue while in neighbouring municipalities the result may well be negative compared to the situation prior to the application of the project. On another topic the result might be the reverse. However, at the regional scale the results are of a different nature. On the one hand, a region can be understood as a summation of single municipalities, while on the other hand, some joint effects (like emissions) cannot be located exactly within the region. In this case, the region as a whole is considered. The model illustrates the effects on these different levels depending on the different kinds of effects.

In what regards municipal revenues the project is focused on two different kinds of effects, namely direct and indirect effects. First, the direct effects of an urban development project are analysed, in particular the effects on the income tax, property tax and equalization payments for all kinds of projects as well as on trade tax and value-added tax (VAT) for projects in companies and in the retail sector. These results will be referred to single municipalities and counties if they are affected by the project.

Additionally, the indirect effects on regional benefits are examined, in particular those that cannot be assigned to individual municipalities. This examination contains

---

5　For further information see: www.regioprojektcheck.de (in German).

the regional value added, job effects, effects on income tax and social subsidies as well as on regional consumer spending. These effects result from economical interconnections with the project explicitly excluding the internal situation of a company. While one-time effects during the construction phase are considered for all types of projects, effects of operational activities are only considered for companies and for the retail sector because they contain economic interconnections. In the context of the project RegioProjektCheck, multipliers and input-output tables following the methods of Kronenberg (2010) and Schröder (2010) are used. These calculations of the indirect effects refer to the region as a whole because they cannot be located on single municipalities. Hence the exact location of a company within a region is of lower interest in the context of the indirect effects.

The results of both kinds of effects are not embedded into the municipal budget, but they describe a delta, meaning the changed revenues, in order to simplify a comparison between projects and municipalities. Both values and evaluations, for instance in traffic light rating systems, should be available for the user who can interpret the results for local and regional planning processes.

The different models of the instrument offer preliminary results. When regarding these results, a distinction between housing areas on the one hand and commercial areas on the other hand has to be made because of different mechanisms of action. At the current level it has to be noticed that the different models are not connected yet, nevertheless preliminary results based on case studies do exist. Interesting trends can be derived, which give a first insight into the possible results of the instrument.

Preliminary Results – Housing Areas

Fiscal calculations for housing areas already exist, but the regional perspective is still missing. The following calculations deal with a housing area in the municipality of Wermelskirchen, a municipality in the case study district of Rheinisch-Bergischer Kreis (RBK). The housing area consists of 55 single family houses of low density (6 housing units per hectare) and the urban development project is currently being implemented. Figure 10.3 shows the case study region, the district of Rheinisch-Bergischer Kreis.

Figure 10.3   District of Rheinisch-Bergischer Kreis

Direct Effects

For the calculation of the direct effects it has to be pointed out that not all residents of a new housing area can be involved. Only the shift in the number of residents is important when calculating the changed revenues (delta). The number of residents in the project area does not form the delta because some people might already have lived in the municipality before, hence they do not cause additional revenues.

The following calculation simplifies the interconnections and only focuses on two municipalities. It includes the assumption that the immigration rate is 30 per cent in a first scenario: 20 per cent of the immigrating population lived in the neighbouring municipality of Kürten and 10 per cent lived outside the district before.[6] The following results (Figure 10.4) describe a cross-section of revenues in 2032 and form a delta to 2012.[7]

The new housing area affects the property and income tax as well as the equalization payments and county rates. Whereas the property tax does not shift between the municipalities because it is independent of the residents and their origin, the income tax shifts depending on the migration of the residents. However, the most important changes result from the equalization payments. Residents moving from Kürten to Wermelskirchen cause this shift in payments. In addition to that, the county rates form a crucial aspect: the county rates of Wermelskirchen are increasing because of its higher taxable capacity and higher equalization payments. Vice versa, the neighbouring municipalities' county rates are decreasing because of decreasing taxable capacity. Furthermore, the

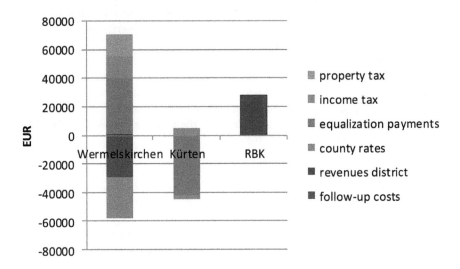

Figure 10.4   Comparison of municipal revenues (housing)

---

6   These assumptions will be replaced by an own model.
7   Additional costs are illustrated as a minus while lower costs are illustrated as a plus.

district receives additional revenues mainly consisting of higher county rates of Wermelskirchen (83.3 per cent) but also of additional equalization payments of the federal state to the district because of more residents.

From a regional perspective, the urban development projects in neighbouring municipalities are of interest for the calculations. Competition between municipalities by developing new housing areas can lead to lower immigration rates because of an oversupply of offers. A modification of the immigration rate in the model also affects the revenues. When the immigration rate is reduced to 15 per cent (10 per cent of the population lived in the neighbouring municipality and 5 per cent outside the district) in a second scenario, the revenues are decreasing as well. But also the county rates are decreasing in comparison to higher immigration rates.

The most crucial aspect for evaluating these effects is the connection with the model for the costs of production and follow-up costs. The costs stay at a relatively constant level, largely independent of the shift in population. While costs are covered in the first scenario by the additional revenues, they do not cover the follow-up costs in the second scenario. From this perspective, the urban development project causes a loss due to the fact that less people move to Wermelskirchen and cause less additional revenues.

As a consequence of these findings, it can be concluded that municipalities might avoid additional revenues due to the fact that they continue developing new areas without coordinating their development strategies with the neighbouring municipalities. If they coordinate and develop just as many dwellings as needed, their development could be more efficient, a condition that local and regional policymakers should consider in this era of fiscal austerity and which should be part of a new governance model to be developed for the post-crisis period.

Indirect Effects

Moreover, the instrument should model the indirect effects of a project. Housing areas only cover the effects of the one-time construction phase because from an economical point of view they hardly contain economic interconnections which lead to an operational phase. In the case study the region receives the following one-time maximum values (Table 10.1).

Table 10.1   Indirect effects of a new housing area in Wermelskirchen (specimen calculation)

	Construction Phase
Gross value added	21 800 000 EUR
Additional income tax	130 000 EUR
Less social subsidies	1 400 000 EUR
Additional regional consumer spending	280 000 EUR

It has to be emphasized that these are only maximum values. The model of input-output tables assumes among other things that the employees are working at full capacity and new employees have to be hired. The determined values have to be readjusted to the local context of the labour market to interpret them.

Preliminary Results – Commercial Areas

In opposition to housing areas, modelling of fiscal effects of commercial areas forms a new and more complex approach. Not only the economic sector of the prospective company is important, but also the fact that it was located in the region before or not. Therefore, forecasts for the prospective need of commercial areas use different probabilities and values for the expected employees distinguishing between these types of companies (Zwicker-Schwarm et al., 2010: 48).

A very important aspect for municipal decision-makers is the trade tax when discussing a new commercial area, because it appears to be the main source of taxes (see above). Yet this assumption is only meant at first sight. According to the German Institute for Economic Research the payments to other administrative levels take 89 per cent of the trade tax on average, which means that additional municipal revenues of 1 EUR cause 89 cents of payment. Consequently, only 11 cents remain with the municipality. In special cases (especially lower fee rate in comparison to the federal states fictitious fee rate) it can rise to 117 per cent (Ifo, 2008: 142–3), which means that some municipalities have to pay more than they receive from the trade tax.

As mentioned in the introduction, the equalization system takes the additional revenues into account. RegioProjektCheck calculates these mechanisms for the different municipalities involved.[8] The results show that the same tentative tax has different effects on neighbouring municipalities because of the equalization system. Figure 10.5 demonstrates these mechanisms on the basis of the district Rheinisch-Bergischer Kreis including the elements trade tax, trade tax levy, value-added tax and county rates. Due to the different fee rates, the same basis of taxation leads to different revenues in the neighbouring municipalities. The fee rates of the trade tax and the county rates have the most important impact. The importance of the region, the district is meant here, is further underlined because it has a strong influence on these effects and takes a large part of the municipal revenues.

The following specimen calculations discuss a commercial area in Rösrath, also located in the case study district of Rheinisch-Bergischer Kreis. Whereas the plot currently is a brownfield, there are plans to develop it into an area for offices, especially for the research and development sector (NACE Rev. 1.1, Code K73) (EU, 2002). Put simply, it is assumed that there will be only new companies from outside the region and that there will be 280 employees, 180 residing in Rösrath and 100 residing in the neighbouring municipality of Bergisch Gladbach. These

---

8   It has to be emphasized that the trade tax, compared with the other taxes, is a much more unsteady tax, because it depends on the companies' yields.

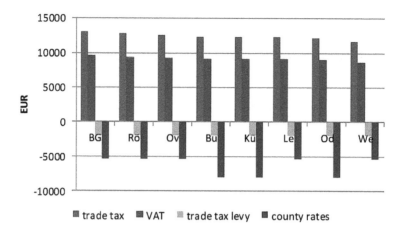

Figure 10.5   Effects of the same tentative tax (trade tax) in RBK

values are based on standard values for areas of employees (Zwicker-Schwarm et al., 2010: 53). Furthermore, it is assumed that about 30 per cent of these employees find a new job after a period of unemployment. The following results describe a cross-section of revenues in 2022 and depict the changed revenues to 2012.

Direct Effects
In this case it can be seen that Rösrath receives additional revenues as well as Bergisch Gladbach (Figure 10.6). The main revenues for Rösrath result from the property tax because of new buildings. Exactly as in the other example, there is no shift between municipalities here. The trade tax compared to the property tax is of minor importance. But Rösrath has to pay additional county rates due to the additional tax revenues. The district has to pay less social subsidies for the unemployed then, which play an important role in the municipal finances and justify the districts' extensive additional revenues.

Positive fiscal effects of commercial areas tend to spread more powerfully on the region than effects of housing areas because all connected municipalities make profit from the project in this case. Thus it can be concluded that the location of a company does not influence the revenues as much as it is often assumed. The most important factors for this calculation are the place of residence of the employees and the number of previously unemployed people.

The topic of follow-up costs in housing (see 3.1.1) can be transferred to commercial areas. Especially concerning commercial areas the time from the start of the construction until the last plot has been developed can take many years. Follow-up costs for infrastructure arise but the amount of revenues is often uncertain.

It can be concluded that a joint and coordinated strategy can contribute to a successful economic development in the region. A coordinated strategy might also

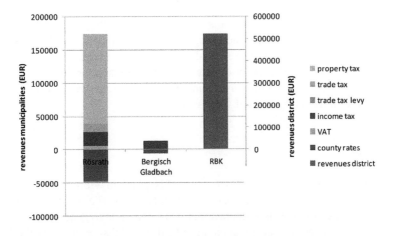

Figure 10.6 Comparison of municipal revenues (commercial areas)

reduce the costs when the area is developed according to the regional requirements on quantity and quality (q.v. ILS, 2006).

Indirect Effects
In commercial projects the one-time indirect effects of the construction phase as well as the annual indirect effects of the operational phase have to be considered. If the company has been located in the region before, the operational phase will not be taken into account. The following table (Table 10.2) shows the maximum results in the context of a gross value added in the expected amount of 23 million EUR for the one-time construction phase and annual 20 million EUR for the operational phase.

Table 10.2 Indirect effects of a new commercial area in Rösrath (specimen calculation)

	Construction phase	Operational phase
Gross value added	23 000 000 EUR	20 000 000 EUR
Additional income tax	135 000 EUR	80 000 EUR
Less social subsidies	1 500 000 EUR	850 000 EUR
Additional regional consumer spending*	285 000 EUR	200 000 EUR

Note: *Additional regional consumer spending also arises in the context of the newly employed regarded in the direct effects, though they form an indirect effect. For these directly employed people the instrument calculates 190 000 EUR annual additional regional consumers spending.

These calculations refer to the region as a whole, because they cannot be located on single municipalities. Hence the exact location of a company within a region will not have an influence on the regional effects. These interim results underline the first conclusions of the direct effects of a commercial area that the benefits spread over the region. A joint development of commercial areas in the region would be useful from this point of view as well.

Conclusion

First of all it can be concluded that a complex point of view is necessary to estimate the fiscal effects of an urban development project. The complex system of municipal financing underlines the fact that it is impossible to generalize effects.

With regard to regional cooperation it can be deduced that positive fiscal effects for the single municipalities considering the topic costs and benefits are probable. The budgets can be used more efficiently if they cooperate in settlement development.

The preliminary results underline that cooperation is useful and that decision support systems can play an important role in regional negotiations because they can increase the transparency of decisions. In addition to that, different alternatives of a project can be juxtaposed, hence discussion processes become enriched by this joint basis of decisions. In conclusion it can be said that planning in regional cooperation and a more objective consideration, for instance by using a decision support system, in a new model of governance can reduce future costs and risks and therefore support a more sustainable way of planning.

The most important factors in these calculations are the employees' place of residence and the number of previously unemployed people. Furthermore, fiscal effects from commercial projects seem to have a much stronger impact on the region and spread more widely than effects of housing areas, thus emphasizing that especially commercial projects need a regional frame of reference.

In the context of the project RegioProjektCheck it can be said that some valuable trends in these first calculations can be observed. Furthermore, the different models still have to be connected with each other. Models for the development of the population and the employees are so important, because they represent the key factors of the entire instrument. Further cooperation with municipalities is required. The examination of the existing instruments has taught that ideas of research and practice do not harmonize in some particular questions, so the importance of exchanging ideas and using case studies is underlined.

Because of its complexity, the instrument should be used by experts. However, the results should also be understandable by planners or politicians. The main objective should be to make all those involved aware of the consequences of their decisions.

The next challenge will be the evaluation of the estimated effects. On one hand, the results within the model have to be calculated, combining direct and indirect effects. On the other hand, they have to be connected with the other models in order to consider ecological and social aspects. Final users have to discuss the results and if possible use them to enrich their decision-making processes. A joint evaluation would be desirable but it still has to be discussed if an instrument like this is able to do this.

References

Bauer, U., Holz-Rau, C. and Scheiner, J., 2005. 'Standortpräferenzen, intraregionale Wanderungen und Verkehrsverhalten. Ergebnisse einer Haushaltsbefragung in der Region Dresden'. *Raumforschung und Raumordnung* 63(4), pp. 266–78.

Bock, S., Hinzen, A. and Libbe, J., 2009. 'Strategische Ansätze zur Kommunikation des Themas Fläche: Fazit und Ausblick'. In Bock, S., Hinzen, A. and Libbe, J. (eds), *Nachhaltiges Flächenmanagement – in der Praxis erfolgreich kommunizieren. Ansätze und Beispiele aus dem Förderschwerpunkt REFINA.* Volume IV: Beiträge aus der REFINA-Forschung.Berlin: Deutsches Institut für Urbanistik GmbH, pp. 203–10.

BMVBS and BBR (Bundesministerium für Verkehr, Bau und Stadtentwicklung and Bundesamt für Bauwesen und Raumordnung) 2007. *Akteure, Beweggründe, Triebkräfte der Suburbanisierung. Motive des Wegzugs – Einfluss der Verkehrsinfrastruktur auf Ansiedlungs- und Mobilitätsverhalten.* Volume 21. Bonn: BBR-Online Publikation.

Burchell, R.W., Downs, A., Seskin, S. and Moore, T. 2010. 'The Costs of Sprawl in the United States 2000 to 2025'. In Danielzyk, R., Dittrich-Wesbuer, A. and Osterhage, F. (eds), *Die finanzielle Seite der Raumentwicklung: Auf dem Weg zu effizienten Siedlungsstrukturen?* Essen: Klartext Verlag, pp. 43–77.

Danielzyk, R., Dittrich-Wesbuer, A. and Osterhage, F. (eds), *Die finanzielle Seite der Raumentwicklung: Auf dem Weg zu effizienten Siedlungsstrukturen?* Essen: Klartext Verlag.

Dittrich-Wesbuer, A. and Osterhage, F. 2010. 'Kostenbewusste Siedlungsentwicklung als Zukunftsaufgabe. Neue Werkzeuge für die Planungspraxis'. In Danielzyk, R., Dittrich-Wesbuer, A. and Osterhage, F. (eds), *Die finanzielle Seite der Raumentwicklung: Auf dem Weg zu effizienten Siedlungsstrukturen?* Essen: Klartext Verlag, pp. 225–47.

Ecoplan 2000. *Siedlungsentwicklung und Infrastrukturkosten. Final report under contract of: Bundesamt für Raumentwicklung (ARE)*, Staatssekretariat für Wirtschaft (seco), Amt für Gemeinden und Raumordnung des Kantons Bern (AGR). Bern.

EU (European Union) 2002. Commission Regulation (EC) No. 29/2002 of 19 December 2001 amending Council Regulation (EEC) No 3037/90 on the statistical classification of economic activities in the European Community.

IHK Region Stuttgart2009. *Wie attraktiv sind Standorte in der Region Stuttgart? Eine Analyse der Verlagerung von Unternehmenssitzen im Zeitraum 2005 bis 2008.* Stuttgart.

IAB (Institut für Arbeitsmarkt- und Berufsforschung) 2008. *Welche Betriebe werden verlagert? Beweggründe und Bedeutung von Betriebsverlagerungen in Deutschland*, Volume 39 Nürnberg: IAB Discussion Paper.

ILS (Institut für Landes- und Stadtentwicklungsforschung und Bauwesen des Landes Nordrhein-Westfalen) 2006. *Interkommunale Gewerbegebiete in Deutschland. Grundlagen und Empfehlungen zur Planung, Förderung, Finanzierung, Organization, Vermarktung – 146 Projektbeschreibungen und abgeleitete Erkenntnisse*, Volume 200. Dortmund: ILS NRW Schriften.

Ifo (Institut für Wirtschaftsforschung) (Ifo) 2008. *Analyse und Weiterentwicklung des Kommunalen Finanzausgleichs in Nordrhein-Westfalen. Gutachten im Auftrag des Innenministeriums des Landes Nordrhein-Westfalen.* München.

IT.NRW 2008. *Gemeindefinanzen in NRW; Ergebnisse der vierteljährlichen Kassenstatistik – 4. Quartal 2008.* Düsseldorf: Statistische Berichte.

Kronenberg, T. 2010. *Erstellung einer Input-Output-Tabelle für Mecklenburg-Vorpommern*, Volume 4. Trier: AStA Wirtschafts- und Sozialstatistisches Archiv, pp. 223–48.

MIK NRW (Ministerium für Inneres und Kommunales des Landes Nordrhein-Westfalen) 2010. *Berechnung der Schlüsselzuweisung, Investitionspauschalen, Schulpauschale/Bildungspauschale und Sportpauschale der Gemeinden im Finanzausgleich 2011 auf der Basis des Gesetzentwurfes zum Gemeindefinanzierungsgesetz 2011.* Düsseldorf: MIK.

Preuß, T. and Floeting, H. 2009. 'Werkzeuge und Modelle der Kosten-Nutzen-Betrachtung – Zusammenfassung und Synthese'. In Preuß, T. and Floeting, H. (eds), *Folgekosten der Siedlungsentwicklung. Bewertungsansätze, Modelle und Werkzeuge der Kosten-Nutzen-Betrachtung, Volume 3: Beiträge aus der REFINA-Forschung.* Berlin: Deutsches Institut für Urbanistik, pp. 159–76.

Reidenbach, M., Henckel, D., Meyer, U., Preuß, T. and Riedel, D. 2007. *Neue Baugebiete: Gewinn oder Verlust für die Gemeindekasse? Fiskalische Wirkungsanalyse von Wohn- und Gewerbegebieten, Volume 3: Edition Difu – Stadt Forschung Praxis.* Berlin: Deutsches Institut für Urbanistik

Schröder, A. 2010. *Regionalökonomische Effekte aus der Nutzung von Windenergie in der Region Hannover.* Kassel: deENet. ed.: Arbeitsmaterialien 100 EE. Volume 3.

Zwicker-Schwarm, D., Grabow, B. and Spath, C. 2010. *Stadtentwicklungskonzept Gewerbe für die Landeshauptstadt Potsdam.* Berlin: Deutsches Institut für Urbanistik.

database enquiry IT.NRW. Available at http://www.landesdatenbank.nrw.de [Accessed 28 May 2013].

database enquiry Regionaldatenbank. Available at http://www.regionalstatistik.de [Accessed 28 May 2013].

Chapter 11

The Economic Crisis Impact on the Social Policy of Ostrava City

Blanka Marková and Iva Tichá

Introduction

Due to an increase in the number of people affected by poverty in the current period of economic stagnation and decline in numerous regions and cities across Europe, social services are increasingly seen as a key component of the European social model. The economic crisis and the subsequent reduction of municipal revenues increased the pressure on the allocation of financial resources to social services in municipalities all over Europe. Social policy in this sense refers primarily to guidelines, principles, legislation and activities that affect the living conditions conducive to human welfare.

In this context, a wider range of actors than before has to be involved in the search for effective policies and tools to handle social problems. The traditional hierarchical system of public administration is increasingly seen as unable to face challenges and problems, and for that reason the hierarchical model of government has gradually been replaced by networks of actors or stakeholders, which are increasingly engaged in the decision-making process at the local level (Ossenbrügge, 2003). This shift can be best described as the move from government to governance, with the basic idea of the governance concept being a partnership and a network of actors for the implementation of a certain common action or project (Héritier, 2002). It includes the formal dimension of the policy process on one hand, that is, public administration and politics, and the informal rules and non-institutional forms of governance on the other hand (Stoker, 1998).

In this new institutional context, the policy tools in the field of social policies can differ geographically and by sector due to the national and local legal framework, the institutional management structures in the area of social services, as well as to the different skills and roles of individual actors, and the different historical process and political leadership of each region or city.

This chapter offers an overview of the development of social services in the city of Ostrava, its actors and external and internal conditions. The goal of the chapter is to analyse the impacts of the economic crisis on the quality of social services in the city of Ostrava. Ostrava is heavily dependent on financial transfers from the state budget (according to the Budgetary Allocation of Tax Act). However, due to the economic crisis and to the decreasing number of inhabitants, the amount of financial resources transferred to the city budget has decreased. The reduction in local financial resources forces local stakeholders to seek savings in all spheres of local government policies. Nevertheless, social services for the elderly and for the poor have been seen by the city government of Ostrava as inevitably necessary, in particular in a period of growing poverty due to the economic crisis. Another aim of this chapter is the description and analysis of the governance model in the field of the social policy in the city of Ostrava.

In this study of the social policy processes in the city of Ostrava we used qualitative research methods, which included participatory observation, semi-structured interviews with actors and experts[1] and the analysis of strategic documents and a literature review.

From the methodological point of view, the basic analytical procedure adopted in this research was the identification of the legal framework of the local social policy and the key actors. This was complemented by the analysis of the local institutional structures and their relevance within the policy-making process, as well as the management structures, as proposed by Van Berkel (2007) and Kazepov (2010).

Governance of Social Services in the Czech Republic

The European Union Background

The European Union (EU) as a dominant actor in the field of social policy determines not only the normative aims that should be reached in this field but also the strategic framework for local policies. The document Europe 2020 adopted by the European Union defines the strategy for an intelligent, sustainable and inclusive growth, and the priorities for EU countries. In the area of social exclusion, the priority is high employment seen to affect social and territorial cohesion and the main initiative included is the establishment of the European Platform against Poverty. Besides this policy document, the EU defined other priorities in the field of social policy in many other documents, such as, for example, the European social charter, the White and Green book for social policy.

Nonetheless, each EU member state has a wide range of their own competencies in this field and for that reason social policies differ not only from state to state but also, within each member state, at the regional or city level due to the different historical contexts (Krebs et al., 1999).

Social Services in the Czech Republic

Social services in the Czech Republic are divided into three main categories: social care, social prevention and social consultancy. Law on social services distinguishes

---

1   A. Adamcová – Association of Shelters in the Czech Republic, Š. Honová – director of elementary schools in socially excluded areas, D. Vrána – Coordinator for Social Inclusion, Regional Authority.

among social services with a full compensation, a partial compensation and without compensation. The governance model in the field of social services in the Czech Republic includes a wide range of actors. The most important one is central government, in particular the Ministry of Labour and Social Affairs, the Parliament (Chamber of Deputies, the Senate) and other entities under the direct control of central government, due to the ability to formulate strategic public policies, which are binding for the other actors. Regional and local self-government are also key players within the governance model in the field of social policy. All these entities claim to act with the aim to reduce or eliminate the negative social impacts of the economic crisis (Großmann, 2012). The task of regional, municipal and local authorities (regions, municipal and village authorities, including consultative bodies) is to provide regional programs and documents, plans and conditions for an implementation of central government policies. Another, a rather secondary actor, is the non-profit sector (for example, charities such as the Salvation Army and so on), universities, entrepreneurs and engaged individuals (Rumpel et al., 2011; Sedláková 2002; Gavlas et al. 2000).

In the Czech Republic, one of the main tools for engaging stakeholders in the discussion and planning of social services is community planning, which significantly strengthens the principles of democracy. The hallmark of the community planning method is the emphasis on citizen engagement in the formulation and implementation of a particular policy issue in a given area. Community planning is a strategic tool to identify needs and the necessary actions in the selected area. Community planning is mostly a medium-term instrument, usually with a three- to five-years horizon (Sedláková, 2002; Krausová, 2008; Šveřepa, 2009).

From the perspective of social services funding, the city and local organizations will always be dependent on external resources, the central government being the main actor in the social services system (Průša et al., 1999). The state defines the structural conditions, issues resolutions and regulations for the whole country, and by these financial decisions influences the decision-making of local actors. This is due to the significance of the Ministry of Labour and Social Affairs' budgets. Less important are the budgets of regions, cities and city districts (municipalities). Their influence stems from the principles of law on budgetary allocation of taxes – for example the regions were originally funded from the state budget, and only gradually, during the public finances reform, were they granted increasingly more significant tax incomes. Among other financial resources there are, for example, the programmes of the European Union (for example, ESF, sectoral operational programmes, regional operational programmes). A growing and more important source of finance are the social services users themselves. From the financing point of view, the typical feature of a social policy funding is its multiple resources character. Providers of social services and related activities thus have an opportunity to obtain funding from the following resources: the city budget (city district budget); EU grants; the state budget (Ministry of Labour and Social Affairs, Ministry of Health); the Moravian-Silesian Region budget; users (payments for services, care allowance);

own economic activity; foundations of OKD, ČEZ, donations; Norwegian funds, Swiss funds and so on.

Case Study: Ostrava City

The Context

The city of Ostrava (306128 inhabitants in 2012) is the largest old industrial city in the Czech Republic. The industrial development was determined by the discovery of coal in 1770s and its industrial processing and the development of closely related industries such as iron, steel industries, metallurgy, the chemical industry, heavy engineering and machinery during the following 150 years. Ostrava is the socio-economic core of the Moravian-Silesian region, located in the north-eastern part of the Czech Republic. Ostrava experienced a long period of economic and population growth between 1828 (1828 being the year of the foundation of Vítkovice ironworks) and 1989, related to the industrialization and urbanisation processes, accompanied by many changes in the administrative and spatial structures of the city of Ostrava. In the period until 1989, Ostrava was a growing industrial city, with a large number of job opportunities and great residential development, and high rates of in-migration and natural population growth due to high birth rates, all responsible for the high population growth registered in that period.

The description of the development of Ostrava city until 1989 is necessary, as it forms a precondition for understanding the development of social policy and the identification of the main problems after 1989. The new elite began, in 1990, with the transformation of the political and economic systems of the former Czechoslovakia, which brought liberalization and opening of the economy to global competition. After 40 years of development behind the iron curtain (1948–89) in the framework of a communist command economy (a centrally planned economy) isolated from global competition, the return to a global trajectory took place and a new stage in the history of Ostrava, as a part of the global economy, began. The competition pressures revealed complex weaknesses in the regional economy of the Ostrava city region and its big companies in old traditional industrial branches. At the same time the city adopted a strategy to adapt itself to the conditions of the global market.

The restructuring process brought high unemployment, especially because of the deindustrialization. Deindustrialization was an inevitable process in the course of economic transformation, which helped the Czech industry to compete globally. The deindustrialization started at the beginning of 1990s and hit the old industrial region of Ostrava very hard. In 1989, the biggest company, OKD (Ostrava – Karvina mines), had 118,000 employees around the whole mining region. However, in 2006, this mining company did not employ more than 18,000. In June 1994, all the collieries and most coke plants on the territory of Ostrava were closed down. The employment in metallurgy and steel industries dropped from approximately 80,000 (1989) to 20,000 employees (2006). In 1998 the blast furnaces of the Vítkovice ironworks were closed down by a political decision by the central government based on environmental reasons such as air pollution. A similar development can be traced in the chemical industry, heavy engineering and other related industries in the territory of Ostrava (for example the chemical plant in Hrušov) (Rumpel et al., 2011).

In the period from 1991 to 1995 the privatization process of these sorts of industrial companies was taking place; mines were being closed (in Ostrava mining stopped in 1994) and metallurgic production was being reduced. These changes brought about the dismissal of many employees and the related growth of unemployment. In 1990 the Ministry of Labour and Social Affairs helped to establish Labour Offices that were registering the unemployed. The legislation of 1991 enabled the unemployed people who registered at a Labour Office to cover their costs of living by money from social benefits financed from the national budget. The benefits (such as jobseeker's allowance) were the main tools that were to stop possible/potential expansion of poverty and social exclusion.

In the period 1990–2010, Ostrava was characterized by a rather small population decrease, which did not have a fundamental impact on the city's development. However, according to population forecasts stating that Ostrava's population might decrease to 280,000 by 2050 (for example Solanský, 2008), or even according to Šotkovský's (2009) negative projection as far as 220,000, it became obvious that problems connected with depopulation will grow if the trend remains unchanged. The shrinkage became a topic of expert discussions, and gradually also a political problem, for which political representation will have to seek appropriate solutions in the form of political initiatives. Shrinkage is not exclusively a problem of Ostrava – this process struck a whole number of Europe's secondary cities, particularly the former industrial hubs, which have been losing their attractiveness notably since the 1970s. In the framework of the case study 'Trajectory of shrinkage of the city of Ostrava', as well as at the stakeholder meeting in Ostrava in September 2010, experts from practice and politicians stated and empirically documented that Ostrava was losing its population, and that the parameters of socio-demographic indicators were changing due to three main reasons: demographic change, deindustrialization, suburbanization.

The Development of Social Services in the City of Ostrava

In the 1980s, there were only residential care services available for the elderly citizens, such as care homes and nursing homes. The city owned these facilities and decided to allocate the places according to waiting lists. The services offered were of poor quality (for example, poor hygienic facilities, many clients in one bedroom, lack of privacy) and the capacity offered did not meet the demand. After 1990, the increasing demands of an ageing population meant also an increase in the offer of services for the elderly. The new services, ambulatory as well as field care, were a result of changes in the legislation (182/1991 Coll.) which enabled the city, districts (established in 1990) and non-profit organizations to provide field services in homes. Regarding the range of field services, the municipalities began to provide services only on weekdays and in usual working hours, so there was open space for non-profit organizations that also offered the services in the evenings, at nights, on holidays and at weekends. After 1990 the NGOs (for example, charities, Salvation Army), which started to establish themselves in the post-socialist countries, came also to Ostrava and started to develop their activities in the city and surrounding areas. In the initial phase, mainly organizations with wide international experience attempted to offer their expertise to the conditions in Ostrava.

In 1992, the Ministry of Labour and Social Affairs approved the regulation concerning home care services, and the Chamber of Deputies of the Czech Parliament passed the Law on Social Security. The regulation mentioned above enlarged substantially the offer of services for older people. City districts, non-profit organizations and individuals became providers of home care services. In 1993, a challenging project was realized by the Archdiocese Charity. It was a foundation of the Přemysl Pittr's Elementary School that was to be a multi-ethnic school. At the same time it was the first elementary school in Ostrava that employed a teacher's assistant who was to help the Romany children.

The expansion of relationships between the public sector and the non-profit organizations is illustrated by the fact that in 1994 there were 9 projects worth 6 million CZK supported from the budget of the City of Ostrava. After the election in 1997, the relationships between the state and the non-profit sector were getting better and the collaboration of the municipality and the non-profit sector was expanding in Ostrava, too. In spite of the growing collaboration and the volume of financial means allocated to the area of social work, the problems in socially excluded areas were escalating after 1997. In Ostrava, the problem of social exclusion was increased by the floods that affected mainly the district of Hrušov.

In the late 1990s projects of non-profit organizations became more common and they were mainly directed at field work with families and prevention of social-pathological phenomena. The development of the non-profit sector was also connected to the increasing volume of financial means allocated for projects in the domain of social inclusion, from means of the state and the city.

In 2000, a higher tier of self-governing entities, the so-called regions, was established. They also joined the planning in the area of social services and gradually began to announce grants that foundations and providers could apply for. Since 2000 and prior to joining the EU, the relationship between the non-profit sector and the city management was stabilized. Another step towards expanding the collaboration was the introduction in 2003 of a community planning method based on the work of expert committees. Nowadays, there are 9 expert committees working and they meet every month. The so-called community plan is approved by the Council of the City of Ostrava for a certain period of time.

In 2007, the Agency for Social Integration – established by the government of the Czech Republic – started its activities in Ostrava. The agency works on the principle of local partnership with all participants. A managerial mistake was that the municipality of the City of Ostrava did not cooperate with the Agency for Social Integration. It was only the management of the district of Slezská Ostrava which saw the significance of the problem and for that reason got involved in that process. Representatives of the district of Slezská Ostrava expected financial resources as part of joining the project of social integration. However, the cooperation process did not proceed in practice in accordance with the strategic plans and expectations of the district. Even so, the cooperation between the municipality and the owners of estates, flats and NGOs did indeed start. As the collaboration was not realized throughout the whole city, it did not produce the expected results. For this reason the Agency for Social Integration concluded its activities in Ostrava in 2011 with a strong belief that the primary collaborations had been started and that it was up to the local participants to take them further or not.

In 2011, the third Community Plan in social services for 2011–14 was approved and its preparation included an increased number of participants. The reason for their activities is the fact that if a priority is incorporated into the Community Plan of social services, it is easier for them to reach financial means of the city, region, state or EU.

Figure 11.1 shows the distribution of social services funding. Financial resources, out of which social services are funded, are coming from the European Union, ministries (particularly the Ministry of Labour and Social Affairs), Moravian-Silesian Region, the city of Ostrava and its city districts, clients and other resources (foundations and so on).

Figure 11.2 also illustrates the comparison of social services funding development between 2006 and 2009. It is possible to see the result of the pressure on clients to finance their social services from their own resources (or from care allowance if they are entitled to it).

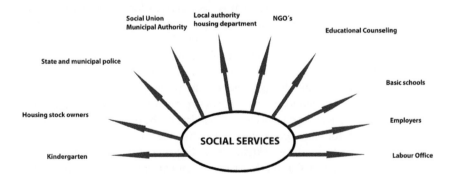

Figure 11.1   Actors of social services in the Czech Republic
Source: authors, 2012.

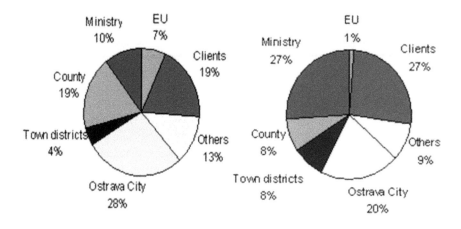

Figure 11.2   Sources of funding for social services, comparing 2006 and 2009

Source: authors, 2012.

The major problem of funding in the sphere of social services is its usual short-term budgeting period (one to three years). The providers are thus suffering from insecure funding for the following years. Particularly the field and ambulatory services are influenced by that fact. Providers operating a long-term or residential service, for example a day care house, should be secured by long-term funding so that elderly people are not unnecessarily worried about the danger of having to search for different accommodation and the subsequent moving then involved.

Conclusion

The sphere of social services in the Czech Republic has been developing dynamically during the past 20 years. Therefore, it was necessary to formulate and to codify the frameworks for the provision and funding of social services. Another part of the changes were real estate transfers in the field of social services in connection with public governance reform. In the case of Ostrava, these changes were not very visible on the outside, because the former county of Ostrava was transformed into the City of Ostrava without changes. In fact, the property transfers were carried out only among the city and its districts. However, the result is that even today the situation is rather unclear for citizens as the founders of the day care houses are city districts, but homes for older people were mostly founded by the City of Ostrava.

Social services are, to a great extent, dependent on the share of funding from the state budget. The fact that the Ministry of Labour and Social Affairs' funds are limited may cause major problems. In this context, the state influenced the planning in the sphere of social services through the legal framework adopted. For example, the law stated that regions are obliged to plan according to a medium-term horizon and the access to EU funds and to the state budget is linked to the real implementation of the community, medium-term or strategic plans. Currently, it is common that cities, municipalities or associations of municipalities, at least on a limited scope, are performing community medium-term planning and not on a day-to-day basis as before. One of the important decisions, which can affect the state in the sphere of social services, is the reduction in funding of care allowances. Cuts in the allowance will probably motivate the citizens to try and arrange social services themselves. The cuts in social welfare benefits pose a problem for the population threatened or struck by social exclusion. At the beginning of 2011, the birth grant for the second, third and following children was cancelled, and unemployment benefit as well as parental allowance was reduced. Such steps are motivated by the government's effort to find space for savings and to create pressure on citizens in order for them to accept whatever work, even if it is badly paid.

Another step which has been recently introduced is the fact that the distribution of social benefits is no longer divided between the Labour Office, the City of Ostrava and city district authorities. Instead, a single place, the Labour Office, was created where all social benefits are administered, including unemployment issues. The results and impacts of this step on the socially excluded groups were not yet known at the time of writing this chapter. Nonetheless, it is possible to conclude from the evidence available that all important actors of social policy decision-making process are cooperating in Ostrava with the common goal to find appropriate sources for social services funding, to maintain the current quality and accessibility to the social services. With the budget cuts on all administrative tiers, the closure of small NGOs is happening while big established agencies are strengthening their position because they have better access to donors, grant schemes and so on. Bigger pressure on the co-financing of social services from social services users is apparent as well. The phenomenon of social entrepreneurship that could bring new impulses to the development of social policy has been introduced to the Czech environment recently.

Acknowledgements

This chapter was elaborated in the framework of the project *Analysis and evaluation of governance of socio-economic development of the Moravian-Silesian Region* (SGS09/PRF/2012), which is financially supported by the students' research grant of the University of Ostrava.

References

Gavlas, M., et al., 2000. *Sociální zabezpečení*. 1. ed. Brno: Masarykova univerzita.
Héritier, A., 2002. *New Modes of governance in Europe Policy Making without Legislating*. Institut für höhere Studien, Wien: Reihe Politik Wissenschaft.

Großmann, Katrin et al. 2013. 'How Urban Shrinkage Impacts on Patterns of Socio-Spatial Segregation: The Cases of Leipzig, Ostrava, and Genoa'. In Yeakey, C.C., Thompson, V.S. and Wells, A. (eds). *Urban Ills: Post Recession Complexities to Urban Living in Global Contexts*, New York: Lexington Books.

Kazepov, Y., 2010. 'Rescaling Social Policies toward Multilevel Governance in Europe: Some Reflections on Processes at Stake and Actors Involved'. In Kazepov, Y. (ed.), *Rescaling Social Policies: Toward Multilevel Governance in Europe*, Vienna: Asghate.

Krausová, A., 2008. *Community Social Work*. Ostrava: Ostravská univerzita.

Krebs, V., et al., 1999. Současný stav transformace sociálního systému ve světle zapojování České republiky do evropských struktur. Praha: VŠE.

Ossenbrügge, J., 2003. 'Wirtschaftsgeographie und Governance'. *Zeitschrift für Wirtschaftsgeographie*, Heft 3. pp. 159–76.

Průša, L., et al., 1999. 'Nad pojetím dotační politiky MPSV'. *Sociální politika*, 25 (9), pp. 1–8.

Rumpel, P., et al., 2011. Working paper, project Governance of shrinkage cities within European context. Ostrava: Ostravská univerzita.

Sedláková, R., 2002. 'Romská problematika v denním tisku'. In *Menšiny a marginalizované skupiny v České republice*, 1 ed. Brno: FSS MU, Georgetown.

Solanský, O., 2008. *Stárnoucí populace Ostravy – současný stav a očekávaný vývoj.* Available at: http://dspace.upce.cz/xmlui/bitstream/handle/10195/38572/SolanskyO_StarnouciPopulace_2008.pdf?sequence=1 [Accessed 3 March 2012].

Šotkovský, I., 2009. 'Population Ageing in the Moravian-Silesian Region'. In: ECON '08.

Stoker, G., 1998. *Governance as Theory: Five Propositions*, UNESCO: Blackwell Publishers. pp. 17–28.

Šveřepa, M., 2009. Nechceme po Komunitním plánování příliš. Available at: http://socialnirevue.cz/item/nechceme-po-komunitnim-planovani-prilis [Accessed 3 March 2012].

Van Berkel, R., 2007. Governance structures in local social policy. Analytical framework and two experiences from municipal elderly care policy in Germany. Paper presented in ESPAnet Conference, Vienna.

Chapter 12
Conclusion

Carlos Nunes Silva and Ján Buček

As this collection of chapters shows local self-government in Europe has been unevenly affected by the global economic downturn and in some countries also by the budgetary and sovereign debt crisis. The variety of experiences and policy responses, both structural, related to the organization of local government, and functional, related to operation of local government, which this book only very partially illustrate, is indicative that we may be near a new wave of local government policies and of a new local governance model in Europe, different from the still prevailing neo-liberal governance model and its new public management principles, although as geographically diverse as previous local governance models in the past have been.

Current trends in the reform of local self-government seem to favour administrative centralization, more strict regulation, a shift of competences and resources from local to central government and a move from forms of networked local governance developed gradually in the last few decades back towards the traditional model of hierarchical public administration, based on arguments of transparency, efficiency and better budgetary control. This is in practice a reinforcement of the power of the old administrative bureaucracy and a loss of influence of non-governmental partners in local government policy issues. Faced with the risk of losing what is seen as advantages of the networked model of local governance, an alternative for the next generation of local governance models seems to be a combination of both models, in an institutional geometry still to be found and experimented, and in which NGOs should have a stronger role to play, as well as, in border regions, a variety of local and regional players on both sides of the border, which have been only marginally engaged so far in regional and local development policies.

The design and implementation of this combined new model of local governance is thus one of the challenges confronting local policymakers in European countries, in particular in those countries within the Euro Zone more affected by the current fiscal austerity measures. Nonetheless, we should bear in mind that, as previous reforms in the territorial governance system show, time and time again, the nature and the impact of these institutional reforms depend more on the specific national and local socio-economic conditions and political and administrative culture than on the institutional model itself, more centralized and hierarchical or more decentralized and networked. In other words, the same governance model will probably have different outcomes depending on these specific national and local conditions.

Another characteristic that emerges from the data collected and examined in the book is the fact that there are large disparities in the financial situation among municipalities and other tiers of local self-government. This facet means that there is a wide variety of policy responses to similar overall external fiscal pressures. Municipalities are not all in the same position when confronted with structural economic adjustment programs, or similar measures, with some of them already confronted with severe indebtedness problems before the current crisis emerged, as the case of Portugal illustrates and the case of Slovakia also confirms to some extent, while many others adopt significant anti-crisis social policies under similar external constraints. The different local conditions, namely the local fiscal capacity and the capacity to access other income sources, explain the differences encountered in the capacity to resist and to react to the hard fiscal austerity measures forced by external institutions, a lesson any new local governance model ought to consider as no single institutional or fiscal solution suits all.

Another feature of the current crisis is the reversal of important aspects of local government autonomy achieved in previous years due to the introduction of a less stable and less predictable public finance environment namely in central-local government relations. The overall context of fiscal scarcity and the increasing dependency on transfers and grants from central government budget and from EU funds reduced the local fiscal autonomy, as the case of Slovakia and Portugal illustrates, and increased the vulnerability to the budgetary or sovereign public debt crisis in the Euro Zone countries. The long-term duration of the current fiscal crisis will place increasingly extra pressure on local governments, which will inevitably force cuts in local public spending, reduction in local investments and a collapse of the local financial reserves, as well as in the potential access to alternative sources. It can also threaten the functioning of local government, and influence the quality and scope of the local services provided.

In some countries, as is the case of Slovakia and Portugal, examined in Chapters 2 and 3 respectively, the economic crisis mitigated many economic and institutional reforms completed earlier and generated contradictory effects, as the pressure for long-term fiscal consolidation forced a shift in priorities and, in Portugal, lead to huge cuts in public expenditure, placing at risk important dimensions of the welfare state and the provision of local public services. In Slovakia it also stopped the decentralization of additional powers and competences to local government tiers, and opened the discussion on whether certain competences should once again be executed or not by the central state.

Governments in countries with small and open economies, extremely dependent on the external economic environment, reacted differently to the economic decline associated with the current economic crisis, as the combined cases of Portugal and Slovakia exemplify, and due to that it is also different the nature and the scope of the local government reforms implemented in these countries. While in Slovakia the responses of central government to the crisis were aimed more at stimulating the economy, and less at reducing public spending, in Portugal the option was almost the opposite, to a large extent as a consequence of the adjustment program established by the MoU between the Portuguese government and the European Commission, European Central Bank and the International Monetary Fund.

While in Portugal and Slovakia both systems of local self-government were outside the direct influence of the financial and economic crisis, as they were not involved in risky financial operations, in Portugal, due to the adjustment program and its impact on public expenditure, the local self-government finance system was affected by the fiscal austerity policy adopted by central government, besides the impact associated with the general economic recession and rising unemployment. Besides general long-term influence of the current fiscal crisis on local finance, numerous local governments have faced also serious internal turbulences related to very unstable financial flows.

The evidence examined in these two countries shows that coordination and cooperation between central and local governments, in this case represented by its main national associations (in Portugal one association for municipalities and another for parishes), were two key factors that helped to smooth the impact of the fiscal austerity in the functioning of local government and in the fulfilment of its functional responsibilities within the local component of the welfare state, and in the definition of the role of each partner in the public finance consolidation process under the tutelage of the structural adjustment program. It documents the important role of well-established nation-wide local government associations in protecting the voice of localities and providing a more realistic view from below.

These case studies also reveal that in general the tendency in the reforms so far implemented has been to avoid radical changes in the structure of local government finance systems and to favour gradual change. A similar trend has been found in other institutional components of the local self-government system. The loss or decline of revenues in some income sources has lead to the search of alternative income sources within the usual portfolio of fiscal measures and less for a rupture in the way local government is financed despite the severity of the fiscal austerity in some of these countries.

The regional tier of self-government has also been impacted by the current context of fiscal austerity. As several chapters in the book show, namely Chapter 6, regionalism is no longer fashionable in many parts of Europe. The role of regions and regional governance seems ambiguous, with not all expectations fulfilled. Regions are no longer seen as the answer for all problems confronting local development processes, which seems to require an entirely new vision of the sub-national governance structures in Europe, distinct from the neoliberal governance model, in order to face the new conditions likely to characterize the post-fiscal austerity crisis period. The long experience of regional reforms in some European countries, illustrated in this book by the case of Hungary, should serve as a reference for those countries new to this kind of reform, as is the case of Croatia and Belarus examined in Chapters 7 and 8, where the reform of the spatial division of power needs to become a central issue in the national political agenda.

In the case of multilevel trans-border regional cooperation, the challenges ahead can be summarized as an option between the implementation of bureaucratic Euroregions, with the aim to attract European funds, as has been done in the recent past, and an alternative system of grass-rooted trans-border regional integration, or, in some contexts, reintegration of what has been divided in the past century or so by the political events that marked the history of the Continent. In other words, the way out of the current austerity period may favour the development of a new process of local cross-border cooperation, beyond the mere reorganization of functional economic, social and administrative units, stimulating instead the reorganization of national and cultural areas beyond the classic nation-state model.

Among the tools the new local governance model can use more widely than before is the partnership between local self-government and Non-governmental Organizations (NGOs), taking as a reference the example of NGOs' operations in developing countries, where they perform a supportive role in managing, implementing and delivering different kinds of policies and programs with very limited financial resources and basic infrastructure, as is shown in Chapter 9 for the case of health policy and health programs. Important can also be the role of NGOs in connecting citizens to local government, facilitating or even encouraging dialogue between different stakeholders, when policy issues get so complex and time-consuming. Also important for a more sustainable local development is certainly the use of innovative policy tools, as is illustrated by the instrument to support fiscal sustainable urban planning examined in Chapter 10. NGOs can play an important and clearly focused and pragmatic role in citizens' participation in social and political life at the local level, in a time when many citizens are dissatisfied and protest against the sort of policy measures implemented in response to the current public finance crisis.

While the findings and insights of this book can be extended to other countries and to other local policy issues, the analysis in each of these chapters confirms that local self-government in Europe is highly differentiated and for that reason no single governance model can be devised for all. In addition, confronted with the challenges raised by the fiscal austerity context, the position and the capacity to react of local self-government in Europe is contingent upon their degree of autonomy, variable from country to country, and over time, as the current reforms in the countries examined clearly illustrate. Local government in Europe does not have the same policy-making autonomy of national governments and neither the full capacity to interact with other tiers of government. It is within these limits, set up differently in each country, and over time, that the capacity of manoeuvre of local self-government to face the challenges of fiscal austerity will be developed.

As a result of this, we are likely to see in the coming years the development and dissemination of a new local governance model, with variable geometry in the tiers or levels of government included, in the role assigned to the private and public sectors in the provision of local public services, in the stakeholders or institutional actors engaged, in the level of citizen active participation and in the innovative policy tools employed to make development more sustainable, to mention just some of the key dimensions of what is certainly a highly complex reform process.

As in previous waves of local self-government reform in Europe, modernization and adaptation of local government to the new circumstances can be carried out by structural reforms, more complex and difficult to implement, and not always successful, or by functional adaptation, which in the past has proved easier to implement.

Index

www.ingramcontent.com/pod-product-compliance
Ingram Content Group UK Ltd.
Pitfield, Milton Keynes, MK11 3LW, UK
UKHW020352010325
455677UK00021B/416